SETTING OUR HEARTS
upon the DEEP

SETTING OUR HEARTS
upon the DEEP

Acknowledging Lament in Christian Life,
Worship, and Thought

HENRY L. NOVELLO

PICKWICK *Publications* · Eugene, Oregon

SETTING OUR HEARTS UPON THE DEEP
Acknowledging Lament in Christian Life, Worship, and Thought

Pickwick Publications
An Imprint of Wipf and Stock Publishers
199 W. 8th Ave., Suite 3
Eugene, OR 97401

www.wipfandstock.com

PAPERBACK ISBN: 978-1-6667-5291-5
HARDCOVER ISBN: 978-1-6667-5292-2
EBOOK ISBN: 978-1-6667-5293-9

Cataloguing-in-Publication data:

Names: Novello, Henry L., author

Title: Setting our hearts upon the deep : acknowledging lament in Christian life, Worship, and Thought / Henry L. Novello

Description: Eugene, OR: Pickwick Publications, 2023 | Includes bibliographical references.

Identifiers: ISBN 978-1-6667-5291-5 (paperback) | ISBN 978-1-6667-5292-2 (hardcover) | ISBN 978-1-6667-5293-9 (ebook)

Subjects: LCSH: Laments in Bible | Laments—History and criticism | Laments | Theology | Suffering—Biblical teaching | Pastoral theology | Prayer—Biblical teaching

Classification: BS1199.L27 N68 2023 (print) | BS1199.L27 (ebook)

DECEMBER 20, 2022 2:41 AM

Dedicated to the suffering faithful whose cries out of the depths are joined to Jesus's cry as they strive to be God's ongoing embodiment in our afflicted world

Lord, on the day I called for help, you answered me.

CONTENTS

PREFACE

THE IMPETUS FOR THIS study comes from my recent monograph titled *Passionate Deification*, in which I argued that the emotions of Christ provide us with a privileged window for gazing upon the process of passionate deification in his person. The congenial emotions of love, compassion, and joy were portrayed as the primary emotions and chief driving forces in Jesus's preaching of the kingdom of God. Yet the Gospels also record non-congenial emotions of Jesus as he confronts the impoverished state of his own people, encounters increasing resistance to his mission, and ultimately suffers the utter rejection of his person on the cross. The emotions of sighing, weeping, grieving, sorrow, dread, and lament all feature in Jesus's journey to Jerusalem and in the agony of his passion. From the standpoint of a cognitive theory of emotion, it was shown that each of the emotions of Jesus has a specific object: the first and chief emotion of ineffable love is directed towards the Father; Jesus's joy is no ordinary joy for it is the ineffable joy that springs from carrying out the will of the Father; Jesus's love of the Father translates into his profound compassion for his people who are like sheep without a shepherd; Jesus sighs at the physical infirmities that afflict his people, and longs for the establishment of the new Jerusalem when sighing will be no more; Jesus sighs at the unbelief of the Pharisees and the spiritual obtuseness and hardness of heart of his own disciples; Jesus weeps bitterly for the impending destruction of Jerusalem due to the rejection of his person and mission; Jesus weeps and grieves at the tomb of his beloved friend Lazarus who had offered him devotion, support, and hospitality; Jesus is deeply distressed in Gethsemane at the prospect of having to drink "the cup"; and from the cry of lament on the cross it becomes apparent that what Jesus dreads in Gethsemane is the prospect of being forsaken by

God as he is handed over into the custody of evildoers, who will execute their ungodly judgment upon him.

It is most significant that Jesus's first and chief emotion of love of the Father culminates in his cry on the cross: "My God, my God, why have you forsaken me" (Mark 15:34; Matt 27:46). It is Jesus's love for the Father and fidelity to his mission as the Son that carries him all the way to the cross. His love for the Father, which translates into unfathomable love for us sinners, ultimately manifests itself in the sacrifice of the cross, which establishes the "new covenant" in his blood. Given that the congenial and suffering emotions of Jesus form an indissoluble unity in carrying out his messianic mission, this implies that the congenial and suffering emotions should also be regarded as forming a composite unity in those who give witness to Christ as "the way, and the truth, and the life" (John 14:6). To imitate Christ, who reveals the pathos of God in relation to the world, involves the *transformation of our emotions* as we allow the Crucified One to become the new object of both our congenial and suffering emotions. The lament speech form is integral to this process of the working out of grace as the transformation of the emotions, and should not be summarily dismissed on the basis of key christological claims. The present world, few would dispute, is just as broken as the world Jesus encountered when he proclaimed the kingdom of God to his own, and the evils and sufferings of our time are just as pervasive as they were in Jesus's day. In the face of the reality of evil in the world, the appropriate Christian response is not to emulate the *apatheia* of the Stoic sage but to acknowledge our sorrow and vulnerability before a troubled world and to openly address God out of the depths of our grieving hearts. The lament speech form is not an opportunity to wallow in self-pity but is a robust form of prayer rooted in the conviction that God, in virtue of the divine pathos, hears our prayers and participates in our situation out of concern and care for us, and will deliver us from our affliction and distress, thereby manifesting the glory of God.

Talk of suffering and lament is inescapable in this world and should not be stifled, yet such talk should not be allowed to overshadow the good news of the gospel and the joy of "new life" in the Spirit. Pope Francis in his apostolic exhortation *Evangelii Gaudium* (The Joy of the Gospel) has reminded Christians that joy is the distinguishing atmosphere of Christian life, and unless our hearts are on fire with the joy of the gospel the church will struggle to effectively carry out its mission in the world. The pontiff acknowledges that at times darkness overwhelms the faithful to such an extent that they question the existence of God, but he urges Christians to rediscover a robustness of joy that adapts and endures through the dark experiences of human existence. All this is well and good; however, a weakness in the pontiff's writings is that he does not specify how this robustness of joy will be rediscovered. The present study seeks to elaborate on the ways in which the practice of lament is indispensable to promoting the robustness of joy that should be the distinguishing character of Christian life. The pontiff strongly urges Christians not to deliberately keep Christ's wounds at arm's length; he is emphatic that Christ wants his followers "to touch the suffering flesh of others."[1] Christians, in other words, must be prepared to embody Christ's diaconal acts of solidarity with suffering humanity. The implication here is that in the church's praxis of selfless service to others, what is at stake is the church's identity and credibility. But without any practice of the lament speech form, how will Christians remain committed to their vocation of imitating Christ as they are confronted by the overwhelming "suffering flesh of others"? If lament was integral to how Christ dealt with his suffering on the cross, how can it not have its place among those who pledge their lives to embodying Christ in the world?

Pope Francis speaks refreshingly of the joy of the gospel, yet by relating Christian joy to Christ's diaconal acts of solidarity with suffering humanity, his exhortation is as daunting as it is attractive. For Pope Francis is asking the faithful to be like Peter in the Gospel story of Jesus's walking on the sea (Matt 14:22–32). Peter says to Jesus: "Bid me to come to you on the water" (v. 28). When Jesus bids him to come, Peter starts walking on the water but quickly begins to sink as fear overcomes him. Needless to say, it is most difficult to step out of ourselves onto that sea, to forsake every safety net that we know, to abandon ourselves to that ineffable divine love that calls us out, and to show unwavering trust in divine providence. Like Peter, we experience an initial astonishing joy in wanting to follow Jesus, but quickly we are besieged by the winds of fear and waves of doubt that threaten to destroy us. It is indeed most challenging *to set our hearts upon the deep* (cf. Luke 5:4) and to leave our familiar safety nets behind in response to the Lord who bids us come. In order to meet this challenge in a troubled world, the present study argues that the church must recover the biblical tradition of lament, which culminates in Jesus's cry on Calvary. The Christian practice of lament, while rooted

---

1. Francis, *Evangelii Gaudium*, §270.

in the Jewish tradition, also displays an element of discontinuity with that tradition. For what is distinctive about *Christian* lament is that the cries of the faithful are joined to Jesus's cry on the cross. This means, according to the line of argument that will be formulated in this study, that since God heard Jesus's cry and was "with" him and "for" him as he suffered on the cross, his followers know that God is "with" them and "for" them in their own cries that are joined to Jesus's cry, and thus redeemed. The present study is motivated by the conviction that Christian life is a journey of ongoing transformation of grief (lament) into joy (praise) as we "put on Christ" (Rom 13:14) and "strain forward" (Phil 3:13) in the expectation of the kingdom of glory to come. The Eucharist, which incorporates lament *into* thanksgiving—for Christ's resurrection is the Father's response to his cry on Calvary—supremely encapsulates this understanding of Christian life as the ongoing embodiment of Christ in a world that remains unredeemed, until that day that Christ comes in glory to consummate all things.

INTRODUCTION

Wrestling with the Problem of Evil

IN A RECENT MONOGRAPH titled *Evil in Modern Thought*, Susan Neiman has argued that the history of European philosophy can be told as the history of thinkers who wrestled with the problem of evil. Enlightenment thinkers such as Voltaire and Rousseau, as well as the great philosophical schemes of Kant and Hegel, all in their respective ways sought to resolve the problem of evil. The notion of progress in history was especially endorsed by Hegel who proposed that the world is advancing by means of a dialectical process: first (*A*), then its opposite (*B*), then a synthesis of the two (*C*), and so on. "Everything was moving toward a better, fuller, more perfect end; and if there had to be suffering on the way, if there had to be problems as the dialectic unwound, so be it; such things are the broken eggs from which delicious omelets are made."[1] Hegel's dialectic was a totalizing dialectic in which the tragic and the logical coincide everywhere: "Something has to die for something greater to be born . . . misfortune is everywhere, but everywhere it is surpassed, to the degree that reconciliation always wins out over dissent."[2] This belief in the rational progress of history was further bolstered by Charles Darwin's *On the Origin of Species* (1859), which is considered to be the foundation of evolutionary biology. Darwin's work was then applied to fields other than biology, as evidenced by the emergence of social Darwinism where the biological concept of natural selection was applied to sociology, economics, and politics.

1. Wright, *Evil*, 21.
2. Ricoeur, *Evil*, 54.

By the end of the nineteenth century the potent combination of Enlightenment thinking, scientific advancement (Newtonian physics), technological achievement (Industrial Revolution), medical advances (germ theory, antiseptic theory, aspirin, quinine, stethoscope, cholera vaccine), Hegelian progressive idealism, evolutionary theory, and the emergence of Western-style liberal democracies (French Revolution) had created a heightened sense of belief in the doctrine of progress. Alfred Russel Wallace's book titled *The Wonderful Century* (1898)[3] captured the heightened mood of optimism that prevailed at the time. Wallace spoke most enthusiastically of the extraordinary technological achievements of the nineteenth century, while expressing concern that the achievements in technological knowledge would be applied to the development of deadlier machines of war. Alexander Sutherland, who in the following year (1899) coined the phrase "the natural decline of warfare," did not share Wallace's concerns and instead proposed that the trajectory of progress would eventually lead to the realization of the goal of eliminating warfare altogether.[4] It was already the case that civilized nations enjoyed a state of peace, and it was only a matter of time, Sutherland believed, before peace reigned everywhere as human history moved into a higher phase of civilization.

From the standpoint of this prevailing air of optimism that fanned heightened expectations at the turn of the twentieth century, we can appreciate the devastating effect that the First World War (1914–1918) was to have on the Enlightenment doctrine of progress and its steady march towards a golden age of prosperity, peace, and high civilization. In the aftermath of the Great War, the mood of optimism was replaced by an atmosphere of crisis. This was especially apparent in the new wave of theological thinking that emerged known as crisis or dialectical theology, which challenged belief in the steady progress of history and the liberal theology founded on the writings of Friedrich Schleiermacher. When Karl Barth wrote his first commentary on the Letter to the Romans in the aftermath of the Great War, his fundamental message was that the time had come to listen afresh to the word of God coming to us from outside, instead of relying on the progress of the kingdom of God within history. The crisis of belief was soon deepened by the further tragic events of

3. Wallace's book conveys the famous *fin de siècle* mood of 1890s Europe. See Danchev, *Fin de Siècle*.

4. See Crook, *Darwinism, War and History*. Sutherland coined the phrase during the euphoria of Tsar Nicholas II's world peace proposals of 1898.

the Second World War (1939–1945) and the horrific happenings of the Jewish Holocaust. N. T. Wright has written that "Auschwitz destroyed, one would have thought forever, the idea that European civilization at least was a place where nobility, virtue and humanizing reason could flourish and abound."[5] Despite the undeniable fact of significant scientific-technological progress in the modern age, Sutherland's belief in the natural decline of warfare has not proven to be well founded. Warfare continues to be a disturbing and troubling feature of the human landscape, and the stockpiling of nuclear weapons, as well as the rising threat of terrorism, have all contributed to an increased sense of the precarious nature of human existence. For all the scientific-technological progress that has been achieved hitherto, moreover, we find ourselves today confronted with the persistent realities of new deadly viruses—e.g., HIV, Ebola, COVID-19—the differential incidence of sickness and death in societies, the ecological crisis and climate change, rising incidences of criminality, and the volatility of the free market economy, all of which have contributed to an age of anxiety and suffering.[6]

Today there are many who contend that the most disturbing thing about our modern age is that "progress itself has turned threatening."[7] Yet despite the mood of anxiety that permeates Western societies, the majority of citizens have opted to retain the belief that the world's problems can be overcome by means of improved education, scientific knowledge, advanced technologies, and the promotion of Western-style democracies. It is remarkable that belief in progress is as strong as it is given the levels of suffering, anxiety, and instability in our world, yet at the same time the doctrine of progress is seriously challenged by various waves of "postmodern" thought.[8] If mainstream European culture could produce

5. Wright, *Evil*, 23.

6. See Dunant and Porter, *Age of Anxiety*.

7. Bauckham and Hart, "Shape of Time," 52. The authors talk of the decline of progress, of the failed metanarrative of historical progress.

8. Postmodern thought is not accepting of basic tenets of modernity regarding the character of rationality, the nature of subjectivity, issues of rights and responsibilities, and the constitution of the political community. Paul Lakeland suggests that the postmodern sensibility is "nonsequential, noneschatological, nonutopian, nonsystematic, nonfoundational, and, ultimately, nonpolitical" (*Postmodernity*, 8). He also offers a basic taxonomy of postmodern thought: "late moderns" regard the project of modernity as unfinished and intend to carry it forward; "true postmoderns" see in the unmasking of modernity's totalizing tendencies the chance to embrace a radical historicism; and "countermoderns" see in modernity's demise the opportunity to return to the securities of an earlier age (*Postmodernity*, 12).

the Jewish Holocaust, then this implies that everything else should be treated with suspicion as well. Postmodern thought is characterized by a culture of suspicion that seeks to "deconstruct" the ideology of "progress." The great masters of suspicion, namely, Marx (everything is about economic forces), Nietzsche (everything is about power), and Freud (everything is about sex), set in motion the train of thought regarding the dissolution of the subject. The Enlightenment's heady notion of human subjectivity—the subject is the seat of reason and the originator of meaning—is rejected by postmodernists who see in this modern idea "the seeds of social and political repression."[9] Thus the postmodern project of the dissolution of subjectivity is "linked directly to the ideal of human emancipation."[10] Also integral to the postmodern project of attaining human freedom is an ethical relativism that rebuffs any claim to external universally imposed moral categories of right and wrong. Postmodernists impose their own moral vision upon the world in the interests of human emancipation.[11] With regard to the political question, this is usually addressed by postmodernity in terms of the problem of "otherness." In times past, otherness was unproblematic by virtue of what Jean-Francois Lyotard calls "metanarratives" that shape a worldview in which the "other" is excluded. The other is the path not taken, the darkness to the light, the chaos that stands over a sense of order, the female to the male, the black to the white, the native culture to the colonial power, the East to the West, the homosexual to the heterosexual, the evil to the good.[12]

Unlike modern thought with its shallow ideology of progress, postmodern thought does acknowledge the deeply flawed nature of humanity and the enduring problem of evil and its power. But because it deconstructs human subjectivity so that there is no longer an "I" or a fixed identity and hence no fixed responsibility, nobody can be blamed for evil. Postmodernity therefore tends to be "dehumanizing" in that there is no moral dignity left since there is nobody left to shoulder the blame.[13] A second major problem is that while postmodernity affirms evil as real

---

9. Lakeland, *Postmodernity*, 20.

10. Lakeland, *Postmodernity*, 20.

11. Lakeland, *Postmodernity*, 25.

12. See Lakeland, *Postmodernity*, 31.

13. Wright, *Evil*, 33.

and powerful, it allows for no redemption and gives no clues as to what we should do about it: "There is no way out, no chance of repentance and restoration, no way back to the solid ground of truth from the quick sands of deconstruction."[14] This readily leads to a nihilistic perspective that fosters a heightened sense of hopelessness. So, what is needed is a more nuanced response to the problem of suffering and evil than that proposed by either the shallow modernist doctrine of progress on the one hand or the nihilistic deconstructive analyses of postmodernity on the other.

What might a Jewish-Christian view of evil and suffering look like in comparison to the modern and postmodern responses to the problem? The task of the present study is to provide a response to this basic question from the vantage point of the tradition of biblical lament, which reaches its zenith with Jesus's cry of lament on Calvary (Mark 15:34; Matt 27:46). In the Bible the problem of sin and evil is introduced very early with the stories of Adam's transgression (Gen 3:6–20), Cain's killing of Abel (Gen 4:8), and God's covenant with Noah (Gen 6:5—9:17). The story of Noah and the flood marks an especially important point in the biblical story, for we are introduced to the all-important notion of the divine "grieving" (Gen 6:6) for the evil workings of humankind. The grieving of God is not limited to his relationship with a rebellious Israel, which the prophets of Israel give ample voice to, but goes back to the early days of the creation. In the covenant that God makes with Noah, he promises to allow the creation to endure in spite of the scourge of human wickedness. This means, though, that the promise to Noah (Gen 9:8–17) necessitates divine suffering. The divine decision to endure the sin and evil of the world necessarily involves a continual grieving as the Lord persists in opening up his heart to that world. Without this definitive decision by God to endure continual suffering on account of human wickedness, the creation would not have a future. This posture of God before the creation takes on another dimension with the introduction of the lament speech form, which first appears when the Hebrew people are living in slavery in Egypt. Exodus 2–15 is presented as a lament form: "The people of Israel groaned under their bondage, and cried out for help, and their cry under bondage came up to God" (Exod 2:23). God then responds that he has seen the affliction of his people and has heard their cry and he will come down to deliver them (Exod 3:7–8). Once deliverance from Egyptian

---

14. Wright, *Evil*, 33.

slavery has taken place, the book of Exodus narrates Israel's murmurings of discontent in the wilderness of Sinai. The people complain to Moses that they would have been better off had they remained in Egypt where they at least "ate bread to the full" (Exod 16:3). God responds by sending quail and manna from heaven (Exod 16:4–30). The divine responses to evil and suffering in the books of Genesis and Exodus already indicate humankind's relevance to God and how God is personally engaged with his creation for the sake of securing its future existence.

Most Christians would have at least heard of the word "lament" and would associate it with the Psalms, since laments far outnumber any other kind of songs in the Psalter. Yet the majority of Christians "would be hard pressed to identify lament as an important aspect of their lives of faith and worship."[15] Oswald Bayer looks beyond the contemporary situation and traces the lack of recognition of lament back to the earliest days of Christianity. He maintains that the influence of Stoic thought has ensured that "the fundamental significance of lament has not been accounted for in the church's liturgy or its theology."[16] Elements of lament are appropriated insofar as the Psalms are prayed in the church's liturgy, but lament does not determine any decisive aspect of systematic theology or Christian ethics. This is quite astonishing, says Bayer, since lament lies at the heart of the paschal mystery: Jesus's resurrection from the dead is confessed as the Father's answer to Jesus's cry on the cross. This Christology of answered lament appears in the Letter to the Hebrews: "In the days of his flesh, Jesus offered up prayers and supplications, with loud cries and tears, to him who was able to save him from death, and he was heard for his godly fear" (Heb 5:7). Since the "new life" in the Spirit of the risen Christ gives praise to God who saves from death and resurrects out of death, this implies that Christian praise of God does not suppress lament but actually makes room for it. The Eucharist, Bayer insists, "incorporates lament *into* thanksgiving."[17] This particular understanding of the intimate connection that exists between lament and thanksgiving is not generally acknowledged among the Christian churches.

There are some contemporary liturgists, it must be said, who do acknowledge a place for lament in Christian worship. The Lutheran liturgist Gordon Lathrop, for instance, talks about the "juxtaposition" or

---

15. Duff, "Recovering Lamentation," 3.

16. Bayer, "Toward Theology of Lament," 211.

17. Bayer, "Toward Theology of Lament," 211; emphasis added.

"apposition" of thanksgiving and lament in Christian worship.[18] But this language is not quite the same as that used by Bayer, who makes a specific point of saying that lament is inextricably incorporated "into" thanksgiving, since the praise of God elicited by the risen Christ makes room for lament. The Roman Catholic liturgist David Power goes further than juxtaposing thanksgiving and lament, and is closer to the view expressed by Bayer. Power says that since there is so much trouble in the lives of the faithful, and given the systemic sin that is oppressive of human life and of nature, hope in God's promises is easily eroded. In light of the obstacles that stand in the way of God's rule, the disturbing and distressing realities of this world have to be named and lamented by Christians, so as "to allow room for open and faithful covenant remembrance."[19] Power talks of "eucharistic lamentation," by which he means that the Eucharist forms the church in the memory of Christ's suffering, into which the memory of all human sufferings and the collapse of the human is gathered.

The writings of Bayer, Lathrop, and Power are notable exceptions to the contemporary neglect of lament in Christian worship and theology. The praise of God necessarily incorporates the lament of Christ's unjust suffering on the cross. In the Eucharist the Crucified One is present as the Living and Risen One; he speaks as the one who has been "heard" (Heb 5:7) by the Father, and together they send the Spirit of new life, which is the power that saves and re-creates out of the midst of suffering and death. As long as we live in the time between the first and second coming of Christ, "we shall lament even as we rejoice . . . the only life we know is entwined with death, and the only joy is inter-laminated with lament."[20] Lament is not a suffering emotion that we experience only occasionally but is constant and durative as long as history is still running its course and we eagerly await the age of glory to come. As the psalmist asks over and again, "How long, O Lord? How long?" (Ps 13:1), which in the New Testament becomes the call *maranatha*: "Our Lord, come!" (1 Cor 16:22; Rev 22:20). The spine of lament, it will become apparent in this study, is eschatological hope that fosters renewed praise of God in the midst of present affliction and distress. This hope is not an empty optimism that things will get progressively better within history but the assurance that evil and death will not have the last word, because they have been

18. Lathrop, *Holy Things*, 55, 57, 164, 208.
19. Power, *Eucharistic Mystery*, 336.
20. Black, "Persistence of the Wounds," 53.

conquered and transformed by Christ's paschal mystery into new life and unspeakable joy. On the understanding, which this study will defend, that God the Father did *not* abandon Jesus the Son in his time of great trial and tribulation, we can confidently say that God is not only "for" us but "with" us in our own cries that are joined to Jesus's cry and therefore redeemed, as we commit ourselves to being God's ongoing embodiment in the world.[21] To live in the Spirit of the risen Christ means that we already experience in the here and now the transforming of grief into joy, we are able to recover a reverence for the "holy ground" upon which we walk, and we eagerly anticipate the coming age of resurrection life out of the present age of affliction and death.

The first chapter of this study will examine the biblical lament literature, which has been described by Walter Brueggemann as a "counter-tradition" within Jewish Scripture, for it stands over against a contractual theology that identifies suffering with sinfulness, and prosperity with righteousness. The laments of the faithful are not meant to be reflections on suffering but simply express the *reality* of suffering. It will be shown that one of the important gains of this form of honest address to God is the maintenance of a truly *dialogical* divine-human relationship, where it is permissible to question divine justice and integrity when life simply overwhelms the faithful servants of God. The problem of undeserved suffering gives rise to the basic question, can God be trusted? This is a vitally important question which inevitably arises when the experiences of historical life fall far short of the expectations associated with the covenant promises of God. The lament speech form, it will be shown, serves an important function in the faith and liturgy of Israel, for it is indispensable to promoting personal communion with God through dialogue, affirming hope in future salvation, and raising expectations of renewed praise of God. A voice that is permitted to speak only praise and doxology, without acknowledging grief and lament, is finally a practice of denial and pretense that fails to recognize the profundity and complexity of the problem of evil and suffering in our world.

The first chapter will not confine itself to human lament addressed to God but will introduce the notion of divine lament, which serves to

---

21. The assertion that God did not abandon Jesus on the cross runs counter to the view expressed by many contemporary theologians who subscribe to the God-abandonment thesis. William Stacy Johnson, for example, says it is time to say no to the God-abandonment thesis and to recover the central conviction of the gospel that because God hears Jesus's cry, our cries also are heard ("Jesus' Cry").

enrich the picture of a truly reciprocal divine-human relationship. The divine lament belongs to the responsiveness of the divine pathos; it gives voice to the pathos of God's suffering and grieving in relation to a sinful and wayward world. It will be argued, following Abraham Heschel, that the concept of divine pathos is not a psychological category but rather a theological category that underscores God's personal relatedness to and ultimate concern for Israel and the world. The depiction of God as grieving and lamenting the state of the divine-human relationship leads to an appreciation of God as internalizing the people's rejection of him as Lord and choosing to suffer for the sake of bringing to fruition the covenant promises. In this perspective there is divine anger or wrath that leads to judgment, but judgment takes on an instrumental role as a necessary prerequisite for God's new redemptive activity: that is, God works good out of a situation of sin and death. By integrating the divine lament materials into the discussion of the human lament speech form, chapter 1 will pave the way for an examination of Jesus's cry on the cross in chapter 3, as well as provide the framework for a more satisfying perspective on the issue of theodicy.

In chapter 2 the discussion on lament shifts from the Old Testament to the New Testament and the Christian theological tradition. It will become evident that with the notable exception of Jesus's lament cry on the cross, there is a perceived absence of lament in the New Testament. Suffering is no longer considered as giving cause for lament, since to suffer in Christ's name takes on the positive aspects of honor and "rejoicing" (Col 1:24). Yet the chapter will also draw attention to the fact that there are various expressions of suffering in the New Testament, such as weeping, mourning, sighing, and groaning. It will be proposed that lament is not so much invalidated as reevaluated as a positive expression of our longing for "adoption as sons, the redemption of our bodies" (Rom 8:23). The second part of the chapter will survey the treatment of lament in the theological tradition. The discussion will be limited to the writings of Augustine, Luther, Calvin, Barth, and Moltmann, which will prove to be more than sufficient in demonstrating a significant narrowing of perspective on biblical lament and a neglect of the tradition of the suffering righteous. The guiding idea in Augustine's thought is that our lament is joined to Christ's lament and that what makes Christians distinctive is their affective attachment to Christ who is the object of their suffering. Lament as a modality of human affect directed to God and anchored in eschatological hope will be affirmed as a step in the right direction. Yet at the same time Augustine will be criticized for treating the lament psalms solely in relation to the problem of personal sin, for using the allegorical method of interpretation, and for regarding Christ as not forsaken by God on the cross, since he himself was God. The discussion on Luther will show that he is very similar to Augustine in treating the lament psalms as penitential prayers, in reducing lament to the problem of sin, and in regarding suffering as a form of pedagogy. Unlike Augustine, though, Luther offers a more satisfactory treatment of the lament cry of Ps 22:1, for it is applied wholly to Christ as the head, who died and suffered as no one else has died or suffered. Luther, contrary to Augustine, has no difficulty in saying that Christ was forsaken by God on the cross, and it will be shown that this is due to Luther's novel perspective on the true communication of properties *in concreto* in the person of Christ. Luther's understanding of the true communion of natures in Christ will be affirmed as a further step in the right direction, for we are able to say that Christ's cry is not merely a human cry but God's cry. In the discussion of Calvin, the intention will be to show that he also sets limits to laments or "murmurings" against God, but these limits are based on his doctrine of God's providential care. He, too, will be criticized for thinking of the afflictions of the faithful as a form of pedagogy related purely to the problem of sin. While Calvin is to be applauded for giving ample voice to the genuinely strong emotions of Christ when he experienced the curse of God on the cross, at the same time shortcomings appear when Calvin says that Christ submitted himself to the will of God with "a composed and peaceful mind." The latter contention, it will be claimed, belies a separation of the two natures in the person of Christ. Unlike Luther's true communion of natures in Christ, Calvin is not able to say that Christ's cry is not merely a human cry but God's cry.

Chapter 2 will conclude with the treatment of lament by the contemporary theologians Karl Barth and Jürgen Moltmann. Barth asserts that Christ's triumph over his enemies on Calvary means that the insoluble question of Job and the psalmists now ceases to be a problem. Suffering is not abolished, though, and now takes on the form of suffering due to membership in the crucified Son. This membership has no room for the continuation of the desperate crying and protests of the faithful in the Old Testament; there is only the "strict matter-of-factness" of those who are called to bear their cross and follow Christ. For Barth, we shall see, obedience to Christ disqualifies the practice of lament as disobedience. Since there can be no question of repetitions of Golgotha, Barth considers all the sufferings of the faithful as completely transcended by the event of Golgotha, in which is revealed the definitive victory of Christ over all sin, suffering, and death. This total victory of Christ leads Barth to set limits to lament, since all our sufferings are to be regarded as already behind us. The eschatological thrust apparent in Augustine, Luther, and Calvin is now replaced by an emphasis on the here and now of Christ's total victory over all the obstacles that prevent us from becoming God's covenant partners. It will be shown that Moltmann, like Barth, also does not allow for believers to be included in Christ's lament cry, for the cry of the Son reveals his act of substitution by means of which the godless are justified and set free to sacrifice their lives for the coming of the kingdom of God. Jesus's lament as the Son is regarded as revealing the cross as an event between God and God, hence Moltmann says that the cross should not be interpreted from the standpoint of the lament tradition in which Ps 22 stands. The chapter will take issue with this perspective, while acknowledging the positive import of treating the cross as a Trinitarian event.

Chapter 3, which is the pivotal chapter of this study, offers a critical interpretation of Jesus's cry on the cross, building on the findings of the previous chapters. The first part of the chapter will examine Ps 22 in light of the Jewish tradition of the suffering righteous, with the intention of showing that the psalm has an intensity and comprehensive in its composition that sets it apart from other prayers belonging to this tradition. It will be argued that the special character of Ps 22 gives us a strong indication as to why Jesus chose to utter the opening verse of this psalm in bringing his messianic mission to completion on Calvary. The suffering righteous one in Ps 22 does not die, though, while Jesus suffers a terrible death by crucifixion. The second part of the chapter will propose that what is missing in Ps 22 is complemented by Jesus's anguished prayer in the garden of Gethsemane, where he pleads with the Father that "the hour" might pass from him and "the cup" be removed from him. In Gethsemane we see that Jesus's impending death is not merely a historical ordeal for him but also an eschatological ordeal that pertains to the final victory of good over evil. This eschatological emphasis which Jesus attaches to his impending death, it will be shown, meshes extremely well with the eschatological hymn of praise that concludes Ps 22. Against the backdrop of Jesus's prayer in Gethsemane and the tradition of the suffering righteous one in which Ps 22 stands, a critical interpretation of Jesus's cry of lament on the cross will be offered.

It will be contended in the third part of chapter 3 that by citing the opening verse of Ps 22 as he breathes his last, Jesus intends to offer a theological—not psychological or juridical—interpretation of his death on the cross, where humanity and divinity are united together in the ultimate agony. The proposed interpretation will affirm both human and divine dimensions to Jesus's cry, which is consistent with the view that Jesus stands in the line of the prophets, who suffered in sympathy with the divine pathos. But Jesus is much more than just a prophet, for he is the eternal Word made flesh, which means that in his person the prophetic life, as well as the figure of the suffering servant of God in Isaiah, is raised to a new key. His humanity is no ordinary humanity, for as the incarnate Word his humanity embodies the fullness of divinity. It will be contended that as human, Jesus's cry stands in the tradition of the suffering righteous one and expresses his solidarity with suffering humanity (God suffers "with us"). And as divine, Jesus's cry reveals how God, in the crucified body of the Son, has internalized and borne the world's sin and rebellion (God suffers "for us"). An important conclusion to the chapter will be the repudiation of the *God*-abandonment thesis. It will be contended that God does *not* hide his face from the Crucified One but is "for" the crucified and "with" Jesus in his cry; hence we know that God is with us and for us in our own cries that are joined to Jesus's cry and therefore redeemed.

The final chapter 4 will discuss some implications of the proposed theological interpretation of Jesus's cry for systematic theology. There is a tendency in systematic theology to quickly reach a happy ending without acknowledging the uncertainties and afflictions of the faithful suffered along the way. The systematic analysis of lament offered in the previous chapters of this study sheds light on its transformative potential for all aspects of systematic theology. Before discussing some of the more important implications, the final chapter will begin by offering a comprehensive definition of *Christian* lament that seeks to encapsulate the various functions of the lament speech form for Christian faith, life, and worship. We shall then proceed to discuss a number of selected topics in order to indicate the transformative potential of lament for systematic theology, namely: (1) the need to keep the theodicy question open, which is deeply bound up with the notion of the suffering of God, hence what is in view is a divine theodicy based on God's self-revelation in Jesus Christ; (2) the need to embrace the apophatic way of unknowing in theology and to view the Spirit as leading us into Christ's relationship with the Father, which is to say that the Spirit leads us out of a provisional existence and into the "adventure of incarnation," which is summed up in the Eucharist; (3) the need to interpret Jesus's cry within the framework of the revelation of God as triune, with a particular emphasis on the interpersonal model of the Trinity as eternal event of kenosis, that is, self-emptying or self-sacrificing love between the divine persons; (4) the need to refute the doctrine of kenosis as surrendered divine attributes in its various nineteenth and twentieth-century formulations and to affirm the fullness of deity dwelling bodily in Jesus Christ; (5) and, finally, some important clarifications will be offered on the issue of God's suffering in his relatedness to the world. The discussion will not be exhaustive, for there are many other topics that normally fall within the ambit of systematic theology that will not be discussed. Nonetheless, the selected topics will effectively serve to indicate lines of thought that impact upon all aspects of systematic theology.

1

LAMENT IN THE OLD TESTAMENT

Reciprocity of the Divine-Human Relationship

R ECENT OLD TESTAMENT STUDY of the lament as a speech form, especially the lament psalm, has revealed the important function that it plays in the faith and liturgy of Israel. Walter Brueggemann has argued that the theological significance of the lament as a form of prayer uttered in a situation of human distress lies in that "it shifts the calculus and *redresses the redistribution of power* between the two parties," so that the petitionary party is truly heard and taken seriously by God who becomes newly engaged in the human crisis.[1] To Brueggemann's mind, the absence of lament from the life of faith involves two dimensions of loss: the loss of genuine covenant interaction inasmuch as the human party has become voiceless; and the stifling of the question of theodicy since there is no capacity to complain and protest that things are not right in the present arrangement.[2] These two dimensions of loss result in the uncritical faith of "structure legitimation," that is, support of the status quo.[3] The genuine covenant interaction that Brueggemann speaks

1. Brueggemann, "Costly Loss of Lament," 59.

2. Brueggemann, "Costly Loss of Lament," 60–62.

3. See Brueggemann, "Shape for Old Testament Theology, I." Brueggemann argues that Old Testament theology fully partakes in the "common theology" of its world and is thus *structure-legitimating,* yet insofar as it struggles to be free of that common theology it is open to the *embrace of pain,* which is experienced in historical situations of distress. These two poles make up the *bipolar* construct that Brueggemann proposes for an Old Testament theology.

about with respect to the lament speech form allows the suffering faithful to articulate feelings of grief and sorrow, thereby "opening the way to a deeper struggle with God."[4] Worship should not be confined to praise and thanksgiving, since a necessary dimension of worship is the acknowledgment that so much of human experience highlights our vulnerability and passivity before the world; we are simply not in full control of our lives, and bad things happen to good people while the wicked prosper through their evil deeds.

Despite the current recognition by Old Testament scholars of the essential role that lament plays in the faith and liturgy of Israel, Brueggemann is concerned that the use of the lament speech form is largely lost in contemporary church usage, and he attributes this fact to the tendency among Christians to disregard the laments on theological grounds, believing they are "superseded by some christological claim."[5] If we are to recover the Jewish practice of lament as a vital and essential part of Christian faith, worship, and theology, then it is important to begin by acknowledging that the lament has a history; that is, it has a historical antecedent as well as a subsequent development.[6] Evidence of the lament as a concrete expression of the real experiences of Israel's life is not confined to the Psalter but is found in the historical narratives, in the prophetic writings, and in some deuterocanonical texts.[7] The lament attests to the fact that "faith and worship deal with and are shaped by life as it comes to us."[8] By integrating the lament speech form into the fabric of Israel's long history of striving with God, it serves as an effective corrective to the type of religious faith that wishes to withdraw from the present struggles of life and lose itself in the detached unreal world of heavenly things. Prayers of protest and lament are uttered in response to the concrete reality of this life, thus they give witness to a robust form of

---

4. Pleins, *Psalms*, 27.

5. Brueggemann, "Shape for Old Testament Theology, II," 401.

6. Westermann, *Praise and Lament*, 168. The rediscovery of lament as a pattern for Christian prayer, worship, and ministries of care has been under way since the 1990s. The rediscovery, however, has occurred primarily within Protestant scholarship and has not received much attention in the Catholic and Orthodox literature.

7. Examples from the deuterocanonical writings include Tob 3:15 and 1 Macc 1:7. Another intertestamental text worth mentioning is 4 Ezra 5:35 (cf. Westermann, *Praise and Lament*, 195n81).

8. Brueggemann, *Psalms and the Life*, 67.

faith that is tested and radicalized in the context of the rough-and-tumble of historical existence with all its ambiguity, injustice, anguish, and death.

It will be shown in this chapter that a major feature of the prayer of lament is that the exchange between the lamenter and the Lord is portrayed as truly dialogical, which allows for newness in the relationship and for the possibility that the Lord can work good out of a bad situation.[9] The lament speech form witnesses to the fundamental conviction that the Lord is "sovereign over the present situation and can work good out of it."[10] At times, however, as will become apparent in this chapter, God's response in bringing good out of a situation of distress is not forthcoming, so that faith is understood as holding to God against God. This more testing form of keeping Torah gives rise to an eschatological approach to the life of faith, where the righteous strive towards a divinely appointed time of final salvation. It is of the utmost importance that the faithful in the throes of suffering and death be allowed to open their hearts in prayers of lament and take initiative with God, for only in this manner can real-life situations be acknowledged and the lament function as a genuine liturgical and theological activity of mourning before God, whose veil of silence often seems impenetrable.

The first part of this chapter will offer a discussion of prayers of lament to be found in Jewish Scripture, from which it will become clear that the practice of lament has a history that well precedes the confessions of Jeremiah, the psalms of lament, and the book of Job. With Moses and the Exodus tradition we already clearly see the lament form of speech in operation as the people experience much hardship and deep uncertainty about their future in the wilderness sojourn. The lament-deliverance structure that is found in the Exodus tradition continues in the book of Joshua and in the history of the tribal period, when the people are no more secure in the land promised to Abraham than in the wilderness of Sinai, since hostile enemies surround them and seek to destroy them. What will become apparent in these historical narratives is the manner in which the Lord listens to the human pleas for divine help and justice

---

9. Roland Murphy, it is worth noting, makes a distinction between "lamentation" and "lament." Lamentation looks backward to an irreversible catastrophe—death of a person, destruction of an area and/or its sanctuary—while lament looks forward to deliverance from a threatening and distressing situation (*Psalms, Job,* 16–17, 41). The lament, then, is an appeal to the Lord's compassion to intervene and transform a desperate situation.

10. Brueggemann, *Psalms and the Life,* 77.

and responds accordingly, so what is in view is a truly dialogical, reciprocal, and dynamic covenant relationship, which culminates in the Davidic
covenant. The discussion will then shift to the confessions of Jeremiah
who brings the lament tradition to intense, personal speech. His prophetic witness brings something new to the lament tradition, for through
his suffering Jeremiah must learn that he embodies the divine pathos
before a rebellious people. The discussion will then turn to the book of
Job, where the lament tradition reaches its apex, and the shortcomings
of the "common theology" of deeds and consequences is exposed. Job
comes to accept that suffering cannot be explained away and has a mysterious dimension, for suffering introduces the just one to a relationship
of personal trust and humble surrender to God, whose sovereignty and
wisdom are simply inscrutable. The book of Job is a prime example of the
wisdom motif of the suffering just (*passio justi*), which is given abundant
voice in the psalms of lament. The latter will be briefly discussed, with
a specific focus on the basic structure of the lament psalms. From the
composite structure of the psalm, it will become clear how the lament
speech form witnesses to a robust faith and functions as the mode by
which hope and trust in the Lord is kept alive.

The second part of the chapter offers a discussion of the all-
important concept of the divine pathos, with special attention given to
the pathos of God's suffering and lament in relation to Israel and the
world. The concept of divine pathos will be discussed from the various
perspectives of three eminent biblical scholars: Abraham Heschel, Walter
Brueggemann, and Terence Fretheim. The discussion will shed light on
the manner in which the notion of divine lament serves to enrich the
picture of a truly reciprocal divine-human relationship, inasmuch as God
enters "into the fray" and suffers with the people so as to make a way into
the future for them. It will become apparent that the concept of divine
pathos is not a psychological category—anthropomorphic metaphors are
not being employed—but rather a theological category that underscores
God's personal relatedness to and ultimate concern for Israel and the
world. The depiction of God in the Hebrew Bible as grieving, suffering,
and lamenting the state of the divine-human relationship implies that
God internalizes the people's rejection of him as Lord and chooses to
suffer for the sake of his unwavering commitment to the covenant and to
bringing to fruition the divine intention for the whole of creation. In this
perspective there is divine anger that leads to judgment, but judgment
takes on an instrumental role as a necessary prerequisite for God's new

redemptive activity: that is, God works good out of a situation of sin and evil, desolation and death. The final, third part of the chapter will offer some important concluding remarks on the theological category of the divine pathos, which will be especially pertinent to the interpretation of Jesus's cry offered in chapter 3 of this study.

Human Lament: Posture of the Faithful before God

The practice of lament as a speech form is not confined to the psalms of the Psalter but can be traced to prayers embedded in early narrative texts that give voice to hardships experienced by the people.[11] The lament is encountered as early as the Exodus tradition. Exodus 2–15 is presented as a lament form: "The people of Israel groaned under their bondage, and cried out for help, and their cry under bondage came up to God" (Exod 2:23). God then says: "I have seen the affliction of my people who are in Egypt, and have heard their cry . . . I know their sufferings, and I have come down to deliver them" (Exod 3:7–8).[12] God commissions Moses to go to Pharaoh, with the task of liberating the Israelites, but instead of improving their plight the situation is worsened, which leads Moses to complain: "O Lord, why have you done evil to this people? Why did you ever send me? For since I came to Pharaoh to speak in your name, he has done evil to this people, and you have not delivered your people at all" (Exod 5:22–23). When God responds to Moses's call for divine justice by performing the miraculous act of deliverance out of Egypt, Moses and the people sing a song of thanksgiving: "I will sing to the Lord, for he has triumphed gloriously" (Exod 15:1).

The Exodus story of God's turning toward an enslaved people in great distress is quickly supplemented by the narrative of Israel's murmurings of discontent in the wilderness of Sinai. The people murmur

---

11. Claus Westermann highlights the laments of Rebekah (Gen 25:22), Moses (Exod 5:22–23), Joshua (Josh 7:7–9), Samson (Judg 15:18), and Jeremiah (Jer 20:18), as examples of complaints against God that are recorded in early narrative texts (*Praise and Lament*, 195–201). Walter Brueggemann also underscores the lament-deliverance structure that is characteristic of Israel's faith, which is found in narrative texts (*Psalms and the Life*, 77–82).

12. It is worth underlining how in the Exodus narrative we encounter the Hebrew notion that God suffers with his people. God "hears," "sees," and "knows" the suffering of the people. The Hebrew God is not a God who sees the suffering from the outside; rather, God sees the suffering from the inside, God is caught up in the distressing situation and makes it his own, and God is moved to take action.

against Moses: "Would that we had died by the hand of the Lord in the land of Egypt, when we sat by the fleshpots and ate bread to the full; for you have brought us out into this wilderness to kill this whole assembly with hunger" (Exod 16:3). The Lord responds to Moses that he has heard the murmurings of the people and instructs Moses to say to the people that the Lord will send quails in the evenings and manna in the mornings. In the following chapter the people again murmur against Moses: "Why did you bring us up out of Egypt, to kill us and our children and our cattle with thirst?" (Exod 17:3). The people find fault with Moses because they have no water to drink, and they put the Lord to the proof by saying, "Is the Lord among us or not?" (Exod 17:7). Not only do the people put the Lord to the proof, they also blatantly turn their backs on him by worshipping the golden calf (Exod 32). The wrath of the Lord burns hot against his people and threatens to consume them; they clearly deserve to be judged and the God of the covenant would be justified in executing judgment. But Moses intervenes and beseeches the Lord: "Why should the Egyptians say, 'With evil intent did he bring them forth, to slay them in the mountains, and to consume them from the face of the earth'?" (Exod 32:12). So that the Egyptians will not think that God is acting for evil rather than good, Moses petitions: "Turn from thy fierce wrath, and repent of this evil against thy people. Remember Abraham, Isaac, and Israel, thy servants, to whom thou didst swear by thine own self, and didst say to them, 'I will multiply your descendants as the stars of heaven, and all this land that I have promised I will give to your descendants, and they shall inherit it forever'" (Exod 32:12–13). The Lord heeds Moses's pleadings and is persuaded to repent of the evil he intended to inflict on his people. If God were to carry through with his evil intent against the people, this would amount to a divine failure to complete the goal of the Exodus from Egypt, and, moreover, it would violate the covenant and undermine trust in the divine character.

Moses's anger against his people, like that of the Lord, also burns hot, which motivates him to destroy the golden calf, and then he turns to the Lord and says: "Alas, this people have sinned a great sin; they have made for themselves gods of gold. But now, if thou wilt forgive their sin—and if not, blot me, I pray thee, out of thy book which thou hast written" (Exod 32:31–32). Moses takes the view that the people should be forgiven for their serious transgression and given the opportunity to turn their hearts back to the Lord; if not, he would prefer to take his leave from the divine-human history of covenant relationship. The wilderness sojourn is truly a difficult and testing time for the Israelites, and Moses expresses displeasure with God and protests that the burden placed on him as the leader of the people is "too heavy" (Num 11:15). Moses feels as if the burden of responsibility for all the people has been placed on him, and he protests to the Lord: "Did I conceive all this people? Did I bring them forth, that thou shouldst say to me, 'Carry them in your bosom, as a nurse carries the suckling child, to the land which thou didst swear to give their fathers'" (Num 11:12). The accusation in Moses's question has a double edge.[13] First, Moses charges that the responsibility for the people properly belongs to God, who gave them birth. Second, while Moses does bear some responsibility as God's designated leader of the people, his abilities are limited, hence he alone cannot carry the people. The "most extraordinary thing" about these narrative texts is that every time Moses is faced with a crisis and honestly addresses God and inter-cedes for the people, it is Moses, not God, who prevails in the dialogue.[14] The protests raised by Moses concerning divine justice are not simply heard by God, but God is truly affected by the complaints and responds accordingly. What Moses has to contribute to the relationship counts with this God. "God has so entered into relationship with him that God is not the only one who has something important to say."[15] With the call of Moses, the Exodus event, and the sojourn in Sinai, it is apparent that God has not chosen the way of *radical* transcendence in his relationship to the creation; instead, God has chosen to relate to the creation in terms of an "immanental involvement."[16] God has entered into the very life of the world and is fully engaged there so as to bring to fruition the divine purposes for Israel and the world. The conversational prayers of Moses

---

13. Balentine, *Prayer in Hebrew Bible*, 127.

14. Brueggemann, "Shape for Old Testament Theology, II," 403.

15. Fretheim, "Suffering God," 113.

16. Fretheim, "Suffering God," 108. The primary "form" in which God engages with the world is in the human form of the theophany—from the call of Moses (Exod 3:1–6), to the crossing of the Red Sea (Exod 14:19), to Sinai (Exod 24:9–11). Fretheim says that this action bespeaks God's: (1) sharing in the human condition; (2) willing-ness to take on a non-divine form and experience what that entails; (3) vulnerability, risking a response in the human encounter that is other than faith and obedience. In all this God does not, though, give up sovereignty. Fretheim argues that in Exodus, God's sovereignty is qualified by God's suffering, and God's suffering is qualified by God's sovereignty. His key proposition is stated thus: "*Suffering and sovereignty are internally related to one another in God, such that the sovereign God is always suffering and the suffering God is always sovereign*" ("Suffering God," 116; emphasis original).

challenge the "party-line" view of divine anger and divinely ordained evil as the just reaction of a just God to the sinfulness of the people.[17]

The protests and complaints do not end once the wilderness sojourn is over and the people finally enter the land of promise. The lament-deliverance structure is quite apparent in the book of Joshua and in the history of the tribal period and the transition to the monarchy, which is narrated in the books of Judges and Samuel. Joshua's honest and frank approach to God is evident when he says: "Alas, O Lord God, why hast thou brought this people over the Jordan at all, to give us into the hands of the Amorites, to destroy us?" (Josh 7:7). God responds that the people have sinned (Josh 7:11), they have transgressed his covenant, and the remainder of the divine response gives instructions for removing the sin. When the people follow the divine instructions, the result is that "the Lord turned from his burning anger" (Josh 7:26). While Joshua's prayer upholds the traditional view that relates suffering to sin, nonetheless the prayer does boldly question the divine character. The pattern of the Israelites "crying out" to the Lord, and the Lord "delivering" them from the hand of their enemies, is especially pervasive in Judges and links the judges to the Exodus event. The use of the structure is especially evident, for example, in the following text: "Whenever the Lord raised up judges for them, the Lord was with the judge, and he saved them from the hand of their enemies all the days of the judge; for the Lord was moved to pity by their groaning because of those who afflicted and oppressed them" (Judg 2:18; also Judg 10:11–12; 1 Sam 7:9). As the narrative develops it becomes clear that "the entire judges period is viewed as a time of distress."[18] The climactic point of this distressing period is the establishment of a king who is presented as the divine response to the lament: "By the hand of my servant David I will save my people Israel from the hand of the Philistines, and from the hand of all their enemies" (2 Sam 3:18). The Lord makes a covenant with David (2 Sam 7:5–17), and by virtue of

17. Balentine, *Prayer in Hebrew Bible*, 128. Moses's pleadings for divine justice reflect the position taken by Abraham who similarly raises questions to God with respect to the divine intention to destroy the wicked city of Sodom (Gen 18:16–33). By virtue of Abraham's pleadings, God turns his focus from the wicked to the righteous and embraces a new notion of what it means for the Judge of all the earth to do justice. Although Sodom is still judged, Abraham has had his say and his pleadings are not ignored: "God remembered Abraham, and sent Lot out of the midst of the overthrow, when he overthrew the cities in which Lot dwelt" (Gen 19:29). God not only receives Abraham's prayer but also heeds it.

18. Brueggemann, *Psalms and the Life*, 79.

this new covenant the people are assured of the enduring character of the Davidic kingdom in the land.

The prayers of Abraham, Moses, and Joshua, which are pleadings for divine justice, are an important dissenting voice to the orthodox teaching concerning the acceptable boundaries of the divine-human relationship. The prayers of these important figures in Jewish history directly challenge God to rethink the issue of divine integrity and to act differently to how God intended to act. "Where else in the Hebrew Bible does one find such bold presentations of individuals standing head-to-head with God, challenging, interrogating, petitioning, and being taken seriously? They not only assault God; at times they even prevail."[19] In these prayers humanity's status is lifted to a new level, for to pray is to become personally engaged with God, to become a partner with God. These bold prayers for divine justice also bring into sharp focus the truly personal dimension of the divine life, which challenges any view of God's activity in the world as "a kind of production, a mere drawing out of what God has always determined."[20] Instead of an unyielding God who imposes monologue without any dialogue, the bold prayers of Moses, Abraham, and Joshua assume that God listens to the human pleas for justice and, moreover, responds freely to the historical predicaments in which the supplicant is situated. While the "embrace of pain" is a minority voice over against the majority voice of the Deuteronomistic tradition, it is nonetheless a crucial voice in the theology of the Hebrew Bible, as Walter Brueggemann has argued.[21] The minority voice serves as a vehicle of theodicy inasmuch as it depicts the divine-human relationship in terms of *genuine reciprocity*. Without this reciprocity at the heart of the relationship between the living God and his people, we would be confronted by "an intolerable inexorability that imposes monologue without dialogue, revelation without response, destiny and fate without hope."[22]

---

19. Balentine, *Prayer in Hebrew Bible*, 142.

20. Fretheim, *Suffering of God*, 44.

21. Brueggemann, "Shape for Old Testament Theology, II," 399. The linking of pain and suffering to human sinfulness, which is perhaps the majority voice in the Hebrew Bible, is the controlling idea in the Deuteronomistic tradition. This major voice espouses a type of contractual theology where suffering is equated with sinfulness and prosperity with righteousness. Prayers of penitence (e.g., Dan 9, Ezra 9, Neh 9) reflect this contractual theology.

22. Balentine, *Prayer in Hebrew Bible*, 145.

Dialogue, response, and hope are integral to a conception of the divine-human relationship in personal and dynamic terms. In the Hebrew Bible the covenant relationship is summed up in the divine words, "I will be their God, and they will be my people" (Jer 31:33). This prophetic text is set within the context of the "new covenant" that God will make with his people. The use of the future tense serves to underscore Israel's sinfulness and rebellion against God, which proves to be a veritable obstacle to making Israel a holy people and a light to the nations. With the writings of the prophets there is a development of thought concerning the function of prayers of protest addressed to God out of a situation of anguish and distress. The personal dimension of the divine life, as well as the reciprocity of the God-human relationship, are still very much in view; but what is new is that the prophet's life of suffering before his people is portrayed as an embodiment of the divine pathos. We will now turn to discuss how the prophet not merely knows about God's attachment to Israel but experiences it intimately from within, so that with the laments of the prophet the focus shifts to the way of suffering as a sign of divine election and closeness to God.

The bold confrontations with God in the prayers of Abraham, Moses, and Joshua are by no means the only witnesses to Israel's tradition of raising protests and complaints to God when faced with disturbing and distressing situations that call into question God's justice. In Jeremiah, Habakkuk, Job, and the Psalter, we find a virtual reservoir of lament literature. With the prophet Jeremiah who lived throughout the catastrophic events that culminated in the fall of Jerusalem in 587 BCE, the lament is heightened to intense personal speech by raising "the issue of divine integrity within the context of a *via dolorosa* [way of suffering]."[23] In the early chapters of Jeremiah we find instances where God laments his rejection by the people and speaks judgments against a sinful Israel (Jer 1:16, 2:1–13, 4:12). Yet when we come to the "confessions" of Jeremiah embedded within chapters 11–20,[24] we find the tables are turned, for the prophet says that he will speak judgments upon God. Jeremiah frames his principal lament with the timeless question: "Why does the way of

23. Crenshaw, "Human Dilemma," 242.

24. Jer 11:18–23; 12:1–6; 15:10–21; 17:14–18; 18:18–23; 20:7–13, 14–18. The short book known as the Lamentations of Jeremiah will not be discussed because it is difficult to credit Jeremiah with the book, and, moreover, the Hebrew Bible groups the short book with the Writings. The Lamentations of Jeremiah are chanted by Jews on the great fast that commemorates the destruction of the temple.

the wicked prosper? Why do all who are treacherous thrive?" (12:1). He also asks: "How long will the land mourn?" (12:4). God stands accused by Jeremiah who "insists on his right to hold God accountable to the same standards of conduct that apply to Israel."[25] What is new in the confessions of Jeremiah is that he is not speaking about God but about himself, about the emotional conflicts he experiences that arise precisely out of his prophetic witness: "they spring directly *ex munere prophetico*."[26] The deep sufferings expressed in the confessions of Jeremiah have to do with the prophetic call and are not to be regarded as general religious expressions that are found side by side with genuine prophetic testimonies. In the case of Jeremiah something new in God's working through the prophet presents itself, for the prophet does not merely proclaim the word of God to a wayward people; rather, Jeremiah's entire life lived in a state of suffering witnesses to the sovereign God. Jeremiah therefore marks "the opening of a new chapter in the stream of prophecy leading to Jesus Christ."[27]

The justice of God is seriously called into question by Jeremiah. Is God reliable? Can God be trusted? So distressing is the situation that the prophet finds himself in—he is like "a gentle lamb led to the slaughter" (11:19) by those who plot his demise—that he is led to utter a profound lament for having to suffer insult on God's account: "Thy words were found, and I ate them, and thy words became to me a joy and the delight of my heart; for I am called by thy name . . . I sat alone, because thy hand was upon me, for thou hadst filled me with indignation" (15:16–17). Jeremiah feels deeply God's indignation towards the people who "stubbornly follow their own heart and have gone after other gods to serve" (13:10). The preaching of a harsh word of impending doom to his people leads Jeremiah to experience much suffering and anguish. "The prophet must learn to feel for himself God's intimate attachment to Israel; he must not only know about it, but experience it from within."[28] The pathos of anger (i.e., righteous indignation) does not stand alone, though, but is intimately intertwined with the emotion of love for his people, which exasperates Jeremiah's state of suffering and anguish. "In his confessions Jeremiah allows us to obtain a glimpse of the fervor of love as well as of

---

25. Balentine, *Prayer in Hebrew Bible*, 153.

26. Von Rad, "Confessions of Jeremiah," 97.

27. Von Rad, "Confessions of Jeremiah," 98.

28. Heschel, *Prophets*, 117.

the raging of anger against the people."[29] Once the nexus between prophetic emotion and divine pathos is appreciated, it is possible to gain
insight into the conflicting emotions of Jeremiah. The words of the Lord
became "a joy and the delight" (15:16) of Jeremiah's heart, but in taking
up his prophetic mission these congenial emotions give way to suffering emotions, to the complaints and laments of having to stand alone
before a wicked people to endure their insults and barbs: "Why is my
pain unceasing, my wound incurable, refusing to be healed?" (15:18)

In his lamentable predicament, Jeremiah experiences no divine
move toward healing his pain, hence he boldly raises the specter of a
divine deception: "Wilt thou be to me like a deceitful brook, like waters
that fail?" (15:18). The response of God to the claim of deception follows
immediately, and it comes as a divine rebuke. *If* Jeremiah returns, and *if*
he utters "what is precious and not what is worthless" (15:19), *then* he
may continue to exercise his prophetic office. The prophet must purge
himself of "worthless" talk directed to God and utter only the "precious"
divine word that is given him. He is required to understand that to be
a mouthpiece of God is a cherished privilege, even if it involves suffering, pain, and sorrow.[30] Jeremiah is given the reassurance that God will
deliver him "out of the hand of the wicked" and redeem him "from the
grasp of the ruthless" (15:21), but this promise is conditional upon the
prophet's repentance. Despite the divine rebuke and call to repentance,
Jeremiah persists with his complaints, he continues to question divine
justice and to accuse God of deception: "Be not a terror to me" (17:17);
"Is evil a recompense for good?" (18:20). The prophet is simply unwilling
to silence his voice in the divine-human dialogue, in the hope of receiving some relief from his anguish and suffering.

However, in the prayers succeeding 15:10–21 there is no longer a
divine response. Jeremiah continues to prosecute his case but God falls
silent, hence the prayers become distinctly one-sided and more intensely
poignant. Despite God's silence the prophet remains committed to the
cause of God, he continues to regard God as his refuge, and he does not
give up on the expectation of a divine deliverance (20:11–13) characteristic of the psalms of lament. Yet the confessions of Jeremiah culminate
in the prophet's profound self-lament which highlights the state of suffering arising from his prophetic call and witness: "Cursed be the day

29. Heschel, *Prophets*, 119.
30. Balentine, *Prayer in Hebrew Bible*, 160.

on which I was born. . . . Why did I come forth from the womb to see toil and sorrow, and spend my days in shame?" (20:14–18). In these culminating verses of Jeremiah's confessions, it is clear that the prophet's quest for divine justice does not receive a satisfactory response. In one of the divine responses to an earlier prayer of Jeremiah, God says that he will have to be prepared to undergo more suffering and affliction (12:5–6), and this reaches its zenith with the prophet cursing the day on which he was born, all of which compels him to rethink traditional theology and "hammer out a new theology."[31] In Jeremiah's confessions we are presented with a veritable collision between faith commitments and their negation, yet "neither achieves ascendancy over the other."[32] In spite of his profound self-lament of coming forth from the womb to see only toil and sorrow, Jeremiah persists in his quest for divine justice, so that he continues to hold to God against God. His prophetic condition is best thought of, according to Abraham Heschel, as "*a state of suffering in sympathy with the divine pathos.*"[33] As God's representative before a sinful people, Jeremiah's suffering reflects the way in which God suffers because of Israel's failure to keep Torah. The prophet's only consolation, which is not found in his confessions but comes much later in the book of Jeremiah, is the divine word addressed to him concerning the coming days when God will give his people a new heart and make a "new covenant" (Jer 31:31) with the house of Israel and the house of Judah. The Lord says to Jeremiah: "I will put my law within them, and I will write it upon their hearts; and I will be their God, and they shall be my people" (Jer 31:33).

The prophet Habakkuk is yet another example of the possibility of embracing a radical dialogue with God. Habakkuk preached after the battle of Carchemish in 605 BCE, where Josiah was killed and Nebuchadnezzar was established as the new world ruler. Jeremiah frames his principal lament with the timeless question, "Why does the way of the wicked prosper?" (Jer 12:1), and Habakkuk also challenges the traditional view of God's justice in history, which is contradicted by the death of Josiah who instigated the period of reforms and covenant renewal. The book of Habakkuk contains two prayers of lament (1:2–4, 12–17), each of which is followed by a divine response (1:5–11, 2:2–4). In the

31. Balentine, *Prayer in Hebrew Bible*, 155.

32. Balentine, *Prayer in Hebrew Bible*, 167.

33. Heschel, *Prophets*, 118; emphasis added. The meaning of this statement will become clearer in the discussion below on the divine pathos.

first lament, Habakkuk asks "how long" must he cry for help (1:2), and "why" does God make him see wrongs and look upon trouble (1:3). The suffering of the righteous at the hands of the wicked (i.e., the Assyrians) is simply a perversion of justice, which results in the weakening of the law (1:4). The prophet complains that the law with its promises of reward for faithfulness is ineffective, and he holds God responsible for the misery and suffering that he has to bear.

The divine response follows the prophet's very serious complaint concerning the paralysis of the law. God announces the coming of the Chaldeans as an instrument for ending the oppression by the Assyrians, but God's proposed solution serves only to "heighten Habakkuk's lament rather than resolve it."[34] Why should a God of holiness (1:12), with eyes too pure to behold evil (1:13), use the savage and terribly violent Chaldeans (1:5–11) to wreak his revenge? The prophet has complained about violence and injustice only to be told that violence is about to increase considerably in order to remedy the situation. Thus follows the second lament (1:12–17) in which Habakkuk complains that God has made human beings "like the fish of the sea" (1:14); they are mere victims of plunder for the fisherman's net. This situation compels the prophet to ask whether the fisherman will continue his merciless plundering "forever" (1:17). Once the heightening of Habakkuk's complaint is complete, the divine response comes in 2:2–4. God avoids altogether the charge of culpability for human suffering and focuses instead on the need for faithfulness in such a situation. The appointed time may "seem slow" in coming, but it will come, "it will not lie" (2:3). The conduct of the righteous is defined by two activities: they are to "wait" (2:3) for the fulfillment of the divine promises, and they are to "run" (2:2) towards this deliverance from their suffering. The righteous are required to "live" (2:4) by God's faithfulness, by the assurance of God's coming salvation, when the wicked will be crushed. The series of five woe oracles against the Chaldeans (2:5–20) serves to underscore this reassurance, and the book ends with Habakkuk's psalm of thanksgiving (3:1–19) for God's ultimate defeat of the wicked. The "why" question does not receive an answer from God, and to the "how long" question Habakkuk is told that he will have to wait expectantly and run assuredly towards the ultimate deliverance. The

---

34. Balentine, *Prayer in Hebrew Bible*, 185.

prophet comes to accept his life as an "eschatological existence,"[35] that is, an existence in time towards a divinely appointed time.

The principal laments of both Jeremiah and Habakkuk relate to the timeless "Why, Lord?" and "How long, Lord?" questions that spring forth from the state of suffering of the righteous. Jeremiah, unlike Moses, Abraham, and Joshua, is rebuked by God for his complaints and protests and is told that his proper vocation is to utter the precious divine word that is given him. The intense personal speech of Jeremiah leaves the reader in no doubt about the extent of his lamentable suffering in the face of much wickedness, yet God responds that Jeremiah's state of suffering pertains to the cherished privilege of being a mouthpiece of the Lord. When Jeremiah persists with his protests and complaints, God then falls silent, and it is precisely at this point that Jeremiah's state of suffering is sympathetically united with the divine pathos. In both Jeremiah and Habakkuk an assurance is given that the day of salvation is coming when the wicked will be crushed, and in the meantime the righteous are to live by God's faithfulness and to wait expectantly for the ultimate deliverance from their suffering and affliction. In the prophetic writings examined, the prophet's existence emerges as a truly eschatological existence towards a divinely appointed time of newness and transformation.

The bold pleadings for divine justice to be found in the historical writings arise out of the multitude of problems encountered by Israel in its infancy as it journeys out of Egypt, through the wilderness of Sinai towards the land of promise, and finally gets established in the land with the advent of the Davidic kingdom. But once Israel is established in the land, new problems emerge, paramount among which is the failure to keep Torah as Israel is seduced by the cultures of the surrounding pagan nations. The prophets preach the word of the Lord in a context of rebellion by the people, so that their laments are born out of affliction for pronouncing a word of impending divine judgment against their own people. The word of impending judgment is meant to stir the people to repentance, but the ineffectiveness of the prophetic word means that doom inevitably awaits the people, which causes further suffering for the prophet. The theme of the suffering righteous, which raises the lament to a heightened level of personal speech addressed to God, is further developed in the wisdom writings, to which we now turn.

35. Janzen, "Eschatological Symbol"; as cited in Balentine, *Prayer in Hebrew Bible*, 188.

The palpable distress expressed in the confessions of Jeremiah reaches its apex with the book of Job.[36] The terrible sufferings of the upright Job compel him to acknowledge that the wicked prosper in their ungodliness, while the righteous suffer and are reduced to a state of helplessness. Job holds God responsible for life's misery and resolutely defies his three friends who regard God's justice as beyond question. Like Jeremiah, Job complains, "Why did you bring me forth from the womb?" (10:18), and he joins Jeremiah in calling God to court (31:35–37). Job demands a lawsuit with God and believes that God cannot justly deny his petition. Thus, the stage is set for God's response, which comes in two lengthy speeches (38:1—40:2; 40:6—41:34). Job has expected answers from God, but instead he receives a multitude of questions, which serve to remind him that he is but a creature whose finite standards are ineffective for judging the creator: "Who is this that darkens counsel by words without knowledge? Gird up your loins like a man, I will question you, and you shall declare to me" (38:2–3).

In the first divine speech the questions concern knowledge and action; "they inquire about Job's qualifications to enter the ranks of the gods, for the knowledge they solicit and the performances they ask about are properties of deity."[37] God is the master craftsman whose handiwork, the cosmos, elicits songs of praise from the celestial beings. The image is one of a well-ordered universe, yet there is resistance to order. Cosmic enemies are real, "but even the most feared personifications (chaos, death, or sea) have limited powers."[38] Job comes to realize that he has taken on more than he ever imagined: "Behold, I am of small account; what shall I answer you?" (40:4). This response is not what the reader expects to hear from Job, who has demanded a lawsuit with the supreme judge. Job continues to profess his innocence, but he is silenced by the series of divine questions that effectively render his own questions irrelevant, and he comes to acknowledge his insignificance in the grand scheme of things.

In the second divine speech God acknowledges that the real issue for Job is the question of justice, not power: "Will you even put me in the wrong? Will you condemn me that you may be justified?" (40:8) God's answer to his own question comes by way of describing the imposing pride of the powerful beasts Behemoth and Leviathan. Job is told that he

36. The book of Job is later than Jeremiah, in postexilic times. The likeliest date is the beginning of the fifth century BCE.

37. Crenshaw, *Reading Job*, 149.

38. Crenshaw, *Reading Job*, 150.

should direct his anger away from God and focus instead on subduing the proud (i.e., the wicked). If Job finds this task of subduing proud humans beyond his abilities, then how will he humble the great Behemoth and powerful Leviathan? Job is therefore led to exclaim: "I know that you can do all things, and that no purpose of yours can be thwarted. . . . I have uttered what I did not understand, things too wonderful for me, which I did not know" (42:2–4). With regard to the question of justice, Job seeks "to rearrange the way the world operates";[39] he thinks he knows exactly how God should run the world and protests that God should have treated *him* better. Job ends up, though, being repentant and conceding that he is no match for the forces of chaos represented by Behemoth (40:15–24) and Leviathan (41:1–34), and only "the arm of God" (40:9) can bring the proud low and tread down the wicked.

The divine speeches in response to Job's plea for vindication come in the form of a divine rebuke. The effect of this rebuke is to silence Job who gives up his role as a litigant in the case against God and comes to admit that he is of small account while God is sovereign and human suffering has a mysterious dimension. "It is of the essence of its message that Job found God *in* his suffering."[40] Job had sought to justify himself by condemning God, but his attitude is converted within a theophany into "a relationship of personal trust and surrender."[41] Job is humbled and repentant before God and enters into *a new consciousness of relationship with God*. Before the divine speeches Job's cry for vindication is based upon a conception of God received from the tradition—"I had heard of you by the hearing of the ear" (42:5)—but once Job is silenced and humbled by God's response, he is now related to God himself in an act of personal faith—"now my eye sees you" (42:5). Job has "become a man of broken and contrite heart, penitent and self-loathing, who, because he knows himself to have nothing and deserve nothing, can most readily cast himself upon God, whose wisdom and omnipotence no longer crush but uphold and uplift him."[42]

Despite Job's repentance before God, he makes no admission of wrongdoing as his friends have consistently urged him to do and maintains his integrity right to the end. Job rejects a world where suffering is

---

39. Crenshaw, *Reading Job*, 154.

40. Rowley, *Job*, 20.

41. Anderson, *Living World*, 559.

42. Peake, "Job," 108.

linked to guilt. With respect to God's own assessment of Job, we read in the beginning of the book: "There is no one like him on earth, a blameless and upright man who fears God and turns away from evil" (1:8). In the epilogue (42:7–14) God speaks a further word concerning Job's integrity and uprightness when he says to Eliphaz: "My wrath is kindled against you and against your two friends; for you have not spoken of me what is right, as my servant Job has" (42:7). This verdict in Job's favor indicates that God values Job's "courage to stand in the face of the Holy One and force the issues in new directions."[43] Because it is Job and not the friends who spoke what was "right," God then says to Eliphaz to go to Job, who will pray for him, and God will accept the prayer of his servant Job so as "not to deal with you according to your folly" (42:8). This folly stems from the common theology of deeds and consequences, which is a barrier to genuine faith because it is incapable of conceiving of the idea of "disinterested righteousness."[44] In the end Job is granted the power of intercession for his friends, which is to say that his prayers, not those of his friends, penetrate the heavens.[45] This is certainly a form of vindication by God, but not the kind that Job had earlier pleaded for. The one who dared to speak to God from the depths of his heart, the one who pushed the boundaries of what tradition had determined as the acceptable response to God, the one who pushed faith beyond simple obedience, "is now invited into intimacy with the Almighty."[46] Through his suffering, Job is granted an encounter with God and comes to experience personal communion with the Almighty. The lesson he learns is that he must deepen his trust in God even though he does not understand the reasons for God's action. It was trust in God that initially enabled Job to dare a lawsuit with God, and after he sees the Lord with his own eyes (42:5) and comes to acknowledge the limits of his human understanding (42:2–3), Job regains his trust in God and continues his journey of faith into the future.[47]

---

43. Brueggemann, "Shape for Old Testament Theology, II," 405.

44. Crenshaw, *Reading Job*, 40.

45. Balentine, *Prayer in Hebrew Bible* 182.

46. Balentine, *Prayer in Hebrew Bible*, 182.

47. Ricoeur interprets Job's answer to the Lord—"Therefore I despise myself, and repent in dust and ashes" (42:6)—as meaning that Job repents the complaint itself, he regrets his lament (*Evil*, 44). But this interpretation is not supported by the preceding verses, which indicate that Job regrets his words because he has now seen the Lord with his own eyes. It is by voicing his lament that the possibility of a dialogue with

In the end, Job still does not know why he suffers, he still does not understand the ways of God, but his ignorance no longer torments him; he has no desire to know, for now he has entered into an existential realm where such problems no longer perturb his soul. Since the process of lament results in the recognition of Job's own ignorance, this recognition changes the criteria for assessing his plight, so that the outcome becomes part of an unfinished project. "Lament cannot be counteracted by a higher knowledge, as knowledge of God only comes about through interaction with God, the outcome of which cannot be anticipated."[48] In the beginning of the book, Job rejects his foolish wife's call to curse God and instead responds to her by saying: "Shall we receive good at the hand of God, and shall we not receive evil?" (2:10). This fundamental attitude of Job is still present at the end of the book, where it has been reinforced as well as transformed by God's lengthy responses to Job. To keep Torah and be upright before God is no longer regarded as a surefire guarantee against suffering. Instead, because it is precisely *in* his suffering that the righteous Job enters into intimate communion with God, suffering introduces the just one to a relationship of personal trust and humble surrender to God, whose sovereignty and wisdom are inscrutable. This new understanding is encapsulated in the wisdom motif of the *passio justi* (the suffering just), which is characteristic of the psalms of lament.

Now that the lament speech form has been discussed through the eyes of Moses, Joshua, the Judges, Jeremiah, Habakkuk, and Job, we can finally turn our attention to the lament speech form in the Psalter.[49] Claus Westermann has observed that only a few lament psalms can be termed "penitential laments" that attribute human suffering to personal sin. Only

---

God is opened up and Job experiences a personal encounter with God, which results in him adopting an attitude of humility and renewed trust in the Lord's sovereignty and wisdom. Since at the end of the book Job comes to love God gratuitously, Ricoeur maintains that lament is superseded by Job's emotional transformation, which leads him to the wisdom of believing in God despite evil and suffering (*Evil*, 68–72). For Ricoeur, the process of emotional metamorphosis initiated by lament means the end of lament itself; he does not have in mind a continuing practice of lament as a form of perseverance in the face of life's sufferings and uncertainties, as an expression of persistent waiting on the journey towards the joyous coming of God's salvation.

48. Welz, "Trust and Lament," 123.

49. The modern study of the psalms, by and large, takes place within the framework established by Hermann Gunkel, who divided the psalms into different literary genres (Gunkel, *Psalms*). Gunkel's student, Sigmund Mowinckel, was not satisfied with literary classification alone and sought to establish the cultic background of the Psalter (Mowinckel, *Psalms in Israel's Worship*).

Pss 38 and 51 have a focus on personal sin, while the other lament psalms make little or no mention of personal guilt.[50] Fredrik Lindström likewise highlights the fact that themes related to sin, guilt, and forgiveness "do not have a prominent place in the psalms."[51] The dominant theme in the lament psalms is the divine absence or hiding, which bears no intrinsic connection with divine judgment as commonly found in the prophetic writings. Something completely different to human repentance is required for the suffering complainant to return to life and to experience once again the gift of the Lord's saving presence. The individual's relationship to God is not constituted by ethical merits but by "the divine saving presence, into which the individual is received."[52] The threat to the sufferer's *conditio humana* as well as to his *conditio divina* comes from the hostile powers allied to death, hence the lament prayers plead for deliverance from the destructive attacks of diabolical force.[53] Traditional philosophical categories such as omnipotence cannot be applied to the God of the psalms, for God's power does not consist of his static omnipotence but of his constant fight to defeat evil. The understanding of divine "power" in the psalms is shaped by the expressive language of prayer and praise: "divine power is revealed in the exaltation of God, in petition to God, in the cry to God, and in the hope for God."[54] The psalmists are not preoccupied with *defending* God and God's rule in the world; rather, they turn to the Lord "from whom one expects everything good and to whom one turns in all tribulations."[55]

When we examine the lament psalms it becomes readily apparent that they display a basic structure made up of five constitutive elements.[56]

50. Westermann, *Praise and Lament*, 273–74.

51. Lindström, "Theodicy in the Psalms," 258.

52. Lindström, "Theodicy in the Psalms," 262. This perspective on human life being constituted by the divine saving presence is an important feature of the temple theology.

53. In the lament psalms, as elsewhere in the Hebrew Bible, evil is frequently seen as having primordial origin. See Levenson, *Creation*; and Novello, "Nature of Evil."

54. Lindström, "Theodicy in the Psalms," 257.

55. Martin Luther. Cited by Lindström, "Theodicy in the Psalms," 257.

56. For the structure of the lament form in the psalms, see Anderson, *Out of the Depths*, 60–62, and Westermann, *Praise and Lament*, 52–81. The basic structure of the lament psalm is a blueprint for constructing lament prayers in relation to particular issues afflicting the faith community. I have provided in a journal article an example of a lament prayer formulated in relation to the scandal of child sexual abuse in the Christian churches (Novello, "Sexual Abuse of Minors," 237–38).

(1) The lament begins with an address to God, either with a poignant cry or a recollection of the saving actions of God in the past. (2) The address is followed by the complaint, which arises out of a situation of distress and anguish caused by a military crisis, threat of enemies, severe drought, prolonged famine, undeserved sickness, injustice, the problem of sin, or fear of death. (3) After the complaint comes a confession of trust. In the midst of a situation of distress and anguish the lamenter recalls God's past saving acts and expresses confidence in God to deliver the afflicted from their anguish. (4) The expression of trust in God is then followed by the petition, which conveys the supplication for divine intervention in the belief that God can work good out of a situation of evil. (5) The psalm concludes with a vow of praise and thanksgiving. In the confidence that God not only hears the lament but is internally related to the suffering of the lamenter and will respond with a new action, the lamenter vows to call upon the name of God and to testify before the community of Israel to God's act of deliverance.

It is of particular importance to stress that the composition is such that the lament never stands by itself, which would amount to a hopeless wallowing in self-pity and misery, and a denial of God's past saving deeds as giving grounds for hope. Instead, like the second movement of a symphony, the initial petition conveyed out of a state of distress moves into the final movement of future praise of God, who alone can vindicate and deliver those who lament from the adverse situation in which they are immersed.[57] No lament directed to God exists "entirely without remembered trust or, finally, expected answer."[58] It is not intended as a reflection on human suffering but as a candid recognition of the *reality* of human anguish and distress, communicated to the Lord in the radical hope that God will respond out of the depths of the divine pathos, so as to make a way into the future for the suffering lamenter. The lament psalm gives heartfelt expression to the existential tension between the experience of human anguish—unrelated to divine judgment and sin—and the yet unfulfilled hope for divine salvation. "It not only articulates that which

---

57. Pss 88 and 39 are exceptions to the rule that the movement of the lament psalm is from desolation to rejoicing, from humiliation to exaltation. See n9 above. These two psalms are hopeless prayers of unrelieved desolation and distress. Roland Murphy has suggested that a distinction be made between a "lamentation" and a "lament"—the former expresses grief over a calamity that is not reversible, whereas the latter is an appeal to God to intervene and change a desperate situation (*Psalms, Job*, 41).

58. Bayer, "Toward Theology of Lament," 216.

is lamentable, but it also invokes that which is desired."[59] What is desired is a reversal from lament to praise, from grief to joy, but since this desire takes the form of hopeful anticipation, the lamenter finds himself in a transitional stage of transformation.

It is important to recognize that some of the psalms of lament, such as Ps 22, reflect a more advanced understanding of the suffering of the faithful. The development of thought consists in interpreting the suffering of those who commit their cause to God as proof of their justice, as the concrete sign of divine election. This mode of thought is especially highlighted in the book of Wisdom (2:10–20). In this deuterocanonical text, the just suffer not *despite* the fact that they are upright and righteous but precisely *because* they bear faithful witness to the living Lord—the sufferings of Jeremiah, discussed above, clearly fit into this category. While the sufferings are still seen as putting the faith of the just ones to the test so that they may be proved to be worthy of God (Wis 3:5), the primary emphasis falls on depicting the suffering endured as proof of their justice: the persecution of the upright by the wicked becomes the sign of divine election. The passage in the book of Wisdom (2:10–20) that purports to be the scornful talk of the impious, and which bears a strong family resemblance to the figure of the suffering servant of God in Isa 52:13—53:12, clearly illustrates this development of thought with respect to the wisdom motif of the *passio justi* (suffering just ones). The impious are irritated by the upright one who is poor and who regards their ways as counterfeit, thus they put the upright one to the test: "For if the upright man is God's son, God will help him, and rescue him from the clutches of his enemies. Let us test him with cruelty and with torture, and thus explore this gentleness of his and put his patience to the test. Let us condemn him to a shameful death, since God will rescue him, or so he claims" (Wis 2:18–20 NJB).[60] In this portrait of the dynamics of cruelty and violence, the just ones are subjected to undeserved suffering at the hands of evildoers purely on the basis of the upright lives they lead. This more developed form of the motif of the suffering just brings to light

59. Welz, "Trust and Lament," 132.

60. This deuterocanonical text represents a principal source of the Gospel narratives of the passion of Jesus. On the cross, Jesus's faith in God is put to a decisive test by his scornful rejectors. The renouncement on Jesus's part of any kind of self-justification before his enemies (Mark 15:29–30), and the acceptance of his unjust suffering unto death without expecting any saving act on the part of God as demanded by those who mock and taunt him (Mark 15:31–32), is thoroughly consistent with the motif of the just one depicted in the book of Wisdom.

the fact that human sin cannot be fathomed by thinking of it simply as weakness in the face of temptation; there is also an element of willfulness in human sin that is often provoked by the mere encounter with virtuous people. The deep-seated character of the reality of sin is manifested in the tendency of humans to treat genuine virtue and goodness as implausible, so that they seek to lay bare the sinfulness of even the just ones by putting them to the test and provoking them to reveal the violence that is in them too. The mystery of sin is nowhere more apparent than in the fact that the human penchant for violence can be elicited by the encounter with virtue.

In this wisdom notion of the just one whose suffering becomes the sign and proof of divine election, both the "existential" view of evil as utterly malevolent and the "instrumental" view of evil as divinely permitted because God works to bring good out of evil, are at play and closely intertwined.[61] For the just one endures suffering at the hands of evildoers who are utterly at enmity with God, yet in this state of suffering the just one represents God before the wicked and trusts that good will triumph over evil, because God is faithful to the covenant promises. In this perspective of the just one who bears faithful witness to God in a world that refuses to allow good to flourish, *suffering takes on a mysterious dimension as vocation of the faithful.* In the book of Job, the upright Job does ultimately come to accept his suffering as having a mysterious dimension ordained by God, but in the book of Wisdom we find a more developed notion of the suffering just: the just one suffers affliction at the hands of evildoers precisely because of his uprightness in keeping Torah, and his innocent suffering is proof of his divine election and his close communion with God.[62]

It is time to draw some conclusions from this discussion of human lament in the biblical literature. Prayers of penitence, which are associated with the majority voice of the common theology of sanctions, are geared to forgiveness, contrition of heart, and submission to God's will.

---

61. See Hick, *Evil and God*, 388–400. The existential view of evil as truly evil is a dualistic and philosophical conception of evil (Augustinian type of theodicy), while the instrumental view of evil as serving God's sovereign and ultimate good for creation is a monistic and theological conception of evil (Irenaean type of theodicy). Hick resolves the paradox of evil by adopting an eschatological perspective.

62. In the book of Wisdom, the just one is put to death by his persecutors, but he is not portrayed as giving his life as a sin offering. Unlike the figure of the suffering servant of the Lord in the book of Isaiah (52:13—53:12), the death of the just one is not seen as justifying many, as bearing the sin of many.

Prayers of lament, on the other hand, which represent a minority voice in Scripture, express an opposing attitude of crying out to God out of the depths of human suffering and anguish. The lament speech form, though, must not be treated as an opportunity to wallow in the sorrow of self-pity, for the lament as an expression of faith performs an empowering function: "Lament gives hope, because embedded in the lament is an appeal that arises out of trust in the God whose love is forever. Lament is the mode by which hope is reborn."[63] From the structure of the lament psalm and the patterns of complaints and protests found in the historical, prophetic, and wisdom texts discussed above, it is clear that the human lament addressed to God in situations of distress witnesses to a robust form of faith. The lament is a frank and honest pleading to God for justice to prevail in a situation of affliction and distress, yet at the same time it is always *an act of faith that assumes and enlivens hope.* The cry of lament is motivated by a deep confidence that the God of Israel not merely hears the cries of his people but is present in the midst of their suffering and displays ultimate concern for them.[64]

Brueggemann has argued that the lament genre is sufficiently pervasive in Jewish literature that it be regarded as a "counter-tradition" to the "common theology" of deeds and consequences.[65] He maintains that the minority voice of this counter-tradition does not supersede or nullify structure-legitimation associated with the common theology of sanctions, "but only lives in tension with it."[66] Recourse is made to the programmatic formulation of Exod 34:6–7, where God takes violators of the covenant seriously on the one hand, and this same God is merciful and gracious on the other, as evidence of this tension which occasions an "incongruity" in God. Talk of incongruity in God, however, is not without its problems, as will be discussed below in the second part of this chapter. Brueggemann is on more solid ground when he asserts that what is redressed by the voice of lament is the *redistribution of power between God and the people.* The lament speech form respects the voice of pain—"How long, O Lord?" "Why, Lord?"—as a legitimate voice in the history of the covenant people. In all the examples of lament examined

---

63. Hicks, "Preaching Community Laments," 79. Hicks gives as an example the "sorrow songs" of African American liturgy, which enabled an oppressed community to persevere and endure through faith.

64. Anderson, *Out of the Depths*, 65.

65. Brueggemann, "Shape for Old Testament Theology, II," 405–6.

66. Brueggemann, "Shape for Old Testament Theology, II," 414.

above, God not only hears the human voice of lament but also responds to it. Yet not withstanding the divine response to the cry of lament, human knowledge and power remain limited and incapable of securing the future. What lament witnesses to is the practice of "limit expression," which gives access to those dimensions of reality that simply defy human attempts to pin everything down in the interests of control, management, and certainty.[67] When God responds in a comprehensive manner to Job's laments, for example, the effect is not to confer greater knowledge or power to Job but rather to humble Job, who no longer seeks to rearrange the way the world operates. The fact that it is precisely *in* his suffering that Job enters into personal communion with God, and is granted the power of intercession for his friends, serves to effectively convey the mysterious dimension of suffering vis-à-vis the inscrutable sovereignty and wisdom of God. In the end, the fortunes of Job are not only restored by God but multiplied, so that the way of innocent suffering and disinterested righteousness is depicted as ultimately leading to the establishment of a new blessed reality as the workings of a righteous and just God.

The foregoing discussion has shown that through the lament form of speech the dynamic between God and his people is changed by virtue of the introduction of genuine reciprocity in the divine-human relationship. The complaints raised against God are a direct challenge to the way God has acted or has threatened to act, hence the protests indicate *a genuine dialogue between God and the protesters.*[68] God not only addresses the human, but the human also boldly addresses God and protests that justice does not have the upper hand in this world. It is precisely this dialogical character of the divine-human relationship that creates room for surprise, for the living of human life as openness to unfathomable mystery, and hence for the reconfiguration of present reality through a new self-communication of God. The reality of suffering, however, as we saw with Jeremiah, may not be relieved at all, for the prophet must come to understand that his state of suffering is in sympathy with the divine pathos. God's suffering due to the rebellion of the people is reflected in the suffering of the prophet, who proclaims the word of God to the people (see below). The prophet not merely knows about God's attachment to Israel but experiences it intimately from within, so that with the laments of the prophet the focus shifts to the way of suffering as a sign of divine

67. Brueggemann adopts Ricoeur's category of "limit expression" as an appropriate category for discussing the psalms. See Brueggemann, "Psalms as Limit Expressions."

68. Miller, *They Cried to Lord*, 70–79.

election and closeness to God. The prophet clings to a radical hope, he does not give up on God's faithfulness to his covenant promises, which become centered on a new covenant that God will make with his people, which will transform their hearts. The anguished life of Jeremiah takes on an eschatological tone directed towards a divinely appointed time of transformation and newness in the land, when God can truly say, "I am their God, and they are my people."

The embrace of pain should be recognized as integral to the life and faith of Israel, yet it must also be acknowledged as *a posture of God* who hears the cries of the covenant people and identifies with them in bringing about a new action to relieve the suffering and create a new future for them. The movement of transformation apparent in many prayers of lament, though, must not be seen as something automatic or orderly. Instead, "it tracks a fierce struggle for faith in God that has its ups and downs and that may last a lifetime."[69] The praise and worship that accompanies the biblical lament does not come cheaply. The hallelujahs are never hollow, for lament gives voice to the enduring struggle to find God in the silence. The stark reality of this world, with its manifold suffering and evil workings, does pose a formidable challenge to faith commitments, yet it is precisely by wrestling with this challenge that faith is radicalized and hope in God is born anew. The embrace of pain and the grief of abandonment is a crucial voice in the history of Israel, and, in the development of the liturgy of the people of God, it runs towards the cross of Jesus the Messiah in the New Testament: "Psalm 22 prefigures a theology of the cross, when God and man are together crucified. They are united in the ultimate agony."[70] Chapter 3 of this study will seek to elaborate on the legitimacy of this statement. In order to lay a solid foundation for this undertaking, the remainder of this chapter will engage in a discussion of divine lament and the all-important notion of the divine pathos, which will serve to firmly establish the dialogical and reciprocal nature of the divine-human relationship.

Divine Lament: Posture of God before the People

It is abundantly clear from the foregoing discussion that the lament form of human speech witnesses to a God who is affected by the cries of the

69. Billman and Migliore, *Rachel's Cry*, 124.
70. Terrien, *Psalms*, 236.

people: God hears their cries, sees their distress, and knows their suffering. To know the suffering of the people implies that God does not merely see their distress but personally enters into their suffering and suffers "with" the people. There are two other dimensions of the suffering of God, however, that are associated not with the human voice of lament but with the divine voice of lament recorded in Jewish Scripture: namely, God suffers "because" of the people's sinfulness and rejection of him as Lord; and God suffers "for" the people in that God bears their sin and is not exacting as to matters of judgment.[71] The discussion in this section will elaborate on these three forms of divine suffering, which not only shed light on the divine pathos but also serve to further enhance and enrich the picture of a truly reciprocal relationship between God and his people.

Before turning to discuss the various types of divine suffering, though, it is necessary to first address the issue of God's emotional life. Does not the presentation of a God who is vulnerable before the world, a God who is affected by historical happenings, indicate the shortcomings of employing anthropomorphic metaphors when describing God? As a first step towards responding to this criticism, it is important to appreciate the Jewish understanding of God as assuming human form in communicating the divine self. The fact that the great majority of divine lament materials are to be found in the writings of the prophets, who had a special closeness to the God of the covenant, illustrates this particular view of divine self-manifestation, as Fretheim explains:

> The prophet had a relationship with God that no other individual in Israel enjoyed; it was of such a character that the prophet's life was increasingly reflective of the divine life. This relationship means that no separation can be made between the suffering of the prophet and the suffering of God. While a distinction between prophet and God must be maintained, the prophet's suffering mirrors the suffering of God before the people. God is present not only in the word which the prophet speaks, but also in the word as embodied in the prophet's life. In a real sense, those who hear *and see* the prophet, hear and see God.[72]

In the Jewish understanding of divine self-manifestation, God assumes human form to appear and to speak. God appears in that which is other

71. Fretheim, *Suffering of God*, 108.
72. Fretheim, *Suffering of God*, 109.

than God; that is, the infinite takes on the finite for the sake of the divine appearance.[73] Rather than the language of separation or identity between the infinite and the finite, the language of distinction is used to convey the notion of God who appears, enfleshed in human form. Many may be uneasy with the use of anthropomorphic metaphors to describe what God is like, but this uneasiness is unwarranted once it is realized that in the Jewish mindset the human being is conceived of *theomorphically*, rather than God being thought of anthropomorphically. The understanding that the human being is created in "the image and likeness of God" (Gen 1:26) implies that we can learn what God is like by observing the human being.[74] The creation of the human being in the image and likeness of God grounds a doctrine of the *analogia entis* (analogy of being), which is highlighted in the commandment, "You shall be holy, for I the Lord your God am holy" (Lev 19:2). In this view, the human form of the divine appearance (theophany) is regarded as bearing "essential continuities with the form which God is believed to have."[75] Thus the life of the prophet is understood as reflective of the life of God. It would be "more proper to describe a prophetic passion as theomorphic than to regard the divine pathos as anthropomorphic."[76] The divine appearance in human form bears witness to a God who shares in the human condition, who is intimately involved in human history, and who makes himself *vulnerable* before the world. This particular perspective attains its consummate expression in the event of Jesus Christ, the Word made flesh, who "dwelt among us, full of grace and truth; we have beheld his glory, glory as of the only Son from the Father" (John 1:14).

A second argument to demonstrate the legitimacy of speaking of the emotional life of God could be formulated by appealing to a cognitive theory of emotion. There is a discernible shift in contemporary philosophical scholarship away from the traditional Western view of emotions as irrational and involuntary towards the recognition of emotions as intelligent and volitional. Martha Nussbaum, for instance, has developed a neo-Stoic cognitive theory of emotion, in which she argues

73. Fretheim, *Suffering of God*, 103.

74. Von Rad, commenting on Gen 1:26, says that "the pattern on which man was fashioned is to be sought outside of the sphere of the created" (*Old Testament Theology*, 1:146). Also, Heschel explains that Gen 1:26 and Lev 19:2 point to a "theomorphic anthropology" (Heschel, *Prophets*, 260).

75. Fretheim, *Suffering of God*, 105.

76. Heschel, *Prophets*, 260.

that emotions "involve judgments about important things, judgments in which, appraising an external object as salient for our own well-being, we acknowledge our own neediness and incompleteness before parts of the world that we do not fully control."[77] According to Nussbaum, emotions always involve thought of an object, combined with thought of the object's salience, and in that sense they always involve appraisal or evaluation. The emotions are always *about* something, which is to say that they have an object, and the object is as an *intentional* object; that is, it figures in the emotion as it is seen by the person whose emotion it is.[78] Emotions are not about their objects merely in the sense of being pointed at them; rather, their aboutness is more internal, it embodies a way of seeing. In grief, for instance, one sees an important object or person as lost to oneself. The emotions embody not just ways of seeing an object but *beliefs* about the object, often a complex set of beliefs. In order to experience fear, for example, one must believe that something bad is about to happen and that one is not entirely in control of warding it off. In order to feel anger, one must believe that some damage has occurred to them or someone close to them, and that the damage suffered was not trivial but significant, and that it was done willingly by the offender.[79] Finally, emotions are concerned with *value*; they see their object as invested with value, as important for the person's own flourishing.[80]

Since emotions register a deep attachment to objects outside our own control, they "record that sense of vulnerability and imperfect control . . . a certain passivity before the world."[81] The experience of passivity before the world is explained by the fact that objects of emotion are people and things, whose activities we do not ourselves control and in whom we have invested a good measure of our own time and well-being. The reason why in some emotional experiences we feel torn apart or, at the opposite end of the spectrum, a marvelous sense of wholeness is that these are subjective engagements with a world about which we care deeply, a world that may complete us or tear us apart. The world enters into the self in emotion, with power to heal or to wound. It enters in a cognitive way, in our perceptions and beliefs about what matters in life.

77. Nussbaum, *Upheavals of Thought*, 19. For a concise discussion of contemporary cognitive theories of emotion, see Novello, *Passionate Deification*, 25–64.

78. Nussbaum, *Upheavals of Thought*, 27.

79. Nussbaum, *Upheavals of Thought*, 28–29.

80. Nussbaum, *Upheavals of Thought*, 30.

81. Nussbaum, *Upheavals of Thought*, 43.

The emotions are subjective, but the *connection with personal biography is what makes emotions subjective.*[82] From the perspective of everyday life, knowledge that matters most is not abstract impersonal knowledge but personal knowledge that is relevant to our way of life and is biographically loaded. The emphasis on personal biography serves to underscore the understanding that emotions have a history. With intellectual reasoning the thinker is more of a detached, objective observer looking for regularities independent of their existence. The logic of emotional reasoning, on the other hand, is different, for emotions are not detached theoretical states but "address a practical concern from a personal and interested perspective."[83] Given this practical engagement with the world from a personal and interested perspective, emotions function as action potentials or *springs of action* in the world. This is apparent from the various interrelated aspects of emotion outlined above: they involve judgments about important objects; they are concerned with value; they embody beliefs about their objects; they have a personal biography of engagement with the world; and they reveal our vulnerability before parts of the world that we do not fully control.

When we come to the emotions of God recorded in Jewish Scripture, a cognitive theory of emotion is useful in illuminating the reality of the divine pathos as integral to the divine character and life. Jewish Scripture attests to Israel's persistent failure to keep Torah in the land. The land is charged with the holy mission of Torah, hence the people are under a specific mandate to live as the people of God. At the heart of Israel's experience in the land lies the dialectic of promise and demand. This dialectic gives rise to the basic tension within the covenant relationship, which provides the setting for the operation of God's emotions. The divine emotions have a distinctly cognitive character in light of the supreme importance and high value placed on their object. (1) God's abiding *love* for Israel, the setting of his heart on Israel, is the basis of his covenant relationship with the people. (2) God's *jealousy* arises out of the exclusiveness of the covenant bond, which forbids the people to worship other gods, for they are called to be a holy people and a light to the nations. (3) When Israel is seduced by pagan gods and fails to keep Torah, God's *wrath and*

82. Calhoun, "Subjectivity and Emotion." Calhoun distinguishes between "epistemic subjectivity" and "biographical subjectivity." The former has a pejorative sense, implying that emotions distort perception, while in the latter the attention falls on one's personal history and social-cultural context.

83. Ben-Ze'ev, "Logic of Emotions," 156.

anger (i.e., righteous indignation) are kindled against the people, for their rebellious conduct undermines the divine purpose of the covenant and the holiness of the divine name. It is because of God's concern and care for his people that his anger may be kindled against them. The pathos of anger is a transient state occasioned by Israel's sin, it is not a basic disposition or attribute of God.[84] Love and mercy are the primary dispositions of God, and in moments of righteous indignation, God's love and mercy remain intact. (4) God *laments* Israel's apostasy and suffers because of the people's rejection of him as Lord. At times the divine suffering takes the form of God choosing to suffer "for" his people, which means that God bears the sins of his people and is not exacting as to matters of judgment. (5) It is with *mercy* and *compassion* that God restores the covenant relationship after Israel has been subjected to suffering and hardship— i.e., judgment understood as God's forsaking of the people to forces of destruction. God is faithful to the covenant he has made with the people and takes redemptive action so as to make a new future possible for them. (6) When the people's hearts are once again turned towards their God, God *rejoices* and *delights* in his covenant partner.

The ontological reality of the emotions of God in relation to the valued and precious object of his covenant partner, is further bolstered by the fact that they are congruous with the commonly recognized communicable or personal attributes of divinity, which are relational properties of God—such as love, joy, freedom, faithfulness, compassion, mercy, righteousness, wisdom, and holiness.[85] In the view that "God is love" (1 John 4:8, 16), the personal attributes of divinity should be regarded as prior to the metaphysical attributes of omnipotence, omnipresence, omniscience, impassibility, immutability, and eternity. Once the history of the Jewish people is recognized as God's special history of engagement with the world for the sake of its salvation, it becomes appropriate to speak of the "biographical subjectivity" of God's emotions. The divine emotions should not be dismissed as mere metaphorical references; they assume ontological significance in the context of God's personal engagement with and steadfast fidelity to the people of the covenant. The covenant operates as a paradigm scenario embedded in Jewish faith, worship, and life, and the divine emotions fit the facts of this paradigmatic narrative. Abraham Heschel writes with respect to the divine pathos:

84. See Heschel, *Prophets*, 279–98.
85. See Schwöbel, *God*, 46–62.

> Is it more compatible with our conception of the grandeur of
> God to claim that He is emotionally blind to the misery of man
> rather than profoundly moved? In order to conceive of God not
> as an onlooker but as a participant, to conceive of man not as
> an idea in the mind of God but as a concern, the category of
> divine pathos is an indispensable implication. To the biblical
> mind the conception of God as detached and unemotional is
> totally alien.[86]

This notion that God can be intimately affected, that he possesses not
merely intelligence and will but also feeling and pathos, "basically defines
the prophetic consciousness of God."[87] The thought of the prophets is
not focused on the self-contained perfection and absoluteness of God
as indeterminate being but on his subjective being; that is, the emphasis
falls on God's expression, pathos, concern, and historical involvement
with his people. An apathetic God of abstraction—e.g., the God of
Aristotle as Unmoved First Cause—is a philosophical conception that
establishes not the dignity and grandeur of God but conveys a sense of
"poverty and emptiness" inasmuch as God dwells in the lonely splendor
of eternity, completely unaffected by anything that happens in his creation.[88] Gottfried Thomasius, writing in nineteenth-century Germany on
how far God could go in his merciful condescension, warned against an
a priori rigid concept of divine immutability that endangers the freedom
of divine love in relation to the world:

> This at any rate knows nothing of a rigid immutability of God
> that would hinder him from doing and becoming what he wills.
> It teaches us rather that even before his incarnation in Christ
> he entered the world of time and space in condescending love,
> that he gave his saving work in the world the form of temporal
> succession, that he lived a history with the world, that in love,
> participation and sympathy he appropriated to himself the af-
> fliction and pain of men—I say appropriated in the literal and
> not in the figurative sense. It is no empty anthropopathism when
> he says of Ephraim, "My heart yearns for him; I will surely have
> mercy on him" (Jer 31:20); no mere figure of speech when "his
> people's affliction touches him to the heart" or when it is said
> that the ungratefulness of men "troubles" him, that he repents
> of punishment or threat. This is rather reality, truth. . . . In all

86. Heschel, *Prophets*, 257.

87. Heschel, "Divine Pathos," 33; *Prophets*, 224.

88. Heschel, *Prophets*, 258–59.

of this we encounter the opposite of that rigid immobility that *must* operate according to its immanent laws. For God there is no other law at all than love, which is one with his holiness.[89]

Instead of thinking of God in terms of an abstract a priori idea of immutability that operates according to its immanent laws of immobility, the prophets "think of God *in the image of personal presence*."[90] The prophets used the language of presence, not essence; they sought not to persuade the reader of the truth of an abstract idea but to make God concretely present and supremely real. The notion of the divine pathos effectively conveys the presence of God in the midst of his people and is not to be thought of as a projection of human traits or attributes into the divine life, as Abraham Heschel explains:

> The idea of the divine pathos combining absolute selflessness with supreme concern for the poor and the exploited can hardly be regarded as the attribution of human characteristics. Where is the man who is endowed with such characteristics? Nowhere in the Bible is man characterized as merciful, gracious, slow to anger, abundant in love and truth, keeping love to the thousandth generation. Pathos is a thought that bears a resemblance to an aspect of divine reality as related to the world of man. As a theological category, it is a genuine insight into God's relatedness to man, rather than a projection of human traits into divinity, as found for example in the god images of mythology.[91]

While the life of the prophet, as an enfleshed form of the divine appearance, is reflective of the divine character, nonetheless the distinction between the human and the divine is always maintained in the Hebrew Bible. God's presence and concern in the midst of his people— i.e., God's immanence—is never emphasized at the expense of sacrificing God's transcendence. The distinction and transcendence of God comes through in many ways. For instance: God's concern for human life, especially the poor and exploited, is an ultimate concern; God is utterly committed to justice and guarantees that justice will reign in the end; God abounds in love and compassion; God is merciful and forgiving and slow to anger; God is not overwhelmed by divine suffering; God is not

---

89. Cited in Welch, *God and Incarnation*, 99. Thomasius was a leader in the development of a kenotic Christology in nineteenth-century German theology. He will be discussed in ch. 4.

90. Heschel, *Prophets*, 275.

91. Heschel, *Prophets*, 271.

embittered by the people's rejection of him as Lord; and God remains steadfast in his ineffable love and seeks to redeem his people so as to create a future for them in the land. The transcendence of the biblical God is always affirmed *within* his relatedness to the people, never apart from or above them.[92] God's immanence is commonly conceived as the divine presence in the midst of the people, while transcendence is thought of in terms of distance, that is, God being above and beyond the historical realm. A dichotomy or polarity is commonly ascribed to immanence and transcendence. However, immanence should be more broadly understood in terms of God's relatedness to his people, of which presence is a significant component, "while transcendence should be stripped of its narrow spatial associations and used to speak of the way in which the Godness of God manifests itself in this 'relatedness'—for God, a permanent state of affairs."[93] A biblical text that is consonant with this perspective is: "for great in your midst is the Holy One of Israel" (Isa 12:6; Hos 11:9; Ezek 20:41, 28:22). In this text, God's holiness, which is a biblical word for speaking of transcendence, does not stand in opposition to God's presence in the midst of Israel. Rather, God is present as the Holy One, which is to say that God's transcendence is manifested by "the *way in which* God is present among his people."[94] While holiness often speaks to the categorical difference between God and his people, it is primarily concerned with expressing the way in which God is present: steadfast in love, merciful and compassionate, patient and slow to anger yet expressing righteous indignation, long-suffering yet not overwhelmed by suffering, committed to justice, unwavering in his redemptive purposes, and having ultimate concern for Israel and the world. As Abraham Heschel concludes on this important issue: "The dichotomy of transcendence and immanence is an oversimplification. For God remains transcendent in His immanence, and related in His transcendence."[95]

92. Brueggemann talks of God as being "above the fray" and "in the fray" ("Shape for Old Testament Theology, II," 406.) These phrases correspond to the traditional distinction between transcendence and immanence. Fretheim views these formulations as problematic because the biblical God is transcendent *within* relationship, never "above" it ("Some Reflections," 74).

93. Fretheim, *Suffering of God*, 70.

94. Fretheim, *Suffering of God*, 70. See also Sponheim, "Transcendence in Relationship."

95. Heschel, *Prophets*, 486.

This view of God as always remaining related in his transcendence is conveyed not only by the notion of the Holy One of Israel dwelling in the midst of his people (Isa 12:6) but also by what Isaiah has to say about the thoughts of God: "For my thoughts are not your thoughts, neither are your ways my ways, says the Lord. . . . For as the heavens are higher than the earth, so are my ways higher than your ways and my thoughts than your thoughts" (Isa 55:8–9). What Isaiah has to say regarding the thoughts of God may equally apply to the divine pathos: For my pathos is not your pathos, neither are your ways my ways, says the Lord.[96] The notion of divine pathos is clearly incompatible with the Greek philosophical conception of a supreme being who is unmoved and unchangeable, for pathos is "a movement from one state to another, an alteration or change."[97] The significance of the divine pathos in all its forms—such as love and anger, grief and joy, mercy and wrath—is that it "reveals the extreme pertinence of man to God, His world-directness, attentiveness, and concern. God 'looks at' the world and is affected by what happens in it; man is the object of His care and judgment."[98] For Heschel, the human is not only an image of God but a perpetual concern of God, and the divine pathos expresses the ways in which God perpetually involves himself with humankind. God is affected by what happens in the world and reacts to events accordingly, all of which serves to shed further light on the dialogical nature of the divine-human relationship. The pathos of suffering and grief in particular highlights the biblical view that we should not focus solely on God's relevance to the human but must also acknowledge the principle of the human's relevance to God.[99]

Walter Brueggemann in his understanding of the biblical God also recognizes the pathos of God, but his conception of divine pathos is different to that of Heschel. For Brueggemann, the divine decision-making process is framed by the dialectical interaction of "structure legitimation" and the "embrace of pain." He regards "contractual" or "common" theology as a tight system of deeds and consequences, and sees the lament speech form as generating changes in this structure: the human

---

96. Heschel, *Prophets*, 276.

97. Heschel, *Prophets*, 260. In the prophetic understanding, God is never thought of as an object or a thing; God is always experienced as Subject, as the "I" who calls, questions, demands, and acts.

98. Heschel, *Prophets*, 483.

99. In *Prophets*, Heschel explicitly mentions God's pain and suffering in several places: 151, 259, 311, 313, 314, and 320.

experience of pain "forces" changes on God's part.[100] The lament prayers of Israel "evoke from God a new posture of relationship."[101] For Israel the issue is whether to be "like the nations" or to be "a holy people," and Brueggemann maintains that Israel's God lived in the same ambiguity; that is, whether to be "like the other gods" or to be "the Holy One in the midst of Israel."[102] This ambiguity refers not to God's external acts but to his interior life: "mutations are going on in the very person of God."[103] God is portrayed as always in the process of deciding, as struggling with decisions about the extent to which he should be defined by the common theology of deeds and consequences. The mutations going on in the very person of God reveal God's own life as troubled, ambiguous, and unresolved. This picture of an unsettled God is clear from Brueggemann's main thesis, which is stated thus:

> Yahweh is a Character and Agent who is evidenced in the life of Israel as an Actor marked by unlimited sovereignty and risky solidarity, in whom this sovereignty and solidarity often converge, but for whom, on occasion, sovereignty and solidarity are shown to be in an unsettled tension or in an acute imbalance. The substance of Israel's testimony concerning Yahweh, I propose, yields a Character who has a profound disjunction at the core of the Subject's life.[104]

For Brueggemann the theme of covenant is transposed into a practice of pathos. Yahweh would be justified in terminating the covenant relationship, but in times of crisis—speaking of the crises of 722 and 587 BCE—Yahweh finds "new measures and depths of positive passion for Israel that were not available to Yahweh until this awesome moment of staying or leaving, of loving or destroying."[105] In times of crisis Yahweh must decide whether to exhibit solidarity with Israel in suffering, and by virtue of such solidarity to sustain a relationship that rightfully could be terminated. This unsettled quality of any resolution to a crisis situation "belongs definitionally to the character of Yahweh,"[106] which means

---

100. Fretheim, "Some Reflections," 75.

101. Brueggemann, "Shape for Old Testament Theology, II," 404.

102. Brueggemann, "Shape for Old Testament Theology, II," 415.

103. Brueggemann, "Shape for Old Testament Theology, I," 35.

104. Brueggemann, Theology of Old Testament, 268.

105. Brueggemann, Theology of Old Testament, 299.

106. Brueggemann, Theology of Old Testament, 303.

that any equation of sovereignty with covenantal love or with pathos is excluded. This leads Brueggemann to speak of God as being both "above the fray" and "in the fray," which corresponds to an incongruity in God: intensification of God's wrath and impatience on account of Israel's infidelity on the one hand and a divine reluctance to enforce the contract and a holding to promises on the other.[107] Brueggemann's treatment of Exod 34:6–7, with its combination of God's merciful love and graciousness and yet taking the guilty seriously, is interpreted as a prime example of the incongruity in God. But why should God's love be regarded as inconsistent with his righteous judgment? Why is a word of judgment "against" Israel incongruous with God's saving will "for" Israel? Is not divine judgment "*always* in the service of God's loving and saving purposes, and their juxtaposition in Exodus 34:6–7 says precisely this?"[108]

Brueggemann asserts that it is the human cry of pain expressed in the lament speech form that "forces" changes in God's character and evokes from God a new posture towards Israel. Fretheim, however, points out that even apart from the lament prayers and appeals to God, "Israel understood that its God was not a simple upholder of the contract come what may."[109] Integral to the covenant that God initiates with Israel is the understanding that within God there is "a leaning towards Israel and being for Israel by virtue of the divine purpose and promises."[110] This is true even in judgment, which is integral to God's faithfulness towards the covenant. Like Heschel, Fretheim maintains that God's wrath issuing in judgment is an exercise of the *circumstantial* will of God, which always stands in the service of God's *absolute* will for life and blessing. Fretheim concedes that God has decisions to make in response to Israel's laments and protests, and God can agonize over such decisions, yet it is important to note that in the biblical texts there are "distinctions among divine decisions."[111] God makes once-for-all decisions within which other decisions are made. The promises to Abraham and Noah are once-for-all decisions that are grounded in an ultimate or fundamental divine will *for* Israel and the world, thus each subsequent decision-making moment or situation does not entail God having to decide "what kind of God to

107. Fretheim, "Some Reflections," 75.

108. Fretheim, "Some Reflections," 77.

109. Fretheim, "Some Reflections," 76.

110. Fretheim, "Some Reflections," 77.

111. Fretheim, "Some Reflections," 78.

be."[112] The various levels of decision making—i.e., God's ultimate or fundamental will, once-for-all decisions that implement that will, and circumstantial decisions—imply that God is both mutable and immutable, and that the divine pathos is integral to God's relation to Israel and the world from the very beginning. God does not change his attitude to Israel in times of crisis because God discovers a depth of devotion to Israel that was not previously available to him. It is more intelligible to hold that the God who is active "in the fray" and embraces pain is so engaged by virtue of a once-for-all decision to be the kind of God who is personally involved with the historical process. This implies that God is transcendent *within* the covenant relationship, not "above" it. The holiness of God, which is a synonym for God's transcendence, is revealed by the *way in which* the living God embraces pain: "steadfast in love, faithful to promises, and unwaveringly willing the salvation of Israel and the world."[113] This particular understanding of the biblical God, who remains transcendent in his immanence and related in his transcendence, emerges with great clarity when we examine the biblical texts concerning God's suffering in relation to his people.[114]

A constant theme running through the Hebrew Bible is that God suffers "because" the people have rejected him as Lord and thus have broken the covenant relationship. The divine laments are modeled on human laments, where the psalmist complains to God of being falsely accused by enemies. The psalmist prays that God vindicate him and deliver his life from the wicked: "Wondrously show thy steadfast love, O savior of those who seek refuge from their adversaries at thy right hand" (Ps 17:7); "May my accusers be clothed with dishonor. . . . With my mouth I will give great thanks to the Lord. . . . For he stands at the right hand of the needy, to save him from those who condemn him to death" (Ps 109:29–31). The psalmist's prayer of lament is occasioned by false accusations leveled against him by his adversaries, and it is this "combination of lament and accusation that is characteristic of much of the divine lament material in this category."[115] Instead of the psalmist, it is now God who

---

112. Fretheim, "Some Reflections," 79.

113. Fretheim, "Some Reflections," 74.

114. In what follows I am guided by the threefold schema of Fretheim in his *Suffering of God*: God suffers "because" of the people's rejection of him as Lord; God suffers "for" the people in that he bears their sin; and God suffers "with" the people when they find themselves in a state of desolation.

115. Fretheim, *Suffering of God*, 110.

stands accused by the people, but God, like the psalmist, is innocent of the charge and laments the miserable state of the covenant relationship.

While the divine lament materials are found mostly in the prophetic writings, the notion of divine suffering is not unique to the prophets, for it is already clearly present in earlier non-prophetic texts. One good example of an early text that speaks of God's suffering is Ps 78:40–41: "How often they rebelled against him in the wilderness and grieved him in the desert! They tested him again and again, and provoked the Holy One of Israel." Here the language of "grieving" is used to express the suffering of God. Given that Israel's rebellion is not a single occurrence but occurs "again and again," it is clear that God suffers again and again due to Israel's faithless character. From the very birth of Israel, God has been grieving for the sins of the people, and the divine grief accompanies both the wrath of God (Ps 78:21) and the compassion of God (Ps 78:38). Another example of a preprophetic text that refers to divine grief is Gen 6:5–6: "The Lord saw that the wickedness of man was great in the earth, and that every imagination of the thoughts of his heart was only evil continually. And the Lord was sorry that he had made man on the earth, and it grieved him to his heart." God's grieving is not limited to his relationship with a rebellious Israel but goes back to the beginning of the world. In the covenant that God makes with Noah, he promises to allow the creation to endure notwithstanding the scourge of human wickedness. This means, however, that the promise to Noah (Gen 9:8–17) *necessitates* divine suffering.[116] The divine decision to endure the sin of the world necessarily involves a continual grieving as God persists in opening up his heart to that world.

The ongoing significance of the flood story is evident in Isa 54:9–10, where God says: "For this is like the days of Noah to me . . . so I have sworn that I will not be angry with you and will not rebuke you . . . my steadfast love shall not depart from you, and my covenant of peace shall not be removed." The grief of God due to Israel's rebellion is necessary to uphold the "covenant of peace." The Noachic promise in Isa 54, it is worth underlining, is juxtaposed to the Suffering Servant Song of Isa 53, which is no mere coincidence, for God's grief "becomes embodied in the world in the life of the servant."[117] The very beginning of the book of Isaiah (1:2–3) clearly sets the tone for all that is to follow; the prophet has

---

116. Fretheim, *Suffering of God*, 112.

117. Fretheim, *Suffering of God*, 113.

in view not the anger of God but the sorrow of God who is forsaken by his "sons." In Jeremiah we find the same divine lament: "My people have forgotten me" (Jer 18:15); "Is Ephraim my dear son? Is he my darling child?" (Jer 31:20) The prophet Hosea uses the image of a long-suffering parent to express the divine lament: "When Israel was a child, I loved him, and out of Egypt I called my son. The more I called them, the more they went from me. . . . I took them up in my arms; but they did not know that I healed them" (Hos 11:1-3). In the book of Micah as well we read: "O my people, what have I done to you? In what have I wearied you? Answer me!" (Mic 6:3). The pathos of God comes through powerfully and movingly in these prophetic texts.

The emotional utterances of God not only show that *God has internalized the people's rejection of him as Lord*, they also seek to elicit a positive response of repentance; that is, the hope that the people will turn their hearts back to God, so that God can hold back from executing judgment upon them: "How can I pardon you? Your children have forsaken me. . . . Shall I not punish them for these things?" (Jer 5:7-9). Yet God says, "Behold, I will refine them and test them, for what else can I do, because of my people?" (Jer 9:7). These questions indicate that while God would be entirely justified in executing judgment upon the people, God's decision is not so clear, for "the people have a role to play in determining what God's final answer to his own questions will be."[118] The clear hope of God is that the people will embrace repentance and restore their covenant relationship with him. God is not legalistic and exacting as to matters of judgment but patiently goes beyond strict justice, because what is at stake is the nature of the covenant relationship (cf. Exod 34:6-7). The grieving of God for the broken state of the relationship implies that "*God chooses to suffer for the sake of the future of that relationship*."[119] The divine suffering is necessary to carry forward redemptive purposes that are consonant with covenant promises given to the forebears of Israel.

From the prophetic texts that speak of God's suffering due to the people's rejection of him as Lord, divine judgment is presented not as the breach of a legal contract and as inflicting a penalty on the people but as the breakdown of an intimate relationship with all its associated effects. From the prophetic standpoint, the effects of this broken relationship are called judgment. The language of judgment is couched in images

118. Fretheim, *Suffering of God*, 123.

119. Fretheim, *Suffering of God*, 124; emphasis added.

of God's forsaking or giving up the people to the consequences of their sin: God "hides his face," or "turns away," or "surrenders" his people.[120] The wrath of God is not understood as irrational or some spontaneous outburst, and the prophet's task is to proclaim to Israel that it must mend its ways. Anger is a reminder that Israel is in serious need of repentance. "There is no divine anger for anger's sake. Its meaning is *instrumental*: to bring about repentance; its purpose and consummation is its own disappearance."[121] The wrath of God must not be treated in isolation from its instrumental meaning, for it must be treated as "an aspect of the divine pathos, as one of the modes of God's responsiveness to man."[122] It is also important to note that divine anger is a secondary emotion, never a ruling passion; it is not an essential attribute of God's relatedness to his people.[123] The wrath of God issuing in judgment is a contingent response to a specific situation, hence it does not go on forever: what goes on forever is God's love and goodness. In the prophetic writings, God makes repeated efforts to heal the breach in his relationship with Israel, and the failure of the people to respond to these persistent efforts means that God comes to the point of allowing destructive forces to have their way with the people. "God's wrath here is his active consent to the working out of human sin into its inevitable consequences."[124]

The contemporary debate on sin and judgment was initiated by Klaus Koch in an article he wrote in the 1950s, in which he challenged the long-held view of a doctrine of retribution in Jewish Scripture. Koch concluded that there is no such doctrine and that instead we find the notion that human actions have built-in consequences.[125] God is not pictured as a higher authority in the juridical sense that he metes out reward and punishment according to an established norm but by facilitating the completion of what previous human action has already set in motion.

---

120. Balentine, *Hidden God*, 143–51. This understanding is shared by Paul in his Letter to the Romans, where he speaks of the divine wrath against sinners in terms of God "giving them up" to the futility of their own desires (Rom 1:24–32).

121. Heschel, *Prophets*, 286; emphasis added.

122. Heschel, *Prophets*, 282.

123. Heschel, *Prophets*, 291; Fretheim, "Some Reflections," 77.

124. Fiddes, *Creative Suffering of God*, 24.

125. Koch, "Doctrine of Retribution." Koch examines Proverbs, Hosea, and the Psalms and concludes that they all essentially teach that human actions have built-in consequences.

Koch describes this state of affairs as "a synthetic view of life."[126] Gene Tucker prefers to call this state of affairs "a dynamistic view of acts and consequences."[127] While Tucker is sympathetic towards Koch's proposal, he does not accept it in its entirety, for he is intent on showing that the prophets adhere to a broadly juridical interpretation of actions as well. He concludes that both a dynamistic view and a juridical perspective are to be found in the prophets. A good example of this is the passage Hos 4:1–3. The first verse says that the Lord has a "lawsuit" against the inhabitants of the land, yet the following verses portray events—the mourning of the land—as corresponding to cause and effect. Thus what we have here is a dynamistic perspective that is brought into the sphere of the dominant legal pattern, so that "the two strands are intertwined."[128] To Tucker's mind the dynamistic perspective provides a rationale for making sense of human experience—why does the land mourn?—yet it is set within the Lord's lawsuit against the inhabitants of the land. Patrick Miller has arrived at a similar position in his detailed examination of the prophetic texts. He finds that there is a general understanding of judgment as related to sin not by external decision but by an internal movement of cause and effect. However, Miller finds that there are a number of prophetic passages that emphasize the idea of correspondence but not consequence. That is to say, they suggest that while there is always a causal effect in the relationship between human action and the judgment received, "that relationship is not necessarily internal but is perceived as resting in the divine decision and not happening apart from that decision or decree."[129] Like Tucker, Miller is of the mindset that "a notion of retributive justice is not incompatible with an understanding of divine judgment wrought out in the process of history."[130]

Irrespective of whether one subscribes to a dynamistic or juridical perspective with respect to divine judgment, what is unambiguously clear in the prophetic writings is that the divine intention is never to give up on the people—judgment is always instrumental—but to restore them out of the depths of their calamity: "How can I give you up, O Ephraim?

126. Koch, "Doctrine of Retribution," 76.

127. Tucker, "Sin and Judgment," 374.

128. Tucker, "Sin and Judgment," 387.

129. Miller, *Sin and Judgment*, 134. Correspondence does two things: (1) it underlines God's judgment as appropriate justice; (2) it sharpens the relation between sin and punishment (136–37).

130. Miller, *Sin and Judgment*, 138.

How can I hand you over, O Israel? . . . My heart recoils within me, my compassion grows warm and tender . . . for I am God and not man, the Holy One in your midst" (Hos 11:8–9). The judgment of the Lord issues from the divine pathos of wrath, but the latter is never divorced from God's merciful love and his *absolute* will for life and blessing.[131] God's judgment is always directed towards redemptive purposes and goals, towards bestowing mercy, compassion, and love upon the afflicted people and creating a future for them by gathering them anew in the land. "We may then make the theological judgment that there is no conflict of love and wrath within God."[132] To state the matter another way, "divine judgment is *always* in the service of God's loving and saving purposes."[133]

In the prophetic texts, divine judgment ensues because of Israel's rebellious character, but it is also intertwined with the category of God's suffering "for" the people. Israel is guilty of unfaithfulness, yet God does not act immediately in judgment but holds back on executing the judgment that Israel deserves. By patiently bearing the sins of a rebellious people, God chooses the road of suffering for the people, rather than exacting strict justice. God holds his peace for a long time, yet despite God's eminent patience it is not perpetual but comes to an end: "The Lord could no longer bear your evil doings and the abominations which you committed; therefore your land has become a desolation" (Jer 44:22); "But you have burdened me with your sins, you have wearied me with your iniquities" (Isa 43:24). The text in Isaiah talks of God being "burdened" with the sins of the people, of God being "wearied" by Israel's persistent iniquities, which serves to underscore the extent to which God internalizes and bears Israel's rebellious conduct.

The divine restraint at Israel's continued unfaithfulness implies a continued intensification of God's suffering, "a build-up of internal forces in God, which finally (though not uncontrollably) burst forth in judgment."[134] The judgment, though—as will become clear below—is a necessary prerequisite to God's activity of salvation, of creating new life out of the midst of desolation and death. The prophet Isaiah uses the image of a woman in travail to express the bursting forth of God's creative

---

131. Cf. Fretheim, "Some Reflections," 77. Fretheim regards divine anger as an exercise of the circumstantial will of God, which always stands in the service of God's absolute will for life and blessing.

132. Fiddes, *Creative Suffering of God*, 25.

133. Fretheim, "Character of God," 297.

134. Fretheim, *Suffering of God*, 142.

activity: "For a long time I have held my peace, I have kept still and restrained myself; now I will cry out like a woman in travail, I will gasp and pant" (Isa 42:14). The restraint of God in the face of Israel's apostasy amounts to an ever-increasing intensification of divine suffering, which must finally burst forth in judgment and the travail of redemptive-creative activity. God's patient bearing of the sins of the people means that God has internalized the people's rejection of him as Lord, and this build-up of internal forces in God has wearied him. There is, therefore, "an intimate relationship to be seen between the continued life of a sinful people and the suffering of God."[135] The suffering of God for the people is not perpetual, though, but builds to the point where restraint is no longer possible, given that what is at stake is the future of God as well as the future of Israel and the world. Judgment does fall on the people, but the desolation that ensues becomes the fertile ground for God's new redemptive activity, for the birthing of a new creation by way of a via dolorosa.

When judgment falls on Israel, the biblical texts portray God as not giving up on the people but as sharing in their suffering, as suffering "with" them and working with compassion towards healing and restoring the covenant relationship: "For a brief moment I forsook you, but with great compassion I will gather you. In overflowing wrath, for a moment I hid my face from you, but with everlasting love I will have compassion on you, says the Lord, your Redeemer" (Isa 54:7–8). This fundamental notion of a God who suffers with his people can be traced back to the foundational event of the Exodus from Egypt: "I have seen the affliction of my people who are in Egypt, and have heard their cry because of their taskmasters; I know their sufferings, and I have come down to deliver them out of the hand of the Egyptians, and to bring them up out of that land to a good and broad land, a land flowing with milk and honey" (Exod 3:7–8). God not only "sees" the suffering of the people but "hears" their cry of affliction and "knows" their suffering. The seeing of God is not a seeing from the outside as though he were looking through a window; rather, "God is internally related to the suffering of the people."[136] The response of God to the people's affliction is one of entering into the situation of the people and making it his very own, with a view to doing something about the situation, since God is not powerless to take action in redeeming his people.

---

135. Fretheim, *Suffering of God*, 143.

136. Fretheim, *Suffering of God*, 128; emphasis added.

When we come to the prophetic texts that speak of God as suffering "with" the people, the language used is not that of lament and accusation but the language of mourning and compassion. The latter are commonly interwoven in the prophetic texts, in the sense that the divine empathy for the people is often presented as *anticipating* the impending divine judgment on fallen Israel. God laments the people's persistent failure to keep Torah and their incapacity to change their ways and turn their hearts back to him: "Can the Ethiopian change his skin or the leopard his spots?" (Jer 13:23). In anticipation of the impending judgment, God takes up a word of lamentation: "Fallen, no more to rise, is the virgin Israel; forsaken on her land, with none to raise her up" (Amos 5:1–2). This is a "funerary lament" in which the fall of Israel is presented as having already occurred, so inevitable is the outcome. The language of mourning, though, is not designed to rest in itself as a final declaration by God of Israel's unholy state of existence but is directed toward the divine exhortation, "Seek me and live" (Amos 5:4; also Ezek 18:32). The purpose of the funerary lament is to startle the people into turning their hearts back to the Lord, so they may have life, not a funeral. "One ought not, however, view the lament as a threat. It is a genuine mourning song. It is not God's threat that is intended to move the people to repentance, but God's sorrow!"[137]

Before the judgment falls upon Israel, God anticipates his response of mourning with those who mourn over the desolation that has visited them. God enters into their suffering and "turns from the role of judge to fellow-sufferer."[138] As fellow-sufferer, God is at work in the situation of death to bring about salvation, that is, new life out of the midst of death. The salvific action of God is regarded as preceding any return on the part of the people: "I have swept away your transgressions like a cloud, and your sins like mist; return to me, for I have redeemed you" (Isa 44:22). The people have sunken to a state in which they are no longer capable of turning their hearts back to God, thus only God can mercifully raise them up out of death and restore them to a life of wholeness that reflects

137. Fretheim, *Suffering of God*, 131.

138. Fretheim, *Suffering of God*, 136. This recalls the view of the process thinker Alfred North Whitehead who wrote in his principal work that God is the "great companion, the fellow-sufferer who understands" (*Process and Reality*, 532). Process thought regards the world not as a hierarchy—as did the church fathers and the medieval Schoolmen—but as a living organism. Whitehead argued that God's actual suffering presence in the world is integral to the ideals by which God influences the world.

the dignity and holiness of the covenant relationship. "In that day I will raise up the booth of David that is fallen and repair its breaches, and raise up its ruins, and rebuild it as in the days of old. . . . I will restore the fortunes of my people Israel, and they shall rebuild the ruined cities and inhabit them" (Amos 9:11, 14).

The judgment of the Lord brings death to the people, but the judgment is viewed as the prerequisite for God's work of salvation that brings new life out of a situation of desolation and death. In the book of Jeremiah, the Lord says, "I am a father to Israel" (31:9), and the exercising of this fatherhood is displayed in the benevolent work of gathering the people and restoring them in the land after they are scattered and displaced by judgment. With the desolation of Israel, moreover, God's suffering is also tied up to some extent with God's own future. The desolation and affliction of Israel causes distress to God in the sense that God is not able to accomplish the divine purpose in the land, which amounts to a denigration of the holy name of God. Therefore, the future for God is different from what it would have been had Israel not committed apostasy and remained loyal to the covenant relationship. Abraham Heschel captures this aspect of divine suffering especially well when he writes: "Israel's distress was more than a human tragedy. With Israel's distress came the affliction of God, His displacement, His homelessness in the land, in the world."[139] Not only are the people displaced as a result of God's judgment, God also suffers the affliction of displacement from the land. The prophet's prayer for divine salvation, then, should be seen as involving not merely the fate of the people but also the fate of God.

Concluding Remarks on the Divine Pathos:
God's Attitude of Perpetual Concern for Humanity

From the perspective of the foregoing discussion, God is not to be thought of as a detached, remote, and impersonal lawgiver who acts legalistically according to a strict standard of justice when the people fail to keep Torah. Instead, the picture that emerges gives us insight into the personal attributes and pathos of God, who, while wounded by the broken state of the covenant relationship, in patience restrains from executing justice again and again, while making efforts to bring about the healing of the relationship. God does not coolly walk away and give

139. Heschel, *Prophets*, 112.

up on Israel but internalizes the existential situation of his people, for the God of the covenant is a *living* God who always maintains an attitude of benevolence and affection towards his people. The three types of divine suffering, moreover, are inextricably intertwined so that one type cannot be thought of without implying the other two: given that God suffers "because" of the people's rejection of him as Lord, yet he patiently holds back from executing judgment, this means that God suffers "for" the people in that he bears their sins; and when judgment does finally fall on the people and they suffer desolation, God suffers "with" the afflicted people and is moved to act in a merciful way that brings the promise of new life for the people in the land: "Behold, I am doing a new thing" (Isa 43:19). In this perspective, judgment is the necessary prerequisite for divine salvation, for God's new action of creating life out of a situation of desolation and death. The divine pathos of anger or wrath, which leads to divine judgment, is never divorced from the divine pathos of merciful love that makes possible the redemption of the people and the creation of a new future for them in the land. The predicament of Israel is never something that does not concern or involve God; the situation of God's covenant partner is also the predicament of God who is affected by events in history. The essential meaning of the divine pathos is that *God participates in the situation of his people.* God is not the Wholly Other but the God of the covenant, the God who is involved in history and who displays ultimate concern for the world. Such concern is the locus of living encounter between the divine and the human.

What is especially noteworthy in this perspective is the understanding that God chooses to suffer for the sake of the future of the relationship. It is not merely the future of Israel, as well as the future of the world, that is at stake but also the future of God. The suffering of God is intimately connected to redemptive-creative purposes, to the ultimate goal of giving the people a "new heart" (Ezek 36:26) with which to dwell in the land as the holy people of God, so that Israel might be "a light to the nations" (Isa 42:6). When seeking to give due recognition to divine lament and suffering, it is important not to lose sight of the fundamental point that divine pathos is not like human pathos, just as God's thoughts are not our thoughts, and God's ways are not our ways (Isa 55:8–9). The divine pathos is rooted in the relational attributes of the divine being, especially God's ineffable love and boundless compassion for his people, which goes hand in glove with God's unwavering faithfulness to the covenant relationship. What is more, God, unlike the human, is not overwhelmed by suffering and is not embittered by the people's rejection of him as Lord but chooses to endure suffering for the sake of the future of Israel and the world. The pathos of God, then, is not to be regarded as a mere projection of human traits or attributes onto the divine, notwithstanding a certain analogy of being between the divine and the human. What the divine pathos brings into sharp focus, as Abraham Heschel has emphasized, is the genuine reciprocity of the divine-human relationship:

> The divine pathos is like a bridge over the abyss that separates man from God. It implies that the relationship between God and man is not dialectic, characterized by opposition and tension. Man in his essence is not the antithesis of the divine, although in his actual existence he may be rebellious and defiant. The fact that the attitudes of man may affect the life of God, that God stands in an intimate relationship to the world, implies a certain analogy between Creator and creature. The prophets stress not only the discrepancy of God and man, but also the *relationship of reciprocity*, consisting of God's engagement to man, not only of man's commitment to God. The disparity between God and the world is overcome in God, not in man.[140]

As a theological category, the pathos of God is a genuine insight into God's relatedness to and personal engagement with humanity and the world. By illuminating the deeply personal dimension of the divine life, the category of divine pathos is able to enrich our understanding of God as choosing to suffer for the sake of the future of the covenant relationship. What happens in God's creation is not external to God, for God internalizes the dismal situation of his people and displays ultimate concern for them, from which springs the recurring initiative to redeem a sinful people and create new beginnings for them in the land as the people of God. By virtue of the divine pathos the world enters into the divine being with the power not only to wound God but, more importantly, to heal and transform the troubled state of the covenant relationship. The glory of God shines forth in the pathos of God, in God's attitude of benevolence towards and involvement with a wayward and suffering humanity.

The relationship of reciprocity between the divine and the human, it has been shown, is especially apparent in the life of the prophet who suffers as a servant of God. Since the suffering of the prophet is directly related to the service undertaken, the prophet is not the suffering

140. Heschel, *Prophets*, 229; emphasis added.

representative of the people, as is often thought. Instead, the special character of the prophetic mission consists in the fact that *the prophet embodies the suffering of God before the people.* The life of the prophet emerges as distinctly theomorphic. From the prophetic writings it is clear that the prophet suffers "because" he is rejected and persecuted by the people. The prophet is one who encounters much resistance in carrying out his mission, to the point that his life is threatened with death.[141] When Jeremiah, for instance, prophesies against the city of Jerusalem, he receives a hostile reaction from the people: "This man deserves the sentence of death, because he has prophesied against this city, as you have heard with your own ears" (Jer 26:11). The people reject not only the word spoken by the prophet—which is a word of God to the people—but his person, that is, the totality of his own life devoted to the cause of God. The laments of the prophet therefore mirror the divine lament over the people's estrangement from God. The sorrow of God finds expression in the laments of the prophet. Just as the people have rebelled against God, they also reject the prophet who is the mouthpiece and personal presence of God in the midst of the people. Abraham Heschel has aptly described the prophet's condition as "a state of suffering in sympathy with the divine pathos."[142]

The prophet suffers not only because of the sinfulness of the people but also "with" the people, which takes on two discernible dimensions in the prophetic writings: the prophet suffers in anticipation of the coming judgment, and he suffers in the aftermath of God's judgment falling on the people, which reduces them to a state of desolation. What is embodied in the person of the prophet is the mourning of God for his people, who are able to see "how God has entered into the anguish of their situation and made it his very own, as in Jer 4:19."[143] In this prophetic passage, both God and prophet mourn in anticipation of the "sound of the trumpet"—see also Ezek 21:6; Isa 22:4; Mic 1:8—and once divine judgment is executed, both God and prophet suffer with the people in their state of anguish and desolation. The prophet suffers as the servant

141. Jesus in the Gospel story clearly acknowledges the people's rejection and persecution of the prophets: "O Jerusalem, Jerusalem, killing the prophets and stoning those who are sent to you!" (Matt 23:37; Luke 13:34).

142. Heschel, *Prophets*, 118. For Heschel, "sympathy" denotes active cooperation with God, identifying one's concern with the concern of God. When the divine in relation to the world is thought of as pathos, the appropriate response is one of sympathy. This notion of religious sympathy underscores suffering as a vocation of the Lord's faithful.

143. Fretheim, *Suffering of God*, 160.

and embodiment of God, who mourns for the situation of his people. The people are homeless when divine judgment falls upon them, yet not only the people but God, too, suffers the anguish of homelessness. This is brought home strongly when Jeremiah is forced to spend his final days in Egypt, so that "the homelessness of God is finally embodied in the homelessness of Jeremiah."[144]

With regard to the prophet suffering "for" the people, this dimension of suffering is less well developed than the previous two dimensions. Jeremiah sees himself as a sacrificial victim, as "a gentle lamb led to the slaughter" (11:19), but there is nothing to suggest that his suffering as the servant of God is vicarious in the sense that he "makes himself an offering for sin" (Isa 53:10–11). Yet given the depiction of Jeremiah as suffering insults from his own people on account of his fidelity to God, there is certainly a sense in which the people's guilt falls squarely on the prophet to bear, hence his profound laments to God. This new mode of thought provides a conceptual framework for further developments of thought. If the life of the prophet is the embodiment of God's relationship with the people, which is characterized by divine pathos, then it is not surprising that such a portrayal of the prophetic vocation gave rise to the formulation of thought to be found in the Servant Songs in the book of Isaiah (42:1–7; 50:4–9; 52:13—53:12), where the suffering of the Lord's servant is raised to a new key. For there the servant's suffering is depicted as distinctly vicarious, that is, as willingly taken up to the point of death for the sake of the redemption of many. The death of the Lord's servant is regarded as a personal sin offering which has universal implications, for it concerns not only the redemption of Israel but the whole world. This notion of the vicarious suffering of the Lord's servant for the redemption of many is ultimately realized in the event of the crucified Messiah. Jesus Christ, the "Holy and Righteous One" (Acts 3:14), who is the consummate embodiment of God in the world, suffers a violent death at the hands of those who reject and mock him, yet through the sacrificial shedding of his precious blood is forged the "new covenant" (Mark 14:24; Matt 26:28) for the redemption of Israel and of the entire world.

In the Hebrew Bible, to sum up, lament as a speech form allows the faithful to acknowledge the disturbing and troubling realities of this world and to communicate their sufferings and pleadings to God "out of the depths," so that the divine-human relationship is no longer envisaged

144. Fretheim, *Suffering of God*, 162.

as a monologue but as a dialogue. The dialogical nature of the covenant relationship means that God is personally engaged in the human crisis and is in solidarity with the sufferers, with the aim of bringing salvation to his people. The lament not only gives poignant voice to a lamentable situation but also invokes the divine salvation that is desired, so that lament is performed out of radical trust in God and serves as a form of perseverance in the journey of faith whose happy ending is hoped for but not yet given. The prophetic laments add something further to this picture by highlighting the divine pathos reflected in the sufferings of the prophet. The prophet's lament is not representative of the sufferings of the people but is a word of God or a posture of God before the people, and not a word of the people to God. The divine pathos effectively conveys the dialogical nature of the covenant relationship by emphasizing the human's relevance to God and not limiting our focus to God's relevance to the human. This perspective of the coming together of human and divine suffering in the life of the prophet reaches its zenith in Jesus's cry on the cross, which will be discussed in chapter 3 of this study.

2

Lament in the New Testament and Theological Tradition

A Narrowing of Perspective

I N LIGHT OF THE persistent voice of lament in Jewish Scripture from the time of the Exodus, through the period of the Judges, to the prophetic and wisdom writings, one would expect the lament speech form to feature also in the New Testament and Christian theological tradition. This expectation is heightened by the answering of Jesus's lament cry by the Father's eschatological act of raising him from the dead in the power of the Spirit. In light of Jesus's answered lament, one would expect to find that Christian praise of God does not suppress or preclude the lament speech form but rather makes room for it because it is "incorporated into thanksgiving."[1] What is more, as long as we live in a world that is still unredeemed, and at times unspeakably evil and plagued by terrible suffering, one would expect Christians to inevitably lament even as they rejoice and give thanks and praise to the God of Jesus Christ. It will become apparent in this chapter, however, that these expectations are not generally realized in the Christian writings, for a variety of reasons.

The first section of this chapter will examine the New Testament writings to determine the extent to which the Jewish tradition of lament continues to receive some form of acknowledgement. The theme of

1. Bayer, "Toward Theology of Lament," 211.

suffering is still very much present in the New Testament; however, the discussion will reveal that the faithful who suffer in the name of Christ have no cause for lament, since their suffering takes on the positive aspects of honor and rejoicing. The tradition of Christian martyrdom highlights this positive approach to suffering. There are various expressions of lament in the New Testament, such as sighing, mourning, and groaning, but it will become apparent that these take on a distinctly eschatological tone, that is, they are portrayed as the pains of awaiting the eschaton. The second part of the chapter will then proceed to offer a critical survey of the theological tradition in order to ascertain the various ways in which the lament literature, especially the Psalms, has been interpreted and incorporated into the development of Christian thought. Augustine, Luther, Calvin, Barth, and Moltmann will be taken as the primary theological figures in tracing the treatment of lament from the patristic era, to the Reformation period, to the contemporary theological scene. What will become evident from the survey of these Christian thinkers is that the Jewish tradition of the lament speech form, which is generally not related to the problem of the lamenter's personal sin—the lamenter suffers as the just one—now becomes centered on the problem of sin in the life of faith. Lament as an appropriate response to physical suffering and illness, or to the loss of loved ones and posterity, or to the suffering of the righteous whose lives mirror the divine pathos in relation to the world, are lost sight of as the focus is reduced to the problem of sin and our utter dependence on the gratuity of grace in Jesus Christ our Savior. While there is a legitimate place for lament in relation to our ongoing wrestling with the tenacity of sin—the practice of lament as penance—we should not lose sight of the enduring significance of lament in the Psalms and in the great biblical figures of Job, Jeremiah, and Jesus of Nazareth.

Lament in the New Testament: Groaning for the Fullness of Salvation in the Risen Christ

When we move away from the motif of lament in the Old Testament and turn our attention to the New Testament, we find that the Christian writings are characterized by the absence of lament. The early Christians certainly did experience much suffering and persecution at the hands of both Jews and gentiles, hence one would expect to find newly written psalms and songs of lament in the Christian writings, but this is not the

case. A number of interrelated reasons have been suggested for this perceived absence of lament.[2] The first important point has to do with the
intimate relation between the accomplishment of Jesus's mission and his
suffering: "For the Son of Man came not to be served but to serve, and
to give his life as a ransom for many" (Mark 10:45; Matt 20:28); "And he
began to teach them that the Son of Man must suffer many things, and be
rejected by the elders and the chief priests and the scribes, and be killed,
and after three days rise again" (Mark 8:31; Matt 16:21). On the basis of
this strand in the Gospel traditions, those who follow Jesus are expected
to willingly undergo suffering and persecution for the sake of his name:
"If any man would come after me, let him deny himself and take up his
cross and follow me . . . whoever loses his life for my sake and the gospel's
will save it" (Mark 8:34–35); "Remember the word that I said to you, 'A
servant is not greater than his master.' If they persecuted me, they will
persecute you" (John 15:20).

These gospel expectations concerning the disciples of Jesus are reinforced and highlighted by the writings of Paul. The apostle saw himself as
having been chosen to suffer in the service of proclaiming the gospel to
the gentiles; he was counted worthy "to suffer dishonor for the sake of the
name" (Acts 5:41). The biography of Paul makes it clear that his calling,
and that of all disciples, is directed toward suffering: "For it has been
granted to you that for the sake of Christ you should not only believe
in him but also suffer for his sake" (Phil 1:29). Suffering is neither to be
avoided nor lamented, for to follow Christ and to suffer in his name take
on the positive aspects of honor and "rejoicing" (Col 1:24). This Pauline
perspective is similar to the understanding of the prophetic condition as
a state of suffering in sympathy with the divine pathos, although Paul,
unlike Jeremiah, does not protest to God that his mission of proclaiming the gospel to the gentiles is too much to bear and he wishes that he
had never been born. Paul's position is more like the response of God to
Jeremiah, when the Lord says to the prophet that he should regard his
suffering as integral to carrying out the sacred work of God in the midst
of his own rebellious people. The prophet suffers dishonor and much
hardship for the sake of the divine name, and Paul regards his mission
in exactly the same terms: he suffers dishonor and hardship for the sake
of Christ's name. Unlike Jeremiah, though, Paul sees no place for lament
in carrying out his mission to the gentiles. Suffering takes on the positive

2. In what follows I am guided by Lakkis, "Have You Any Right," 177–80.

elements of honor and rejoicing, thus lament plays no part in the life of faith and the rebirthing of hope amidst the trials and tribulations of Christian discipleship.

In addition to the Pauline writings, the letters of Peter also highlight the aspect of rejoicing in the calling to share in Christ's sufferings (1 Pet 4:13). At the same time, however, a distinction is drawn between suffering for the sake of Christ's gospel (which meets with God's approval) and general suffering due to a multitude of human perversions (which meet with God's disapproval). "But let none of you suffer as a murderer, or a thief, or a wrongdoer, or a mischief-maker; yet if one suffers as a Christian, let him not be ashamed, but under that name let him glorify God" (1 Pet 4:15–16). Neither of these forms of suffering is thought of as cause for lament, for Christian suffering meets with divine approval, while wrongdoing rightly leads to suffering. The New Testament notion of Christian suffering as meeting with divine approval is further underlined in the extracanonical literature concerning the Christian martyrs. A good example is the martyrdom of Perpetua and Felicity in the very early third century. After having been sentenced to a violent death by wild beasts in the arena for refusing to participate in the practice of emperor worship, Perpetua writes that she and the others "went down cheerfully to the dungeon."[3] The suffering of these martyrs is cheerful because it is seen as sharing in the suffering of Christ, through which comes the anticipated glory of resurrection life. By the end of the second century, "the early church had already idealized this approach to suffering and persecution, holding up the lives of the saints as the normative example to be emulated by all Christians."[4] The practice of martyrdom as the idealized approach to suffering precluded any practice of lament as appropriate to Christian discipleship.

There are scholars who, while acknowledging that the New Testament is characterized by the absence of lament, nonetheless maintain that we should not overlook certain events and experiences that provoked even the early Christians to lament. Markus Öhler, for instance, writes that what we find in the New Testament is "neither a general repudiation nor a denial of lament, mourning, and other expressions of the experience of suffering."[5] Lament is expressed through various genres and the topic is

---

3. Lakkis, "Have You Any Right," 180.

4. Lakkis, "Have You Any Right," 181.

5. Öhler, "To Mourn, Weep, Lament," 150. The author examines the topic of lamenting death in the Gospels, the positive assessment of lament in the Letter of James, lament in an apocalyptic context, and "sighing" and "moaning" in the Pauline writings.

treated from diverse perspectives. In the Gospels, for instance, "to weep" is often associated with death: people weep over the death of the young daughter of the ruler of the synagogue (Mark 5:39); Jesus weeps over the death of Lazarus (John 11:35); Mary Magdalene weeps over the death of Jesus (John 20:11); as Jesus walks to his place of execution women weep for him (Luke 23:27), but Jesus says to them that they are not to weep for him but for themselves and their children (Luke 23:28); Jesus weeps bitterly as he approaches Jerusalem (Luke 19:41–44) because of the judgment that will descend upon the people due to their rejection of his messianic mission; and Jesus utters a cry of lament on the cross (Mark 15:34; Matt 27:46) so that lament and mourning appear not solely in relation to the death of human beings but also take on a christological perspective. When we move away from the Gospels and turn to the Letter of James, lament plays a role in a vastly different context: "Cleanse your hands, you sinners, and purify your hearts. . . . Be wretched and mourn and weep. Let your laughter be turned to mourning and your joy to dejection. Humble yourselves before the Lord and he will exalt you" (Jas 4:8–10). The context here is a call to humility and penance in the interests of transforming the "passions" (Jas 4:1–3). Christians must acknowledge their state of wretchedness with mourning and weeping, which results in nearness to God and purity of heart. The framework within which James operates is that of Jewish penance, classically expressed in the lament psalms that focus on individual sin (e.g., Pss 38 and 51).[6]

In addition to the lamenting of death in the Gospels and the practice of lament as penance in the Letter of James, the New Testament also depicts lament in the apocalyptic context of the book of Revelation.[7] The basic structure of the apocalypse genre serves to effectively put the problems of the present age in perspective: "It provides a view of the world that will be a source of consolation in the face of distress."[8] In the

6. Öhler, "To Mourn, Weep, Lament," 153. Psalms 38 and 51, it should be noted, have the lamenter's sin and iniquity in focus and are therefore exceptions to the main theme of the divine absence or hiding—unrelated to sin—in the other psalms of lament.

7. Ever since the discovery of the Qumran Scrolls and the Nag Hammadi texts around the middle of the twentieth century, there has been a resurgence of interest in Jewish apocalyptic writings and an increasing recognition of their significance for Christian theology generally and systematic theology in particular. See Koch, *Rediscovery of Apocalyptic*. Koch refers to the seminal thought of Ernst Käsemann and Wolfhart Pannenberg on this topic.

8. Collins, *Daniel*, 22. The basic structure of the genre is that a revelation is given by God, through a mediator (angelic agency), to a seer, concerning future eschatological

context of deep conflict, the central question that occupies the mind of the apocalyptist is how to overcome the discrepancy between what is and what should be: "Why is faithfulness to the God of the Law rewarded by persecution and suffering?"[9] Central to the apocalypse genre is the questioning cry to God—"How long?"—which we find repeatedly in the psalms of lament. In the book of Revelation this lament is associated with the martyrs whose souls cry out with a loud voice from under the heavenly altar: "O Sovereign Lord, holy and true, how long will it be before you judge and avenge our blood on those who dwell upon the earth?" (Rev 6:10). While this lament cry is attributed to the souls of the dead martyrs, its articulation actually arises from the living faithful who are being tested by persecution, and it serves to encourage them to remain steadfast in their faith because universal judgment and eschatological salvation must soon take place: "And behold, I am coming soon" (Rev 22:7, 12, 20). True to the genre of the apocalypse, Revelation does not end with lament but with the vision of the "new heaven and new earth" (Rev 21:1), when time is fulfilled and God will "wipe away every tear from their eyes, and death shall be no more, neither shall there be mourning nor crying nor pain any more, for the former things have passed away" (Rev 21:4). In the full-blown apocalyptic of Revelation, lament as the cry to God—"How long?"—is portrayed as integral to the life of the faithful who are persecuted for the sake of Christ and yearn to partake of the glory of the eschaton.

When we examine the Pauline writings, in two passages Paul speaks of a specific form of lament, namely, "groaning" or "sighing." In one passage the focus is on the Christian life (2 Cor 5), while in the other Paul refers to the state of creation (Rom 8). The apostle displays in his writings ideas that reflect the influence of apocalyptic thought. The frequency of "flesh" language in particular is evidence for "the pervasiveness of the apocalyptic framework in Paul's thinking, since 'flesh' means the sphere over which the power of Satan holds sway."[10] Those who are in the "flesh" (*sarx*) are not free to realize the good because they serve the "law of sin" (Rom 7–8). While humans are free to choose the good, they experience themselves as inclining towards the gratification of "the desires of the

---

events that will finally establish God's universal reign in "a new heaven and new earth" (Isa 65:17; Rev 21:1).

9. Beker, *Paul's Apocalyptic Gospel*, 30.

10. Marcus, "Evil Inclination," 17.

flesh" (Gal 5:16).[11] The only thing that can break the evil inclination of the flesh is the universal redemptive power of the crucified and risen Christ. To belong to Christ is to live "according to the Spirit" (Rom 8:5), that is, the new life that is God's triumph over the powers of death (both within and without). For Paul, the paschal mystery of Christ is "*the* apocalyptic event,"[12] for it signifies the setting free of the creation from the powers of death: "We know that the whole creation has been groaning in travail together until now; and not only the creation, but we ourselves, who have the first fruits of the Spirit, groan inwardly as we wait for the adoption as sons, the redemption of our bodies" (Rom 8:22–23). The present age is characterized by longing for our "heavenly dwelling" (2 Cor 5:2) when we will be "further clothed, so that what is mortal may be swallowed up by life" (2 Cor 5:4). Death is the mark of the present age, and life is the hallmark of the age to come.[13] The groaning of which Paul speaks is inseparable from his longing in the Spirit to be clothed in resurrection life. Paul does not regard sighing and groaning as expressions of weakness and despair that do not befit Christian discipleship but affirms these genres of lament as integral to life in the Spirit, which evokes in Christ's followers such eager longing for "adoption as sons, the redemption of our bodies" (Rom 8:23). Therefore, "it is not that lament is invalidated, but is rather *re-evaluated as a positive expression of our longing*."[14] To be heirs with Christ implies that we must "suffer with him" (Rom 8:17; Phil 1:29), which takes on the positive aspects of honor and "rejoicing" (Col 1:24).

11. This Pauline thought regarding the desires of the flesh bears a strong family resemblance to the *yeser* theory of rabbinic theology. See Otzen, *Judaism in Antiquity*, 89–90. The Hebrew word *yeser* conveys the sense of "striving" or "will," but it takes on a primarily negative meaning inasmuch as it refers to the evil impulse that the individual must endeavor to bring under control by adhering to the law. The *yeser* theory pertains to ethical dualism, which is implicit in the basic religious structure of Judaism: "I have set before you life and death, blessing and curse; therefore choose life, that you and your descendants may live" (Deut 30:19); "Behold, I set before you the way of life and the way of death" (Jer 21:8); "In the path of righteousness is life, but the way of error leads to death" (Prov 12:28). To the Jewish mind, the individual is poised between the two worlds of evil (death) and good (life), and adherence to the law brings the blessings of life.

12. Marcus, "Evil Inclination," 18; emphasis original.

13. The doctrine of the two ages refers to an eschatological dualism: it is a dualism on the temporal plane since it expresses a contradiction between that which presently is and that which is to come; and it is eschatological because it concerns the final replacement of this age by the age to come.

14. Öhler, "To Mourn, Weep, Lament," 165; emphasis added.

Paul, therefore, does not lament his suffering with Christ but rather sighs and groans out of his eager longing to be glorified with Christ.

The foregoing discussion has shown that while the only explicit use of the tradition of Jewish lament in the New Testament is to be found in the Gospel account of Jesus's cry of God-forsakenness on the cross, nonetheless upon closer examination of the Christian writings various forms or expressions of lament come to light, such as groaning, sighing, mourning, and weeping. Paul in his writings proffers a particular understanding of groaning and sighing as positive expressions of our longing to be glorified with Christ, while he repudiates any expression of lament in association with suffering in the name of Christ, for Christian suffering takes on the positive elements of honor and rejoicing. But if Christ's suffering for the sake of the godless culminates in his lament cry on the cross, and he was heard by the Father, why should lament be precluded among his followers who are placed before God by him and undergo suffering as the ongoing embodiment of God in the world? Lament should not be regarded as unwanted, unbidden prayer but has a right to be voiced since it functions as *a form of perseverance* in the journey of Christian life, whose happy ending is hoped for but not yet given. The last word of Christian faith—i.e., nothing can separate us from the love of God that is in Jesus Christ our Lord (Rom 8:38)—should not be made the first, which is to say that the journey towards the hoped-for happy ending is ineluctably marked by much anguish, many uncertainties, and various sufferings (guilty and innocent).[15] Insofar as lament gives expression to our manifold sufferings and brings them before God who listens to our burdened hearts and sympathizes with us through the exercise of the divine pathos, lament can be thought of as *"the persistent waiting for God's saving presence."*[16] Instead of thinking that lamentable situations are to be endured silently without complaint—which recalls the Stoic ideal of extirpating the disturbing emotions—a theology *de profundis* (from the depths) encourages Christians to view the lament speech form as integral to the process of entering into genuine dialogue with God, renewing hope, persevering in faith, and transforming grief into joy as

15. Welz, "Trust and Lament," 135. Welz acknowledges the argument put forward by Oswald Bayer that too often Christian theology reaches a happy ending much too quickly and does not take seriously the uncertainty and hopelessness along the way.

16. Welz, "Trust and Lament," 135; emphasis added.

they journey towards the hoped-for happy ending of sharing in the glory of Christ's resurrection from the dead.[17]

Lament in the Theological Tradition: Neglect of the Biblical Notion of the Suffering Righteous

When we turn our attention from the New Testament to Christian theology, we find that there, too, lament generally plays little or no part in the development of theological thought. In the patristic period the one notable exception to this neglect of lament is Augustine, while Luther and Calvin in the Reformation follow Augustine in granting legitimacy to lament in Christian faith and worship. But the overarching view in the tradition of Christian theology, both in the East and in the West, is that Jesus's cry on Calvary expresses *our* forsakenness and brokenness—in no way can the cry be interpreted as the Son being forsaken by the Father. The appropriate human response to God's grace revealed in Jesus Christ is not complaint, or protest, or lament, but praise and thanksgiving for what God has done for us in the crucified and risen Christ. The main forms of prayer in the Christian tradition are prayers of thanksgiving and penitential prayers that acknowledge the ongoing problem of sin and the continual growth of Christian life as a "straining forward to what lies ahead" (Phil 3:13). Gregory of Nyssa, for instance, introduces the key doctrine of eternal "progress" according to which one becomes "God's friend"[18] through a process of progress in the life of virtue. The essence of the Christian faith is participation in the divine nature, which implies that it is necessary to show by our life that "we ourselves are what the power of this great name [of Christ] requires us to be."[19] Gregory is influenced here by Paul's statement, "It is now no longer I that live, but Christ lives in me" (Col 2:20). The Christian life cannot be the partaking of both light and darkness, for the stronger of the two must destroy the weaker. Virtue will have victory over evil only when the enemy gives way to it completely. The practice of lament would be unbecoming of Christian life understood as an imitation of the divine nature, that is, our sharing in

17. Against Ricoeur who maintains that the process of transfiguration initiated by lament means the end of lament—Ricoeur interprets Job's repentance at the end of the book of Job as a repenting of the complaint itself—Welz argues that the process of transfiguration is ongoing until the hoped-for happy ending is attained.

18. Gregory of Nyssa, *Life of Moses*, 137.

19. Gregory of Nyssa, "On Perfection," 95.

the "lofty ideas"[20] that such imitation implies. Gregory does acknowledge that in moments of misfortune and loss—such as the untimely death of bishop Meletius of Antioch, who presided over the First Council of Constantinople in 381—it is appropriate to "burst out with a voice of lamentation adequate to the greatness of the distress,"[21] but his writings do not promote a practice of lament as integral to Christian faith, worship, and theology. At the end of his *Funeral Oration on Melitius*, Gregory intimates that the faithful should console one another by sharing in the Eucharist: "Give your wine to those that are in sorrow . . . thus our grief may be turned to joy and gladness."[22] It is by the shedding of the blood of Christ that the grief of our human existence is transformed into joy and gladness. But for Gregory the cry of the Savior cannot be God's cry, it cannot be the cry of the divine Son; rather, the Savior was appropriating our personality when he cried out "My God, my God, why have you forsaken me?" It was the humanity of Christ speaking, not his divinity, as he appropriated our forsakenness in order to bring about our regeneration. Given that it was not the divinity of Christ that was speaking when he uttered his dying cry, it follows that Christian life, as a participation in the divine nature, cannot include the practice of lament.

It is important to appreciate the close connection between the patristic and medieval axiom that the divine nature is not subject to suffering (*apatheia*) and the neglect of the practice of lament in Christian faith and worship. Christ, as the incarnate Word of God, could be conceived as suffering only according to the flesh. And even this suffering of his flesh was seen as under the control of Christ's perfect self-mastery as the Word made flesh. All of Christ's passions are depicted as under the spontaneous guidance of his reason as the Logos, so that Christ displayed perfect virtuous behavior, which serves as a model for us sinners. Even Cyril of Alexandria, who more than any other theologian of his time stressed the personal unity of Christ—"one incarnate nature of the Word"[23]—could not manage to acknowledge Christ's lament cry on Golgotha as the cry of the divine Son. Instead, Cyril says that *Christ is calling to the Father for us and not for himself.* John of Damascus asserts the same thing in his interpretation of Christ's prayers in Gethsemane and on the cross: he says

---

20. Gregory of Nyssa, "On What It Means," 84.

21. Gregory of Nyssa, *Funeral Oration on Melitius*, 513.

22. Gregory of Nyssa, *Funeral Oration on Melitius*, 517.

23. See Cyril of Alexandria, "Second Letter to Succenus," 87–89.

that Christ offered these prayers "as appropriating our personality."[24] The prayers of Christ are seen as nothing more than lessons for his followers to ask God to help them in times of trial and to always prefer God's will to their own. Christ's cry does not and cannot mean that he as the Son was forsaken on the cross; rather, it was we who were forsaken and disregarded. Following the orthodox norms of his time, John of Damascus refuted any suggestion that Christ's divinity suffered in the flesh. He writes that Christ "endured all in the flesh, while His divine nature which alone was passionless remained void of passion."[25] This view remained axiomatic in medieval theology. Thomas Aquinas, for instance, held that Christ's passion did not relate to the divine nature that was incapable of suffering, and his suffering was always under the spontaneous control of his superior reason as the Word of God.[26] In the perspective of these orthodox teachings on Christology, Christ's cry on the cross is strictly attributed to his flesh, for the divine Son assumed our flesh in order to make atonement for sins and to restore sinners to union with God. Now that sinners are reconciled to God by Christ's suffering in the flesh, Christians have no cause to utter cries of lament to God, hence patristic and medieval theology in general precluded reflection on lament as a theological topic.

The basic problem with patristic and medieval theology is that the incarnation is thought of as the "taking up" of humanity by the Word of God—with a corresponding emphasis on Christ's humanity as sharing in his divinity—rather than the descent or real participation of divinity in the human temporal realm (i.e., kenosis of divinity), which requires us to acknowledge the genuine human becoming and development of the incarnate Word. Within the framework of a truly kenotic Christology, each nature is understood as *advancing through the other* in the authentic historical life of the incarnate Word, which implies that Christ is conscious of his divinity through his humanity, and he is conscious of his humanity through his divinity.[27] With respect to Christ's prayers in Gethsemane and his lament cry on the cross, he does not offer these prayers "as appropriating our personality," but is petitioning the Father for himself as he finds himself in the clutches of agonizing dread, distress, and death. All of *Christ's actions are at once both human and divine*, for he acts as the

---

24. John of Damascus, *Exposition of Orthodox Faith*, bk. 3, ch. 24, 71.

25. John of Damascus, *Exposition of Orthodox Faith*, bk. 3, ch. 26, 71.

26. Aquinas, *Summa theologica*, III, 15.2, 15.3, and 15.6.

27. See Novello, *Passionate Deification*, 149–59.

Son of the Father when he acts as a human, and as a human when he acts as the Son. The two natures progressively actualize themselves as the one and the other as they encounter and address each other in the person of the incarnate Son. The cry on Calvary is truly the anguished cry of the Son addressed to the Father, which has both a human element in keeping with the Jewish tradition of the suffering righteous, and a divine aspect in that as the Son who is forsaken by his Father, we see the extraordinary manner in which God bears the people's sin and internalizes their rebellion—the divine pathos—so as to bring to fruition the fullness of the covenant of grace. In this perspective, *human suffering and divine suffering, while distinct, are inseparable, and their ultimate unity in the person of the crucified Christ is integral to God's work of divinizing humanity and the world.* The following chapter 3 will elaborate at some length on this particular perspective.

When we turn our attention to Augustine's writings, we find that his thought is quite unique in the patristic era in that he accords a central place to lament in Christian life. In his *Enarrationes in Psalmos*,[28] Augustine offers his reflections and sermons on the book of Psalms and engages at length with lament as a theological topic. The topic of lament is not limited to Augustine's writings on the Psalter, though, for lament clearly forms the atmosphere of another of his major works, namely, *Confessions*, which is patterned after the book of Psalms.[29] In that work, Augustine describes his profound wrestling with God, for unlike Gregory of Nyssa, he magnifies the Lord's name as a sinful and wretched man, not as someone whose virtuous life gives testimony to the great name of Christ. By the time Augustine sat down to write the *Confessions* he had given up on the optimistic goal of attaining perfection through a Christian Platonism, since he continued to struggle with his own temptations and the weight of his sins: "He would never achieve the wrapt contemplation of the ideal philosopher."[30] In his reassessment of the human condition, Augustine came to affirm the compulsive force of habit (*consuetudo*) in the human will, which drags the baptized Christian down and sucks him back into everyday common things.[31] Saint Paul's depiction of a basic tension between "flesh" and "spirit" resonated with Augustine's experience of

28. See Augustine, *St. Augustine on Psalms*; and Brock, "Augustine's Incitement to Lament."

29. Studer, *Grace of Christ*, 45.

30. P. Brown, *Augustine of Hippo*, 147.

31. Augustine, *Confessions*, §10, 40.

the lingering weight and burden of his sins. There could be no complete break for the baptized Christian from the past: "In the last resort, the individual Christian, like the Church, remains deeply infected with sin."[32] Baptism does not cure the Christian all at once from his past sinful life but launches him on a lifelong process of convalescence, sustained by the love of God's mercy and consoled by occasional inward glimpses of God as sheer delight.

For Augustine nothing else but delight can motivate the human will; to act is to be affected by an object of delight. Augustine uses the language of erotic longing to underscore the emotions as acknowledgements of the truth of our profound neediness. Unlike the Stoic doctrine regarding the need to extirpate perturbing emotions such as desire, fear, grief, sorrow, and sadness, the crucial point for Augustine is the rightness of the object of the emotions: the Christian who feels appropriate emotions will desire eternal life, fear eternal punishment, feel sorrow for sins committed, feel gladness at performing good works, feel compassion for fellow sinners, grieve for the redemption of the body, and rejoice in the hope that death will be swallowed up in victory.[33] Since baptism does not represent a clean break from one's past history of sin, Augustine thinks of Christian life as an ordeal to be endured in the hope of being completely filled by God in the age to come. The entire ethos of the *Confessions* is one of profound lament for the ongoing burdens that Augustine endures as he yearns deeply for the bliss of eternal union with God as his hoped-for final end.

It is in his *Enarrationes in Psalmos*, however, that Augustine elaborates at length on lament as a theological topic. The Psalter is given a christological reference by Augustine, and he often makes a scriptural argument for why Christians should pray the psalms. David is considered a prophet and the author of the psalms, and according to Jewish prophecy the Messiah will come from his seed. So, Christ is David's son according to the flesh and his Lord according to his divinity. "David both *represents* Christ, and more importantly, is a *member* of his kingdom, of the *totus Christus*."[34] As a prophet, David is held to be a participant in Christ's body, hence his words are the words of Christ. The places in the Gospel story where Christ appears vulnerable and weak, namely, his anguished

---

32. Markus, *End of Ancient Christianity*, 54.

33. Augustine, *City of God*, §14, 9.

34. Brock, "Augustine's Incitement to Lament," 191.

prayer in the garden of Gethsemane and his cry of God-forsakenness on Calvary, guide the manner in which Augustine understands lament in the Psalter. Christ was not above human weakness and vulnerability but has assumed our lament and borne the cries of human frailty before the Father: "Just as he freely took on real flesh so he freely took on real sadness."[35] This he has done in order that we might reconfigure the object of our emotions; that is, that we may desire eternal life, fear eternal punishment, feel sorrow for sins committed, feel gladness at performing good works, feel compassion for fellow sinners, grieve for the redemption of the body, and rejoice in the hope that death will be swallowed up in victory. Central to Augustine's thought on lament is the guiding idea that *our lament is joined to Christ's lament in his passion.*[36] The remembrance of Christ's passion is required to transform believers, and this remembrance is secured by participating in Christ's passion. Augustine writes, "By listening, understanding and groaning with the Psalm let us be changed."[37] By praying the psalms, Christians come to understand that the eyes of the Lord are upon them and they are heard, and that their groaning is an expression of the anticipated joy of life in the age to come. It is through suffering in faith and hope that Christians come to know intimately the divine person of Christ as the object of their suffering.

What makes Christians distinctive is their affective attachment to Christ and the way they make use of the things of this world only to secure eternal happiness. Worldly things are to be used (*uti*) rather than to be enjoyed (*frui*). For Augustine only love of God can satisfy the deep longings of the human heart, thus happiness cannot be sought in earthly things that can never satisfy the heart's yearnings. The way of Christian life is the way of detachment from earthly things, which is the way of making our Passover and cleaving to Christ in the mighty hope of attaining

35. Cited by Brock, "Augustine's Incitement to Lament," 193. While Augustine states that Christ took on real sadness, it is worth noting, however, that he mistakenly interprets Stoic first movements or "prepassions" (*propatheia*) as actual passions, with the result that the suffering emotions of Christ are not accorded any real depth and Christ appears as a Stoic sage. See Novello, *Passionate Deification*, 125–28.

36. Brock, when discussing Allen Verhey's contemporary individualistic account of lament, points out how Verhey conceives of lament in terms that are quite the opposite to Augustine's intention: "In lament we do not join Christ's suffering; Christ takes up human cries of suffering" (Brock, "Augustine's Incitement to Lament," 202). Verhey maintains that Christ made the human cry of lament his own cry, and God raised him up; this is the good news of the gospel.

37. *Enarrat. Ps.* 68 (1.)2. Cited by Brock, "Augustine's Incitement to Lament," 194.

beatific union with God. God should not be praised when things go well and cursed when things go wrong; rather, praise is due God at all times, since whether feeling happy or suffering distress believers are being educated by God and prepared for an eternal inheritance.[38] Augustine therefore affirms the worth of endurance in suffering (cf. Rom 5:3–5) as essentially purgative. The Christian martyrs exemplify this basic attitude of forfeiting earthly things in order to seek the beauty of virtue and to prepare for eternal happiness. Within this framework of Augustine's pedagogy of lament, a definition of lament can be proposed: "*Lament is a modality of human affect directed to God, and anchored in eschatological hope.* . . . Lament is the expression of the pains of awaiting the eschaton."[39] The eyes of faith perceive with clarity the "groaning" (Rom 8:18–24) of this troubled age and look with anticipation to the glory of "the things that are unseen and eternal" (2 Cor 4:17–18). Christians must be taught this pedagogy of lament in their pilgrim life of ascent towards God.

Augustine's ontology of lament is centered on an account of Christ's sorrow on the cross. What Christ laments in his passion is human resistance against him, not God-forsakenness. His mission as the good physician was to bring people health, but they resisted him and "thrashed about savagely, and this was the source of sorrow to the doctor."[40] Believers, who possess the first fruits of the Spirit, are those who seek to detach themselves from earthly cares by initiating the practice of lament that transforms. Lament performs a transforming function by reorienting prayers of the faithful so that they conform to Christ as members of his body, rather than attempting to manipulate Christ for earthly gain.[41] In contrast to modern sensibilities where people lament the loss of bodily integrity, material possessions, and loved ones, Augustine suggests that the loss of these things is only "the *occasion* for the loss that is truly lamentable: of affective attachment to Christ, of virtue and charity."[42]

38. Cf. *Enarrat. Ps.* 54.2. Cited by Brock, "Augustine's Incitement to Lament," 186.

39. Brock, "Augustine's Incitement to Lament," 186; emphasis added.

40. *Enarrat. Ps.* 68 (2.)5. Cited by Brock, "Augustine's Incitement to Lament," 195.

41. Brock, "Augustine's Incitement to Lament," 196.

42. Brock, "Augustine's Incitement to Lament," 184; emphasis original. See Juvin, *Coming of the Body*, for a treatment of what people today lament about. Juvin contends that the trinity of Western ideals—i.e., liberty, equality, and fraternity—is being replaced today by the new trinity of health, security, and pleasure. People are becoming increasingly obsessed with longevity, maintaining youthfulness, maximizing pleasure, and ensuring their security by eliminating all hazards, risks, and chance. It is the loss of any of these things that gives cause for lament to contemporary modern people.

He never reflects on human lament in abstraction from Christ's cry of dereliction on the cross as he seeks to determine "what precisely is truly lamentable to Christian faith."[43] By insisting that a Christian judgment about the things that are truly lamentable be determined from the vantage point of inclusion in *Christ's* lament, "Augustine remains instructive for a contemporary systematic theology of lament."[44] His reflection on lament in terms of affective attachment to Christ makes an enduring contribution to a Christian theology of lament, "not least by demanding that it be conceived in fundamentally social and redemptive terms."[45] Against modern accounts of suffering and lament that tend to have an anthropological and individualistic focus,[46] Augustine's account highlights the need to allow Christology to serve as a basic criterion.

What is especially positive about Augustine's account is that lament is portrayed as bringing humans to themselves, as a modality of human affect directed to God and anchored in eschatological hope. Since the laments of the faithful are included in the lament of Christ, lament is seen as leading the faithful out of the abyss of futile desires and the quagmire of sin and into a new transforming focus on Christ as the object of the soul's true aspiration. There are, however, also weaknesses in Augustine's account. The first obvious limitation is that lament is acknowledged *only in relation to the enduring reality of sin*. Any sustained expression of grief or lament over worldly losses, including loss of loved ones, betrays

---

43. Brock, "Augustine's Incitement to Lament," 184.

44. Brock, "Augustine's Incitement to Lament," 200.

45. Brock, "Augustine's Incitement to Lament," 201. One of the ethical implications of Augustine's view of lament is that it orients Christian mission by inducing affective attachment to nonbelievers, to the profligate, to those who are lost and in need of rescue from futile desires. Lament, in other words, engenders compassion towards nonbelievers.

46. Brock offers the example of Allen Verhey, who describes suffering as the breakdown of one's self-perception; that is, suffering consists in alienation from the body, isolation from social existence, and the loss of the ability to express one's experience. Verhey sees Job and the lament psalms as giving the suffering voice and allowing them to begin to reconstruct their identity. Suffering has no pedagogical purpose in Verhey's anthropological account, since lament does not include sufferers in Christ. Most striking, though, says Brock, is that Verhey appears to have no understanding of lament as speech *to God*, hence there is no room for petitioning God to respond to the human cry for help. Verhey talks of "owning" our suffering, but Brock insists, following Augustine, that we are to *relativize* our suffering (i.e., join our suffering to Christ's suffering, so that we may know the person of Christ as the object of our suffering).

a disordered soul.[47] The piety of detachment from worldly things and affective attachment to Christ means that God alone is the object of the Christian's delight and joy. Only God should be loved in a way that if lost, due to sin, would cause grief and lament. Hence the psalms are treated as penitential prayers of the sinner, never as complaints to God or as expressions of feeling abandoned by God to terrible affliction and suffering.

A second questionable area of Augustine's thought has to do with his account of suffering as a form of pedagogy. The distress of innocent suffering or expressions of protest raised up to God in the face of terrible injustice have no place in Augustine's view of biblical laments. The problem is that Augustine adopts a purely allegorical interpretation of the psalms, which are given a completely christological reference: everything is read through the lens of the spiritual life, of the soul's longing for the peace of the heavenly Jerusalem. Augustine's adoption of the allegorical method means that he does not treat the psalms in their historical context. For instance, with regard to the cry of Ps 13—"How long, O Lord"—Augustine writes, "How long wilt thou hold me back from understanding in a spiritual manner this Christ who is the Wisdom of God and the true end of the soul's every aspiration?"[48] Similarly, following the dictates of patristic thought that were highlighted earlier, the cry of abandonment in Ps 22 is interpreted as the words of the crucified Christ on behalf of sinful humanity. What the cry on the cross signifies is "the old self whose mortality He had assumed. Together with him, then, our former nature has been nailed to the cross."[49] When Augustine prays this psalm, the prayer he utters is "not that of a righteous man but of one laden with sins. He who thus prays nailed to the cross is indeed our old self who does not even know why God has forsaken him."[50] What is more, with respect to what Christ meant when he uttered the cry on the cross, Augustine writes: "*God had not forsaken Him, since He Himself was God. . . .* Why were these words used, if not because we were present there, because the Church is Christ's Body?"[51]

47. Billman and Migliore, *Rachel's Cry*, 50.

48. Augustine, *St. Augustine on Psalms*, no. 29, 151–52.

49. Augustine, *St. Augustine on Psalms*, no. 29, 201.

50. Augustine, *St. Augustine on Psalms*, no. 29, 201.

51. Augustine, *St. Augustine on the Psalms*, no. 29, 210; emphasis added. The view that God had not forsaken Christ because he himself was God goes hand in glove with the patristic teaching on the impassibility of the divine nature. The proposition that Christ suffered not in his divinity but only in his humanity enabled the church fathers

The thesis of God-abandonment, which has risen to the level of an axiom in some theological circles, receives no support from the writings of Augustine, nor from the writings of the church fathers in general.[52] In his commentary on the creed, Augustine makes it plain that Christ suffered abandonment at the hands of his own people, "those insulting ones"[53] who ridiculed him on the cross, not at the hands of God. The cry of abandonment is a prayer on behalf of our sins, that is, Christ spoke those words for the sake of the members of his body who are sinners and who fear death. Christ's dying cry is not addressed to the Father, for it is impossible that he as God could be forsaken by God, hence Augustine asserts that the lament cry was not the cry of the head but of the members of his body. He as the Son was not petitioning the Father for himself but merely appropriating our human predicament. But is there not a real sense in which it can be said that Jesus *is* forsaken by God, namely, in the sense that the Father abandons or hands over the Son into the custody of evildoers? This particular interpretation is well founded in the New Testament (Rom 8:32; cf. Rom 1:18–32), and it need not give rise to the God-abandonment thesis as long as we understand that since the Father also abandons himself in the handing over of the Son, the Father is not absent but present on the cross as the interiority of the event. The Father, in other words, speaks the Word even in the final silence of the cross, which speaks of the fecundity of God's love for the world.[54] This will be elaborated in the following chapter 3.

When we turn to Luther's writings on prayer and lament, we find that his thoughts are similar to Augustine's in many respects, although there are some notable differences as well. The leaven at work in all of

---

to hold two fundamental doctrines together; namely, God's presence or solidarity with Christ on the cross and the impassibility of God. The prayers of Christ in Gethsemane and on Calvary are thus attributed to his humanity, not his divinity.

52. Athanasius, for example, interpreted the ominous signs that accompanied Jesus's cry on the cross—the trembling of the earth, the rending of the veil of the temple, the eclipse of the sun, the splitting of the rocks, the opening of the tombs, and the centurion's confession—as evidence of the Father's presence on the cross. See Athanasius, *Four Discourses against Arians*, 424. John Chrysostom went a step further by interpreting the numinous events that accompanied Jesus's death as signs of Christ's might and power—"I have power to lay down my life, and I have power to take it again; and this charge I have received from my Father" (John 10:18)—and of God's wrath against the wicked who put Christ to death. See Chrysostom, *Homilies on the Gospel*, 520–21.

53. Augustine, *On the Creed*, 373.

54. See McIntosh, *Mystical Theology*, 158–59.

Luther's writings is his doctrine of justification by grace through faith, as well as his theology of the cross and his teaching regarding *Anfechtung* (temptations or trials).[55] These doctrines provide the context for appreciating Luther's thought on prayer and lament. Luther views spiritual trials as rendering believers capable of receiving the gifts and works of God in Christ. In his commentary on chapter 8 of the Letter to the Romans, Luther says that whenever we pray to God for something, God contravenes all of our ideas and tears them down before we can receive his good things (cf. 1 Sam 2:7). Only when we have ceased making our own plans— which is a form of idolatry—and have become purely passive before God are we capable of receiving God's counsels and works: "Therefore, when everything is hopeless for us and all things begin to go against our prayers and desires, then those unutterable groans begin. And then 'the Spirit helps us in our weakness' (Rom 8:26)."[56] Before God can come to our aid, God performs his "nihilizing work" (*reductio in nihilum*), that is, God makes us "empty" and "nothing" so as to overcome our efforts to make ourselves gods and to justify ourselves.[57] It is only by passing through this agony that Christians achieve true knowledge of themselves (*cognitio sui*) and become capable of receiving God's grace in Christ (*capax Dei*). It is through trials that we grow in humility before God, that we come to know ourselves as weak and easily tempted to sin, and therefore dependent upon divine grace to win the victory over our trials. When we pray, we should not tempt God or presume to prescribe God's response. Luther writes: "We should not determine the when and where and why, or the ways and means and manner in which God should answer our prayer. Rather, we must in all humility bring our petition before him who will certainly do the right thing in accordance with his unsearchable and

55. In discussing Luther, it must be noted that there is a new Finnish interpretation of Luther, which takes issue with the Kant-Ritschl-Herrmann line of Luther-interpretation that has dominated Protestant theology of the last century. The Finnish school—headed by Professor Tuomo Mannermaa—has undertaken a careful rereading of Luther's works, and its research has revealed the ontological concepts in Luther's thought and how Luther's teaching on justification converges with the Orthodox view of salvation as theosis. According to the forensic model of justification, it is *as though* sinners are righteous. But the Finnish school argues that Luther clearly speaks of how the faithful participate in the person of Christ, who communicates the righteousness, blessing, and life of God, which means that we *really and inwardly* receive the righteousness and life of God in a real exchange of properties. See Braaten and Jenson, *Union with Christ*.

56. Luther, *Lectures on Romans*, 365.

57. See Braaten and Jenson, *Union with Christ*, 10.

divine wisdom."[58] Luther here appeals to the text of Isa 55:8–9: "For my thoughts are not your thoughts, neither are your ways my ways, says the Lord." The hiddenness of God's working, which is contrary to what our minds can grasp, is confirmed by Luther's theology of the cross.

Since Christ was humbled on the cross and has borne our sin, our death, and our hell, so that we might know that God is a God of salvation, not damnation, we should not think it strange that we, too, have to endure suffering and affliction in our pilgrim lives. Conformity to Christ is something that takes shape in the context of the sufferings and sorrows of the present age. Commenting on Ps 51, v. 17—"The sacrifice acceptable to God is a broken spirit"—Luther says that the stubborn and the smug understand nothing of spiritual matters and that faith in Christ pertains to "the afflicted, miserable, and despairing . . . they accept Christ the Physician who teaches that 'this is not an illness unto death' (John 11:4) but a most joyful sacrifice to God."[59] God finds no sacrifice more pleasing than a contrite and humble heart, therefore a Christian should "walk in the midst of death, in the remorse and trembling of his conscience, in the midst of the devil's teeth and hell, and yet should keep the Word of grace, so that in such trembling we say, 'Thou, O Lord, dost look on me with favor.'"[60] Prayers raised up to God are expressions of faith by which we humbly allow God to deal with us according to his gracious saving word revealed in Christ, who has won for us the definitive victory over sin, death, and hell. Prayer and petition are required to keep Christians aware of their insufficiency in the face of distress and weakness and to enable them, in the Spirit, to experience God's power in weakness and in suffering.[61]

Genuine prayer gives expression to the fierce struggle of the life of faith, which is powerfully recorded in the lament psalms of the Hebrew Bible. The psalms were for Luther second only to the Lord's Prayer in instructing Christians how to pray.[62] In his commentary on Ps 6:3—"My

---

58. Luther, *Devotional Writings*, 230–31.

59. Luther, *Selected Psalms I*, 405.

60. Luther, *Selected Psalms I*, 405. The Finnish school of Luther interpretation contends that justifying faith does not merely signify a reception of the forgiveness imputed to sinners by Christ's cross (Christ as *favor*, God's favor) but also a real participation in Christ and therefore a participation in the divine nature (Christ as *donum*, as God's gift). See Braaten and Jensen, *Union with Christ*, 33.

61. Cf. Lehmann, *Luther and Prayer*, 129.

62. Billman and Migliore, *Rachel's Cry*, 51.

soul is sorely troubled"—Luther asserts that "no one who has not been profoundly terrified and forsaken prays profoundly."[63] Psalm 13—"How long, O Lord?"—also gives voice to a troubled soul who feels forsaken by God, and Luther appeals to this psalm when he contends that God gladly hears those who cry and lament but turns away from those who feel smug and proud. Our weeping and groaning in the journey of faith is the humble recognition of our helplessness before God, of our inability to save ourselves from our sinfulness and misery. Our willingness to suffer in the Christian life, in other words, is our recognition that before God all we can do is but wait on God's grace. The modus of Christian life, then, is always *passio*, that is, the faithful are neither inwardly nor outwardly active but only experience what God affects in them.[64] This basic disposition of waiting on God's grace means that Luther, like Augustine, gives an eschatological orientation to Christian prayer, which sustains our waiting in hope for the final establishment of God's kingdom of righteousness and life in the age to come. Also similar to Augustine is the manner in which Luther is preoccupied with experiences of anguish and sorrow that are of a different order than ordinary losses, such as the loss of a loved one. At the center of Luther's thought is the awareness of the total helplessness of the sinner before God, and the accompanying terror of utter abandonment and rejection by God. As with Augustine, Luther regards Christ as "the Physician" who consoles the afflicted soul by the workings of grace, and suffering is portrayed as a form of pedagogy—we are wholly dependent upon divine grace to win the victory over our spiritual trials.

The one area where Luther differs markedly from Augustine concerns his interpretation of Jesus's cry on the cross. Augustine offers an allegorical interpretation, according to which the cry is not the cry of the head but of the members of his body. Luther, on the other hand, offers a more literal interpretation, since he holds that the cry of Ps 22 is to be understood wholly of Christ. What underpins this view is Luther's notion of Christ as the "greatest sinner" (*maximus peccator*). The Word did not take upon himself merely human nature as such, in a "neutral" form, but sinful human nature. He assumed, in other words, adamic flesh. This means that Christ bears the sins of all *in a real manner* in the humanity he has assumed. He is thus the greatest sinner, not in the sense that he committed sins, but in the sense that he took these sins, committed by us,

---

63. Luther, *Selected Psalms I*, 141–42.
64. Cf. Braaten and Jenson, *Union with Christ*, 39.

upon his own body, in order to make satisfaction for them with his own blood.[65] Christ is a kind of collective person or, as Luther says, the "greatest person" (*maxima persona*), in whom all are united in a real manner. This idea of Christ as the greatest person culminates in the notion of Christ as the "only sinner" (*solus peccator*). By virtue of the Word becoming flesh, he immersed himself in all sins, all sins are immersed in him, and there is no sin anywhere that is not in his person. As a human, Christ is the greatest sinner of all; as the Word, he is God, that is, perfect righteousness, blessing, and life, and these divine attributes fight against sin, death, and curse—which also culminate in his person—and overcome them.[66] Hence there is no sin or death or curse anymore because "all sin is gathered together" in Christ, making him the only sinner.[67]

What is more, Luther uses the traditional phrases "according to his human nature" and "according to his divine nature" to uphold the distinction of the natures, but his usage of them no longer displays the dualism that sees divinity and humanity as unreconcilable opposites. In the person of Christ this separation of the two natures has gone: "We may not speak of the divinity separated from the humanity, or of the humanity separated from the divinity."[68] For Luther, the properties of the two natures are communicated to the *concretum* of his person. An important distinction is made between a communication *in abstracto* and *in concreto*.[69] When divinity is thought of in a philosophical and abstract manner, God does not suffer; however, since the Son of God has *in concreto* assumed humanity in the person of Jesus Christ, divinity does suffer, hence the chasm between creator and creature has been overcome. In Christ the two natures are united in such a way that they have *true communion* with each other, otherwise the Chalcedonian formula would be seriously undermined. In light of this true communion of the natures, Luther writes: "God dead, God's passion, God's blood, God's

65. Cf. Braaten and Jensen, *Union with Christ*, 29–30.

66. We get a real sense in Luther's writings that the two natures in Christ are not statically juxtaposed to one another but are thought of in dynamic terms as truly encountering and addressing each other in carrying out his divine work. The divine really participates in the human, in order that the human may participate in the divine. A real exchange of natures is in view. There are no indications of Stoic influences in Luther's thought. The same cannot be said of Augustine.

67. Braaten and Jensen, *Union with Christ*, 31.

68. Nagel, "Martinus," 47.

69. See Lienhard, *Luther*, 337, 339; and Ngien, "Chalcedonian Christology," 62–64.

death. According to his nature God cannot die, but since God and man are united in one person, it is correct to talk of God's death when that man dies who is one thing or one person with God."[70] Luther does allow a place for expressions of grief in Christian life, but our grieving should not be primarily focused on our own suffering; instead, if we are going to grieve "we should grieve over Christ's death . . . *Christ died as no one else died or ever will die.* . . . Why aren't you weeping and lamenting over Christ your Lord, whose death was so much greater and more horrible than that of all [others]?"[71]

On the basis of Luther's doctrine of the communication of the two natures *in concreto* in the person of Christ, we can appreciate why Luther regards Christ's cry on the cross as the cry of the head and not, as Augustine contends, the cry of the members of his body. Luther allows that Christ's cry be interpreted as God's cry, to which the cries of the faithful are joined in an ontological fashion. A potential weakness in Luther's thought, however, is that because Christ's cross was much heavier to bear than any cross his followers will ever have to carry, Luther teaches that the grief of the faithful must be moderate lest the cross of Christ is lost sight of. The limits that Luther places on Christian lament have given rise to the criticism that his theology of the cross instructs Christians to passively and submissively bear the suffering that comes their way, no matter the cause, and not complain or protest their suffering.[72]

We turn our focus to Calvin, who shares Augustine's and Luther's high regard for the Psalter as the primary prayer book of Christians. Calvin calls the book of Psalms "An Anatomy of all the Parts of the Soul,"[73] for there is not an emotion of which anyone can be conscious that is not represented in the Psalter as in a mirror. All the griefs, sorrows, fears, doubts, hopes, cares, and perplexities of historical life are brought to light in the

---

70. Tappert, *Book of Concord,* 599.

71. Luther, *Sermons I,* 234. Cited in Billman and Migliore, *Rachel's Cry,* 54; emphasis added.

72. In response to rebellious peasants who were accusing their rulers of perpetrating injustices against them, Luther instructs the peasants: "Suffering! Suffering! Cross! Cross! This and nothing else is the Christian law!" (Luther, *Christian Society III,* 29; cited in Billman and Migliore, *Rachel's Cry,* 55). Luther expected the peasants to passively endure and suffer wrong; pray to God in their need; and not, like the heathens, seek to force rulers to conform to their impatient will. Clearly such an instruction is open to abuse by the privileged and powerful who exonerate themselves while expecting sufferers to submit to and welcome their suffering.

73. Calvin, *Commentary,* 1:xxxvii.

psalms.[74] Earnest prayer, according to Calvin, proceeds first from a sense of our need and second from faith in the promises of God, and "whatever may serve to encourage us when we are about to pray to God, is taught us in this book."[75] While the psalms are replete with the precepts that frame the life of the people of God, Calvin considers them as principally teaching and training Christians to bear the cross as a genuine proof of obedience. Through the obedience of the cross we renounce the guidance of our own affections and "submit ourselves entirely to God, leaving him to govern us, and to dispose of our life according to his will, so that the afflictions which are the bitterest and most severe to our nature, become sweet to us, because they proceed from him."[76]

The psalmist, and those who pray the psalms, voice real doubt and an acute sense of abandonment by God in times of affliction, yet Calvin sets limits to such intense feelings; they must not become "murmuring" against God. The setting of boundaries to lament logically follows from the fundamental importance that Calvin attaches to his doctrine of *God's providential care*.[77] He acknowledges the difficulty of perceiving divine providence in the midst of history, and this admission allows for the legitimacy of lament in the life of faith, but Calvin insists that the expression of lament must be regulated and moderate.[78] Writing on Ps 13, Calvin says that while David complains to God that he is weighed down by calamities and he feels neglected by God, "yet by this very complaint he gives evidence that faith enabled him to rise higher, and to conclude, contrary to the judgment of the flesh, that his welfare was secure in the hand of God."[79] The opening words of the psalm—"How long, O Lord?"—already indicate how apparently contrary affections are held in unity by David;

---

74. Calvin's high esteem for the Psalter is reflected in the fact that this was the only Old Testament book from which he preached on Sundays (Selderhuis, *Calvin's Theology of Psalms*, 24).

75. Calvin, *Commentary*, 1:xxxvii.

76. Calvin, *Commentary*, 1:xxxix.

77. Billman and Migliore, *Rachel's Cry*, 59.

78. Calvin comments that Ps 88 is an example of a lament that is excessive and improper. With respect to the book of Job, Calvin regards Job as essentially in the right, but he considers Job culpable for using excessive and immoderate language in his complaints to God. Calvin finds the heuristic key to the book of Job in the Pauline statement "Now we see in a mirror dimly" (1 Cor 13:12), which underscores the need for trust in the governance and order of divine providence. See Schreiner, "Through a Mirror Dimly."

79. Calvin, *Commentary*, 1:182.

he feels neglected by God, yet by faith apprehends God's "invisible providence" and encourages himself in the "exercise of patience."[80] Patience
requires believers to stretch their view as far as possible into the future, so
that present grief may not deprive them of hope. Here we see the manner
in which Calvin reads and expounds the psalms in their Old Testament
context; he recognizes the actual historical context in which they were
composed, unlike Augustine's allegorical method. Faith as expressed in
the psalms does not allow itself to be determined by what is visible but
patiently endures the greatest darkness by clinging to the light of God's
promise. Calvin's exposition of Ps 137 shows both his recognition of historical context and the manner in which lament and hope are intertwined
in the lament psalms. Commenting on the Israelites who sat down by the
rivers of Babylon and wept when they remembered Zion, Calvin says that
the intention of the psalmist was to ward off the danger that the exiled
Jews might lose their faith in a foreign land. The writer of the psalm drew
up a form of lament, "that by giving expression to their sufferings in sighs
and prayers, they might keep alive the hope of that deliverance which
they despaired of."[81] Calvin here affirms the Jewish understanding of
lament as the mode by which hope in the promises of God is reborn and
kept alive.

Calvin's exposition of Ps 22 makes much the same point about faith's
exercise of patience and the interweaving of lament and hope. The psalmist, says Calvin, begins with a distinct confession of faith when he twice
refers to God as "*my* God," and then proceeds to pour out his heart to
God.[82] According to the judgment of the flesh, the psalmist thinks he is
forsaken by God, yet he apprehends by faith God's grace which is hidden
from the eye of sense and reason: "And thus it comes to pass, that contrary
affections are mingled and interwoven in the prayers of the faithful."[83]
Faith calls the afflicted back to the divine promises, and teaches them to
wait patiently and to trust in God, and keeps all their thoughts and feelings "under restraint, that they may not break beyond due bounds."[84] Thus
while the afflicted are permitted to express their strong sense of being
forsaken by God, this should not be allowed to become "murmuring"

80. Calvin, *Commentary*, 1:182.
81. Calvin, *Commentary*, 5:189.
82. Calvin, *Commentary*, 1:357; emphasis original.
83. Calvin, *Commentary*, 1:358.
84. Calvin, *Commentary*, 1:359.

against God but must remain within the bounds of submission to God's providential care. Humility, patience, and moderation in sorrow are the virtues that Calvin commends to the afflicted. When the faithful patiently bear the cross of their afflictions and sorrow, God is either punishing them for their sins or purifying them for closer communion with him. As with Augustine and Luther, Calvin affirms suffering as a form of pedagogy and limits expressions of lament to the problem of sin. The suffering of the righteous faithful at the hands of the wicked, or the mourning for the loss of a loved one, or the groaning to God due to extreme illness are not given any acknowledgement by Calvin.

With regard to Jesus's uttering of the first verse of Ps 22 on the cross, Calvin writes that although David bewails his own affliction, "this psalm was composed under the influence of the Spirit of prophecy concerning David's King and Lord."[85] Jesus's cry on the cross, though, sets up an apparent contradiction: if he was the only begotten Son of God, how can he have been so penetrated by grief as to cry out that God his Father had forsaken him? Calvin says that Christ was not altogether exempt from the terrors which the judgment of God strikes into sinners. Although Christ was without sin, he became "our representative" and took upon himself our sins, so that he had before his eyes "the curse of God."[86] Being a real man, Christ was truly subject to the infirmities of our flesh,[87] yet given the perfect purity of his nature, the human affections were perfectly regulated in him and never became sinful through excess. His profound grief on the cross, therefore, "could not so weaken him as to prevent him, even in the midst of his most excruciating sufferings, from submitting himself to the will of God, with a composed and peaceful mind."[88] At this point, though, Calvin appears to fall into the traditional tendency, unlike Luther, of separating the two natures in the person of the God-man.[89]

---

85. Calvin, *Commentary*, 1:362.

86. Calvin, *Commentary*, 1:361.

87. Calvin acknowledges the strong emotions of Christ exhibited in his passion as evidence of his being subjected to the infirmity of this life. See *Institutes*, 3.8.9, where Calvin says that Christianity has nothing to do with Stoic philosophy.

88. Calvin, *Commentary*, 1:372.

89. Calvin does affirm a real communication of attributes of both natures but to the person of Christ, not between the natures themselves as in Luther. The problem with this view—which is basically the position held by Pope Leo in his *Tomus ad Flavianum*—is that it usually results in the separation of the natures since the person is seen as the connecting link between the natures, which are irreconcilable. The actions of Christ therefore appear to be divided up into human and divine actions, as if there

Since Christ "our representative" was a real man who was subject to the infirmities of our flesh, we can say that on Calvary he experienced the terror that proceeds from a sense of the curse of God; yet, on the other hand, given his divinity as the Son, he submitted himself to the will of God with "a composed and peaceful mind." But is it warranted to hold that Christ's prayer in Gethsemane and his lament cry on the cross are indicative of his submission to the Father's will with a composed and peaceful mind? Is it not clear from the Gospel narration of Christ in Gethsemane and on Calvary that he as the Son is petitioning the Father for himself, that he is extremely troubled as he finds himself in the clutches of agonizing dread, suffering, and death? Where Calvin falls short—as does Augustine but not Luther—is in his failure to acknowledge that the actions of Christ the Son are at once both human and divine, for he acts as the Son of the Father when he acts as a human, and as a human when he acts as the Son. This means that the profound grief of the man Jesus as he hangs on the cross is the grief of the Son who is truly distressed by his ordeal; he does not endure his agony with a composed and peaceful mind in obedience to the Father. The strength of Calvin's thought lies in his understanding that Christians, by giving expression to their pain, suffering, and sorrow, are united with Christ who clothed himself with our flesh, so that we might be "more fully clothed" (2 Cor 5:2–3) with the blessed inheritance of Christ's life and glory.[90] Calvin exhorts the faithful to patiently and trustingly bear their trials and sufferings, but a potential weakness in his thought is that Christian lament must not be immoderate lest God's providential care be called into question. But was Christ's lament moderate, notwithstanding his complete submission to the Father's will?

When we move from the Reformation period to contemporary theology, Karl Barth is one eminent theologian who has given serious consideration to the place of prayer, including the lament prayers of the Bible, in Christian life and worship. Barth understands prayer as essentially petition. He acknowledges that prayer has dimensions of praise, thanksgiving, adoration, and confession, but the heart of prayer is asking, for the Son of Man teaches the community of believers to pray and therefore to ask. "The Son of God became the Son of Man, and passed through

---

were two persons in view, not one. Luther also says that the properties of the two natures are communicated to the *concretum* of Christ's person, but he does not envisage a separation between the natures because the person is the principle of the true communion of the natures—the person is the one person of the God-man.

90. Calvin, *Institutes*, 3.9.5.

the narrow archway of asking, in order that He who takes and receives the divine gift and answer might be the Representative and Substitute for all others."[91] The petition of the Son of Man is a petition on behalf of those who cannot ask for themselves and are not in any position to take and receive. The community assembled by Jesus Christ affirms his intercession as that of the great high priest, thus it has the freedom to ask. However imperfect and perverted the asking of the faithful may be compared to Christ's, it will be at his side with its own asking. The following citation captures Barth's thought on prayer as petition:

> And both with heart and mouth the asking of the community which is elected together with Him will be a true and genuine asking, because and in the very fact that it is merely a repetition of His petition, that it is enclosed in His asking. . . . It will ask . . . that it may really be His community; that it may not be in vain that it is founded and maintained and ruled by Him; that it may not be in vain that it is separated from the world and sent out into the world. It will ask for His love, that in a new way it may be united within itself; for His Word, that in a new way it may hear and know it; for His witness, that in a new way it may be effective both in its life and on its lips. It will ask for all that it requires as His community, and therefore as the light of the world which He has kindled.[92]

To Barth's mind, since the will of God that we humans become his covenant partners is fully realized in Jesus Christ, our petition is enclosed in the petition of our Representative. Barth's treatment of the prayer of lament is thus given a thoroughly Christocentric interpretation. The old

---

91. Barth, *Church Dogmatics*, III/3:276. With regard to the Son of God becoming the Son of Man, it is worth highlighting that this event is, in the first instance, the participation of the divine in the human, and only then can it be a participation of the human in the divine (cf. *Church Dogmatics*, IV/2:78, 87). Barth acknowledges the real participation of the divine in the human—i.e., the humiliation of the Son of God who descends into the realm of adamic flesh—which is ordered to the exaltation of the Son of Man—i.e., the participation of the human in the divine. Barth talks of a "mutual participation" of natures in the person of Christ: the twofold movement from above to below (humiliation) and from below to above (exaltation) is conceived in historical terms as an *operatio* between God and adamic flesh (cf. *Church Dogmatics*, IV/2:75). Barth regards the divine and human essence united in the person Christ as working together, as communicating with one another, so he is able to avoid a dualistic Christology that ends up separating the two natures. Barth's Christology is therefore more developed than Calvin's.

92. Barth, *Church Dogmatics*, III/3:277-78.

aeon of sin and death has been overcome in Jesus Christ who "took it in His body to the cross and bore it to the grave."[93] Since the triumph of Christ over his enemies means that the old aeon has been done away with, the program of the Old Testament has been carried through to a completion in the passion of Christ. We cannot, says Barth, fail to see in Jesus's cry on the cross "the answer to the insoluble question of Job and the Psalmists."[94] The problem of the suffering of the righteous now ceases to be a problem in light of the Christ event.[95] Those who are called and converted to Christ must be prepared to suffer and even sacrifice their lives for the sake of Christ, but such suffering due to membership in Christ, our Representative and Substitute, is emphasized in quite a different way from the Old Testament:

> And that is why now there can be no further continuation of the series of prophets and servants of God, or of desperate crying and protest and unbelief, but only the strict matter-of-factness of those who are challenged to bear their cross and follow Christ. The fact that Christ's disciples and also His communities must suffer is important only in connexion with Christ, but in itself it is actually a trifle. . . . The New Testament answer to the problem of suffering—and it alone is the answer to the sharply put query of the Old Testament—is to the effect that *One has died for all.*[96]

Clearly for Barth the question of the suffering righteous, expressed by Ps 22, has been resolved once and for all on the cross, and the appropriate attitude of the followers of Christ is one of "strict matter-of-factness" in bearing their cross and partaking in suffering for the sake of Christ. The practice of lament is not seen by Barth as appropriate to the *communio sanctorum*; what the members of the community of saints must do is "to recognize, and continually recognize, that He [Christ] is the regulative law of their relationship to Him, and therefore to be obedient to Him."[97] The requirement of *obedience to Christ disqualifies the*

---

93. Barth, *Church Dogmatics*, I/2:106.

94. Barth, *Church Dogmatics*, I/2:107.

95. It should be noted, however, that in the last volume of his *Church Dogmatics* (IV/3.1:383–88; 398–408; 421–34; 453–61) Barth offers a commentary on Job where he defends Job's freedom to grieve his afflictions and to protest to God. This represents a possible advance on the theology of lament espoused in earlier volumes. See Billman and Migliore, *Rachel's Cry*, 63.

96. Barth, *Church Dogmatics*, I/2:108–9.

97. Barth, *Church Dogmatics*, IV/2:682.

practice of lament as disobedience. The followers of Christ must subject themselves obediently to the Holy One who has borne the powers of sin and death by his cross and descent into the grave. Hence the complaints and laments of the righteous in the Old Testament are now silenced in the New Testament, although suffering is not abolished but now takes on a different form as partaking in the suffering of Christ.[98] Our suffering is not like the suffering of Christ, though, for no one but the Crucified One has ever known "the true breadth and depth, the true essence and darkness, of human misery. What we see and note and know and more or less painfully experience of it is only a shadow of His cross touching us."[99] However severely we may be buffeted by historical existence, says Barth, "there can be no question of repetitions of Golgotha."[100] All the content of our own experience is completely transcended by the event of Golgotha, hence Barth places restrictions on expressions of lament.[101]

It is clear that Barth sets limits of lament on the basis of his understanding of the definitive victory of Jesus Christ over all sin, suffering, and death. His thought on suffering and lament, however, is not without its dangers, as many critics have already noted.[102] So strong is Barth's emphasis on the complete victory already won in the person of the crucified Lord that the distinction between the "now" and the "then" (1 Cor 13:12) tends to disappear as all our sorrows and losses are already put

98. Barth's position is very much like that of St. Paul, which was discussed in the first part of this chapter.

99. Barth, *Church Dogmatics*, IV/2:487.

100. Barth, *Church Dogmatics*, IV/2:487. Barth's understanding of Christ's passion recalls Luther's perspective, which was cited earlier in this chapter: "Christ died as no one else died or ever will die . . . Christ your Lord, whose death was so much greater and more horrible than that of all [others]?" For Barth, the humiliation (kenosis) of the Son of God reaches its climactic point in his suffering hell on the cross, which is at the same time the climactic point of the exaltation of the Son of Man—the movement from above to below and from below to above is not a matter of two different and successive actions but of a single action, because the "going out of God" aims only at the "coming in of man" (*Church Dogmatics*, IV/2:21). Here we see how Barth, in contrast to the inherited theological tradition, does not allow abstract metaphysical concepts of God to be superimposed upon the Gospel story. Since the fullness of divinity dwells bodily in Christ, Barth asserts that the suffering of the Son of Man is at the same time the suffering of the Son of God.

101. The boundary that Barth sets to the expression of lament in Christian life can be seen in his sermon delivered at the funeral service for his son Matthias. Barth acknowledges his grief and loss, but he views his sorrow as already overcome by Jesus's victory over sin, suffering, and death. See Billman and Migliore, *Rachel's Cry*, 64–65.

102. Cf. Billman and Migliore, *Rachel's Cry*, 66.

behind us, so as to allow the light of Christ to already shine in the darkness of historical existence. What's more, Barth tends to minimize human suffering and misery when he contends that there can be no repetitions of Golgotha, that is, our suffering can never match the depths of Christ's suffering on the cross. While it is a step in the right direction to insist that the breadth and depth of Christ's suffering on Golgotha is qualitatively different to ours—"One has died for all"—nevertheless Barth's thought tends to be insensitive to the plight of many who find themselves in the clutches of great anguish, misery, and injustice in this life and cry to the Lord out of the depths. Calvin places limits on lament primarily on the basis of his doctrine of divine providence, although at the same time he recognizes the positive function lament performs in keeping hope alive as the faithful patiently bear their sufferings in their ascent towards God. Barth, in contrast, sets boundaries to lament on the basis of his theology of Jesus Christ as the victor over all sin, suffering, and death.[103] So complete and total is this victory that all our sorrows and sufferings are already fundamentally behind us as we live our Christian life in obedience to Christ our Representative. There is no room in this perspective for according lament the positive functions of fostering mutual dialogue with God and rebirthing hope as the faithful "strain forward" (Phil 3:13) in their adoption as sons and daughters of God in Christ the Son (filii in Filio).

Another eminent contemporary theologian whose writings are instructive for illustrating how key christological claims preclude a practice of lament is Jürgen Moltmann. Moltmann's journey of faith began when he stumbled upon the psalms of lament while exiled in the Norton prisoner-of-war camp in Scotland. Weighed down with the grief of war, Moltmann discovered the words of the lament psalms that resonated with "the words of my own heart and they called my soul to God. Then I came to the story of the passion, and when I read Jesus' death cry . . . I knew with certainty: this is someone who understands you. . . . I began to summon up the courage to live again, seized by a great hope."[104] This personal journey of faith, together with the theological influences of Dietrich Bonhoeffer's writings from prison and Abraham Heschel's theology of the divine pathos, have all been instrumental in making the theme of

103. Insofar as Christ's victory over all sin, suffering, and death is taken as evidence of God's providential care of his people, Barth and Calvin can be seen as similar in their thinking on the limits to lament.

104. Moltmann, Source of Life, 4–5.

the suffering God central to Moltmann's theology. He offers a strong critique of the traditional doctrine of divine impassibility, which he insists
is incompatible with the biblical picture of a passionate and living God
who becomes vulnerable to suffering out of steadfast love for his people
and the world. In *The Crucified God*, Moltmann develops a theology of
the cross that is centered on Jesus's lament cry on Calvary. Every theology
that claims to be Christian "must come to terms with Jesus' cry on the
cross. Basically, every Christian theology is consciously or unconsciously
answering the question, 'Why hast thou forsaken me?'"[105]

In light of the primary place accorded to Jesus's lament cry in
Moltmann's thinking, it is somewhat surprising that he does not seek
to explore the lament tradition in which Ps 22 stands, in order to shed
light on Jesus's use of this psalm. Instead, Moltmann asserts that it is "not
right to interpret the cry of Jesus in the sense of Ps. 22, but more proper
to interpret the words of the psalm here in the sense of the situation of
Jesus."[106] The reason Jesus's cry is not interpreted from the perspective of
the cry of the psalmist is that Moltmann regards the cross as "an event
between God and God."[107] In the case of Jesus the Son, the "my God" of
Ps 22 does not refer to the covenant God of Israel but exclusively to "my
Father"; and the "I" who has been forsaken is not the righteous person
faithful to the covenant but is in a special way the "I" of the forsaken Son.
This assertion is problematic, though, for it is plain from the Gospels
that the God whom Jesus addresses as Father is most assuredly the God
of Israel. The fact that Jesus views himself as the one proclaimed by the
prophets is sufficient in itself to establish that in the case of Jesus the
"my God" of Ps 22 does refer to the God of the covenant. In the second
century, Irenaeus of Lyons wrote the following in relation to this issue:
"If, therefore, the self-same person is present who was announced by
the prophets, our Lord Jesus Christ . . . it is plain that the Father also
is Himself the same who was proclaimed by the prophets, and that the
Son, on His coming, did not spread the knowledge of another Father."[108]
In combatting various heresies of his day, Irenaeus taught that there is
but one God, the creator of the world, who delivered the Israelites from
slavery in Egypt, who gave the law to the people, who sent the prophets,

---

105. Moltmann, *Crucified God*, 155.
106. Moltmann, *Crucified God*, 152.
107. Moltmann, *Crucified God*, 253; also 154.
108. Irenaeus, *Against Heresies*, 475.

and who in these last times sent his own Son, in whom all things are summed up.[109] Another important figure of the second century, Justin Martyr, bolsters this view regarding the identification of the Father with the covenant God of Israel, when he treats Ps 22 as predicting the entire passion of Christ. So important is this psalm in interpreting Jesus's death that Justin Martyr deems it necessary to cite the whole of it "in order that you may hear His reverence to the Father, and how he refers all things to Him, and prays to be delivered by Him from this death."[110] Both Irenaeus and Justin Martyr regarded Ps 22 as a hermeneutical key for interpreting Jesus's death, and they understood that in the case of Jesus the "my God" of Ps 22 refers to "my Father."

Moltmann disregards these traditional perspectives in relation to Jesus's cry on the cross in order to pursue his interest in modern atheistic protest.[111] He is keen to emphasize that the abandonment on the cross is a *God*-abandonment that separates the Son from the Father: "The cross of the Son divides God from God to the utmost degree of enmity and distinction. The resurrection of the Son abandoned by God unites God with God in the most intimate fellowship."[112] The God of classical theism, a God who is not involved with history and is incapable of being affected by the pervasive suffering and injustice in this world, is a loveless being who is indifferent and not concerned with his righteousness in the world. This type of theism gives rise to protest atheism where God is rejected as a highly dispensable and superfluous being. "A man who experiences helplessness, a man who suffers because he loves, a man who can die, is therefore a richer being than an omnipotent God who cannot suffer, cannot love and cannot die."[113] So as to effectively respond to protest atheism, Moltmann contends that the concrete "history of God" in the crucifixion of Jesus "contains within itself all the depths and abysses of human history. . . . All human history, however much it may be determined by

---

109. Irenaeus, *Against Heresies*, 514, 547, 550.

110. Justin Martyr, *Dialogue with Trypho*, 248. The significance of Ps 22 in relation to Christ is expounded over several pages (248–52). Tertullian also regards Ps 22 as a prediction of Christ's passion (Tertullian, *Against Maricon*, 337).

111. Moltmann, *Crucified God*, 226–35.

112. Moltmann, *Crucified God*, 154–55. Father and Son are united not only by the resurrection but also by the Holy Spirit. By the Spirit, the cross as the separation or gulf between Father and Son is also their most intimate union in love.

113. Moltmann, *Crucified God*, 230.

guilt and death, is taken up into this history of God."[114] While one might readily sympathize with Moltmann's endeavor to address the real issues raised by protest atheism, nonetheless it is questionable whether one is justified in holding that the cross of the Son "divides" God from God.[115] The God-abandonment thesis proposed by Moltmann is in the service of a somewhat extreme theology of creation. Taking his cue from the Jewish kabbalistic doctrine of *zimsum*, Moltmann asserts that "it is only a withdrawal by God into himself that can free the space into which God can act creatively, . . . *creatio ex nihilo* only comes into being because, and in as far as, the omnipotent and omnipresent God withdraws his presence and restricts his power."[116] The space that comes into being by God's self-limitation is "a literally God-forsaken space."[117] Thus it follows that if Jesus is to occupy our place in this God-forsaken space, so as to bring about the eschatological renewal of all things, then the Son must suffer God-abandonment on the cross. What is apparent in Moltmann's thinking is that his "philosophical presuppositions drive his exegesis."[118] His exegesis of Jesus's cry is not in any way guided by the Jewish tradition of the just ones who suffer because of fidelity to God and whom God will *not* abandon. Like Barth, Moltmann "does not allow for believers to be

114. Moltmann, *Crucified God*, 255.

115. Moltmann's assertion that Jesus died as one rejected by his Father, which precipitated a divide or rift in the very life of God, is predicated on his conception of the Trinity as three subjects or individual centers of consciousness; and it is in the service of his rather extreme theology of creation, according to which God in creating the world "withdraws" to make room for the creature, which means that the created world is a God-forsaken space. Barth, in contrast, resisted any suggestion of a division or separation within God himself in light of Jesus's death as God-forsakenness. Barth was concerned to preserve the unity of God: God cannot contradict himself within his own inner life, but he can suffer a history of contradiction when the Son takes on human flesh for the sake of our being reconciled to God and having fellowship with God. Barth's theology of creation, moreover, is nowhere as extreme as Moltmann's, as is apparent in Barth's axiom that the covenant is the internal basis of the creation, and the creation is the external basis of the covenant. Hans Urs von Balthasar, in his conception of the Trinity as the eternal event of self-emptying love between the divine persons, does speak of a "distance," "difference," and "distinction" between Father and Son in the Godhead, which becomes manifest in salvation history in the form of a "separation" on the cross that goes to the extent of abandonment. But this distance between the Father and the Son on the cross can never be separation in the true sense, since the Spirit constantly bridges the distance between the Father and the Son.

116. Moltmann, *God in Creation*, 86–87.

117. Moltmann, *God in Creation*, 87.

118. W. Johnson, "Jesus' Cry," 84.

included in the lament of Christ," since the act of substitution revealed by Jesus's cry is a one-way street: God appropriates the suffering of the godless and the forsaken and removes their burden from them. Amen![119] This view of Jesus's cry as a one-way street is also in evidence when Moltmann asserts that all human history is taken up into this "history of God," so that there is "no suffering which in this history of God is not God's suffering; no death which has not been God's death in the history of Golgotha."[120] The appropriate response to being justified by the event of Christ's passion is to work selflessly for the coming of God's kingdom by imitating the sacrifice of Christ. The latter implies a willingness to share in Christ's sufferings, hence, as with Barth, Moltmann regards suffering in the name of Christ as no cause for lament.

It is time to sum up the second part of this chapter. We have seen various approaches and understandings of lament in the theological tradition and in contemporary theology. Augustine's view of lament is guided by his anthropology of desire, according to which our longing must be freed from worldly attachments and directed instead toward an affective attachment to Christ, the Physician, in whose person we cleave to the hope of beatific union with God in the age to come. Lament is conceived as a modality of human affect directed to God and anchored in eschatological hope. Lament brings humans to themselves and performs a transforming function by reorienting our prayers so that they conform to Christ—our lament is joined to Christ's lament—rather than attempting to manipulate Christ for earthly gain. For Augustine, through lament we come to know the divine person of Christ as the object of our suffering. This is all well and good, insofar as Augustine seeks to underscore the hoped-for happy ending of the earthly life of toil and paints a vivid picture of the struggle over sin as the cause of much grief and sorrow in Christian life. But we have also drawn attention to a number of limitations in Augustine's perspective, namely: he acknowledges lament only in relation to the problem of sin, hence prayers of lament are regarded as penitential prayers; grief and sorrow over the loss of a loved one or the laments of the suffering righteous who bear the injustices of the wicked do not feature in Augustine's thinking; he treats the psalms according to the allegorical method of interpretation and fails to recognize the historical context in which the psalms were written; and Jesus's dying cry is not

---

119. Harasta, "Crucified Praise," 207.
120. Moltmann, *Crucified God*, 255.

seen as addressed to the Father, for it is impossible that Jesus as the Son could be forsaken by the Father, hence Augustine claims that the lament cry was not the cry of the head but of the members of his body who are sinners and fear death. But this begs the question, how does our lament perform a transforming function if Jesus's cry was not the cry of the head, if it is was not also God's cry before an estranged humanity?

We saw that Luther follows Augustine in regarding Christ as the Physician who consoles the afflicted soul with the word of grace. Lament is associated with the spiritual trials of the sinner, with the awareness of the total helplessness of the sinner before God and the accompanying terror of abandonment and rejection by God. Luther is even more radical than Augustine with respect to this experience of the human condition, which means that he, too, reduces Christian life to the problem of sin and regards prayers of lament as penitential prayers. The prayers are given an eschatological orientation, which is well and good, for they sustain our waiting in hope for the glory of the promised age to come. Where Luther differs markedly from Augustine is that Ps 22 is understood wholly of Christ, who died as no one else has died or ever will die: Christ's cry is affirmed as the cry of the head and not, as Augustine contends, the cry of the members of his body. The notion of Christ as the "only sinner," together with the novel understanding of the communication of the two natures *in concreto*, allows Luther to affirm Christ's cry as God's cry, to which our own cries are joined in an ontological fashion.[121] All this represents, to my mind, a further step in the right direction. What is more, Luther contends that because Christ's cross was much heavier to bear than any cross his disciples must carry, our grief and sorrow due to our wrestling with the problem of sin must be moderate lest the cross of Christ is lost sight of. While this type of thinking does positively serve to underline the uniqueness of Christ's redemptive suffering as the head of his body of disciples, at the same time caution must be applied in order to avoid the potentially problematic teaching that Christians must passively bear the suffering that comes their way, no matter the cause, and not complain or protest their suffering to God. More problematic, though, is that Luther, following Augustine, says that experiences of anguish and sorrow arise solely in connection with the awareness of personal sin and belong to a different order than ordinary losses, such as the loss of a loved

121. Luther, unlike Augustine, does not think of Christ as a Stoic sage who quickly overcomes his suffering by the exercise of his perfect reason as the Logos. See Novello, *Passionate Deification*, 125–30.

one or innocent suffering. But are the sufferings of Job and Jeremiah, who are righteous and upright figures in the Bible, of a lesser order than a sinner's anguish and sorrow?

It was shown that Calvin also sets limits on lament, but unlike Luther the limits are determined by his doctrine of divine providence and the corresponding piety of patience. The trials of the faithful give rise to lament, but our lament must not be immoderate or constitute murmuring against God, for such a form of unregulated lament would call into question God's invisible providence of history. When Calvin examines the lament psalms, he finds that apparently contrary affections are held in unity; the psalmist feels abandoned by God yet by faith apprehends God's invisible providence and commits himself to the exercise of patience. Patience requires believers to stretch their view as far as possible into the eschatological future, so that present grief may not deprive them of hope. Calvin shares the eschatological approach to grief which is given abundant expression in the writings of Augustine and Luther. With respect to Christ's cry on the cross, Calvin affirms that Christ was not exempt from the terror that the divine judgment strikes into the heart of sinners, yet, on the other hand, in the midst of his terrible sufferings he submitted himself to God with a composed and peaceful mind. But is it legitimate to say that Christ on the cross submitted himself to the Father with a composed and peaceful mind? Does not the anguished state of Christ in the garden of Gethsemane indicate otherwise, notwithstanding his obedience to the Father? Is the psalmist's lament in Ps 22 the cry of a righteous person with a composed and peaceful mind, notwithstanding the psalmist's trust in God's providence? It would seem that while Calvin does seek to uphold Christ's terrible suffering in having borne the divine judgment against sin, at the same time Christ's divinity implies that his suffering was endured with a composed and peaceful mind. In such a perspective what is lacking is the affirmation of a real participation of divinity in the humanity of Christ, or, to state the matter another way, Calvin does not share Luther's understanding of a true communion of natures *in concreto* in the person of Christ. Unlike Christ who possessed a composed and peaceful mind as he suffered on the cross, Calvin says that we sinners must display courage and strive to maintain patience and keep hope alive through prayers of lament. As with Augustine and Luther, Calvin regards suffering due to sin as a form of pedagogy in the journey of ascent towards God. Suffering on account of sin certainly does serve to educate the faithful to become wholly dependent on God's merciful grace in Christ, but are there not also other forms of suffering that perform a pedagogical function? Is not the calamitous suffering of Job due to loss of livelihood, loss of family, and the pain of loathsome sores that cover his entire body a form of pedagogy since it is precisely in his innocent suffering that Job realizes true humility and enters into personal communion with God? Is not the mission of Jeremiah, whose prophetic condition is a state of suffering in sympathy with the divine pathos, a form of pedagogy in which the prophet comes to learn what it means to embody the word of the Lord in a sinful and perverse world?

We saw that Barth, too, contends that there are limitations on lament, but unlike Luther and Calvin he arrives at this conclusion from the standpoint of the complete victory of God's grace in Christ over all sin, suffering, and death. In the writings of Augustine, Luther, and Calvin, prayers of lament have an eschatological orientation, they are directed toward the much-hoped-for there and then of the age to come. But with Barth the focus is much more on the here and now of Christ's definitive victory over sin, death, and hell, so that all our sufferings are to be thought of as already behind us. For Barth the question of the suffering righteous expressed by Ps 22 has been resolved once and for all on Golgotha, hence any lament of ours must be truly restricted because already transcended by Christ's lament which expresses his unique sacrificial suffering as our Representative and Substitute. There can be no question of repetitions of Golgotha. The appropriate attitude of Christ's disciples is one of "strict matter-of-factness" in bearing their suffering and subjecting themselves obediently to the Holy One who has borne the powers of sin and death by his cross and descent into the grave. Moltmann, it was shown, is certainly similar to Barth's thinking on the uniqueness of Christ's lament of God-forsakenness and in not allowing believers to be included in the lament of Christ. The cry of the Son cannot be interpreted in terms of Ps 22 and the Jewish tradition of the suffering righteous, because the event of Golgotha is a unique event between God and God, which renders the act of substitution a one-way street. The godless are justified by Christ's act of substitution, and those who are incorporated into Christ, through the activity of the Spirit, are set free to work for the coming kingdom of God, which inevitably involves a sharing in the suffering and sacrifice of Christ.

With respect to the theological positions of both Moltmann and Barth, what is especially noteworthy and praiseworthy is that they unreservedly affirm the suffering of God: the divine Son has suffered and died and descended into the grave. In a manner that recalls the thinking of Luther, no separation of the two natures is entertained; there is no desire to uphold the traditional doctrine concerning the impassibility of God. The Son of God in his humiliation addresses his lament cry to the Father, which means that the cry on Golgotha is interpreted as an event between God and God. This, to my mind, is certainly a step in the right direction. What is questionable in both Moltmann and Barth, however, is that they view Christ's lament as a one-way street: since God appropriates the suffering of the godless and the forsaken and removes their burden, the justified have no right to lament. Augustine, Luther, and Calvin all acknowledge, in varying degrees, the role that lament plays in the practice of repentance and penance, but Barth and Moltmann display a different mindset. There can be only a strict matter-of-factness of those who are called to bear their cross and follow Christ, which recalls the position of St. Paul discussed in the first section of the present chapter. This raises an important critical question, which Eva Harasta states in the following words: *"If lament has its place in how God incarnate deals with suffering, how can it not have its place amongst those who are placed before God by him?"*[122] The point of origin for the lament of Christ's followers is his cry on the cross, which is "inseparably intertwined with his praise of God as the resurrected one."[123] Moreover, in light of the fact that we live in the time between the first coming of Christ and his second glorious coming when the fullness of salvation in him will be made manifest, given that history is still running its troubled course and we are therefore still subject to manifold evils and tribulations, how can the lament speech form not be accorded a rightful place in Christian life and worship?

The writings of Oswald Bayer are most instructive on this fundamental question. Bayer contends that since the Father's response to the Son's lament cry comes by way of Jesus's resurrection, this implies that the thanksgiving of the new being in the Spirit of risen Christ gives praise to God who resurrects out of death. Jesus's resurrection from the dead as the Father's response to his cry on Calvary means that Christian praise of God "makes room" for lament, it does not suppress it. This is not a matter of a juxtaposition or an apposition of praise and lament; rather, the Eucharist is to be understood as incorporating lament *into*

---

122. Harasta, "Crucified Praise," 208; emphasis added.

123. Harasta, "Crucified Praise," 209.

thanksgiving.[124] The scholar Matthias Wüthrich, who has analyzed Barth's christological theodicy and is critical of Barth for suppressing lament, is fully accepting of Bayer's Christology of answered lament and seeks to highlight the current state of systematic theology where an appreciation of lament "is almost completely missing."[125] Following Bayer, Wüthrich asserts that systematic theology must not hastily strive towards a happy ending while failing to seriously take into consideration the dead ends of the journey of faith with all its anguish, uncertainties, and sufferings.

Another reason why lament should be incorporated into thanksgiving is that Jesus's resurrection from the dead does not mean that God wiped away his wounds and lacerations (see Luke 24:39): God did not eradicate the scars of his crucifixion but vindicated the Crucified One as the Holy and Just One in whom God has embodied himself for us, for our salvation, for the making of the new creation.[126] This embodiment of God in the crucified body of Christ is fully consistent with the discussion in the previous chapter of this study, where it was argued that the lament literature positively serves to underline the dialogical-reciprocal nature of the divine-human relationship: the laments of the faithful portray Israel's life in the presence of the Lord, and, conversely, the divine pathos and laments of God paint "a picture of divinity in the presence of humanity."[127] In the event of Golgotha, human lament and divine lament are uniquely joined together in an ultimate agony that transforms suffering and grief into ineffable joy, and sin and death into the glory of eternal life and eternal praise of God. The following chapter will endeavor to shed more light on this christological mystery, so as to further illustrate why systematic theology must not suppress lament but rather allow it to shape all decisive aspects of Christian faith, life, and worship.

---

124. Bayer, "Toward Theology of Lament."

125. Wüthrich, "Lament for Naught," 60. In the last thirty years, the absence of lament in systematic theological reflection has been repeatedly noted by Old Testament scholarship.

126. Black, "Persistence of the Wounds," 56.

127. Terrien, *Psalms*, 45.

3

JESUS'S CRY OF LAMENT
Humanity and Divinity United in the Ultimate Agony

T HE FIRST CHAPTER OF this study shed light on the extent to which current Old Testament scholarship recognizes the essential role that lament plays in the faith and liturgy of Israel. Despite this recognition in Old Testament scholarship, the previous chapter has discussed several reasons why lament is not generally incorporated into the faith and liturgies of the Christian churches. Walter Brueggemann attributes the loss of lament in church usage to the tendency among Christians to disregard the laments on theological grounds, believing they are superseded by key christological claims.[1] The first chapter, which discussed the Jewish perspective of lament and thanksgiving as closely interwoven, already indicates legitimate reasons why Christians should not disregard lament on christological grounds. The cry of lament lifted up to God is motivated by the belief that the God of Israel is a God who hears the cries of the people, who is personally engaged with them, and who shows mercy and compassion in redeeming the people and making a way into the future for them. The initial petition to God born out of a situation of distress

---

1. Brueggemann, "Shape for Old Testament Theology, II," 401. The basic tenet that forgiveness of sins and reconciliation with God are attained through Christ's atoning death gives rise to the view that praise and thanksgiving are the appropriate response to the cross of Christ. Eberhard Jüngel, for instance, asserts that "the appropriate response to the cross of Jesus Christ is the hymn of praise and thanks, not the lament; it is hope, not resignation" (*God as the Mystery*, 374).

never stands by itself but moves into a final movement of future praise of God. The lament speech form is a poignant acknowledgment of suffering, loss, and failure, yet at the same time it is portrayed in the Hebrew Bible as an act of faith that assumes hope and radicalizes hope in the God of the covenant, who displays ultimate concern for his people. It is important that the faithful in the throes of injustice, suffering, and death be allowed to open their hearts in prayers of lament and take initiative with God, for only in this manner can real-life situations be honestly acknowledged and the lament function as a genuine liturgical and theological activity of pleading for help from God, whose veil of silence seems impenetrable at times.

When the focus shifts from the Hebrew Bible to the realm of Christian faith, why should Christians regard the practice of lament as having no appropriate role to play in their pilgrim lives as followers of Christ? Is not Christian life, no less than Jewish life, a "straining forward" (Phil 3:13) to the future good of the "new creation" revealed in the person of the risen Christ? In the biblical view that the followers of Christ, together with the whole of creation, are "groaning" (Rom 8:22–23) for the fullness of salvation, is not the lament a legitimate form of speech that expresses our fundamental longing for the fullness of the "new creation" anticipated in the risen Christ? To state the matter a little differently, if incorporation into the body of Christ, through baptism, means that Christians always carry in their bodies the afflictions and redemptive death of Christ so that the life of the Savior may be manifested to the world in their mortal flesh (2 Cor 4:7–11), how is it possible to ignore the legitimate role played by prayers of lament in Christian life, worship, and theology? If lament plays a central role in how Jesus Christ, the incarnate Word, deals with his suffering on Calvary, how can it not have its place among his followers who are placed before God by him? If Jesus's resurrection from the dead is the Father's response to his cry on the cross, does this not mean that God will hear our cries also because they are joined to Jesus's cry?

In this chapter the task will be to offer a composite interpretation of Jesus's cry of lament, taking into consideration the discussion and findings in the previous chapters of this study, as well as contemporary scholarship on the topic. As the Messiah who had an intimate knowledge of the Scriptures, there can be no doubt that Jesus was fully cognizant of the role of the lament speech form in the maturing of Jewish faith and the radicalizing of hope in the God of the covenant. This means we cannot ignore the fact that Jesus on the cross deliberately chose to utter the opening words of Ps 22 as his last words in his dramatic struggle with sin and evil. A fundamental assumption made in this chapter is that on the cross Jesus himself cried out, "My God, my God, why have you forsaken me?" (Mark 15:34; Matt 27:46). As Donald Senior writes in his study of Jesus's passion in Mark's Gospel, "It is surely not impossible that Jesus himself in the crisis of death would have prayed this classical prayer of the tormented Israelite."[2] This possibility is supported by the manner in which the other evangelists seek to modify this word from the cross, from which "we can be fairly certain that the cry from the cross was one of the clearest memories of the first communities."[3] Even if Jesus did not actually utter the opening words of Ps 22, they may still be regarded, as Kenneth Grayston explains, as true: "The sayings of Jesus from the cross may be 'true' not because he said them but because they *truly* indicate a possible interpretation of his death."[4] Irrespective of whether Jesus himself uttered the opening verse of Ps 22 or whether the evangelists Mark and Matthew placed the words on Jesus's lips, the last words of Jesus assume special significance. As Raymond Brown remarks in his comprehensive study of the death of the Messiah, "In any good drama the last words of the main character are especially significant. It is important for us, then, to ask how literally we should take, 'My God, my God, for what reason have you forsaken me?'"[5]

The life of the one who had proclaimed the eschatological nearness of God culminates in his agonizing death as one rejected by his own people and forsaken by his Father into the hands of evildoers. Those who adhere to the thesis that Jesus on the cross suffers *God*-abandonment, all follow the line of argument that Jesus's nearness to God gives way to exclusion from God's nearness. In order to uphold this argument, Ps 22 is not considered in its entirety but is restricted to the opening verse, which is uniquely applied to Jesus as the Son of God. Hans Urs von Balthasar, for example, maintains that the cry of abandonment "directs us to the unique point which is Jesus, and in no way to the beginning of a psalmic recitation which finishes with the glorification of the suffering individual."[6]

---

2. Senior, *Passion of Jesus*, 123.

3. O'Donnell, *Mystery of Triune God*, 62.

4. Grayston, *Dying, We Live*, 222.

5. R. Brown, *Death of the Messiah*, 2:1045.

6. Balthasar, *Mysterium Paschale*, 125. For Balthasar, the episode in Gethsemane shows that all expectation of glorification is walled off—a narrow perspective is in view, in which the will of the Father is loved for its own sake; Jesus does not look to anything beyond the sacrificial death he is about to suffer (*Mysterium Paschale*, 106).

Jürgen Moltmann also takes issue with an interpretation of Jesus's cry of abandonment offered by the history of tradition, arguing that it is "not right to interpret the cry of Jesus in the sense of Ps. 22, but more proper to interpret the words of the psalm here in the sense of the situation of Jesus."[7] Gérard Rossé is of a similar mindset when he writes that "it is not enough to interpret Ps 22:2 in the light of the Old Testament; one must give it a new content that proceeds from the reality that Jesus himself is."[8] And Raymond Brown sees in Jesus's lament cry simply a statement of Jesus's real suffering and terrible agony on the cross, and nothing more.[9] Contrary to these views, it will be argued in this chapter that the God-abandonment thesis is marked by serious exegetical and theological flaws. In order to gain insight into how Jesus himself interpreted his agonizing death, the whole of Ps 22, which forms a composite unity, must be taken into consideration. As James Mays points out, "Citing the first words of a text was, in the tradition of the time, a way of identifying an entire passage."[10] This perspective will be bolstered in this chapter by highlighting the manner in which the Gospel narrative—in Mark and Matthew—meshes well with Ps 22 in its entirety.

The first part of this chapter, which examines the tradition of the suffering righteous, will draw attention to a number of sources to substantiate the claim that citing the first words of a text implied the remainder of the text. There can be little doubt that Jesus would have been well versed in the use of psalms in the liturgical setting of the local synagogue and the temple in Jerusalem. The primary objective of the first section of this chapter, however, will be to demonstrate that Ps 22 has an "intensity and comprehensiveness"[11] in its composition that is not found in other prayers belonging to the tradition of the suffering just. Once the special character of Ps 22 is recognized, it becomes clearer why Jesus would have chosen to cite the opening verse of the psalm as his final words in bringing his messianic mission to completion. An appreciation of the intensity and comprehensiveness of Ps 22 in comparison to other writings in the tradition of the suffering righteous is not in itself sufficient, however, to fathom the death of the Messiah. In Ps 22 the suffering just one does

7. Moltmann, *Crucified God*, 152.

8. Rossé, *Cry of Jesus*, 61.

9. R. Brown, *Death of the Messiah*, 2:1050.

10. Mays, "Prayer and Christology," 322.

11. Mays, "Prayer and Christology," 324.

not actually die, but in the case of Jesus he is fully conscious of the terrible death that awaits him, which leads him to pray that the hour might pass from him (Mark 14:35) and the cup be removed from him (Mark 14:36). What is lacking in Ps 22 is complemented by the Gospel narration of Jesus's prayer in the garden of Gethsemane. The second part of this chapter will examine the episode in Gethsemane, arguing that the emphasis in the narrative falls not on Jesus's pleading with the Father that the cup be removed from him but on the Son's determination to be perfectly obedient to the Father as a decisive manifestation of his unity with the Father in unfathomable love. The acute suffering of the crucified Son must be contemplated in this light. At the same time, the discussion will also consider a proper interpretation of the cup that Jesus must drink. While it will be contended that the cup of the new covenant does mean that the Son bears or assumes the sin of the world, his passion will not be thought of in the sense that Jesus, who is without sin, is the object of God's wrath against sin or suffers extreme separation from God. Rather, his vicarious suffering unto death will be portrayed as taking place in the apocalyptic context of the great struggle of last times when God's kingdom overcomes the powers of evil in our world. The death of Jesus is not just a historical ordeal for him but also an eschatological event that pertains to the cosmic struggle of good over evil. This perspective fits in perfectly well with the conclusion to Ps 22, which is an eschatological hymn of praise (vv. 27–31) that envisages all the families of the earth worshipping before the Lord. Once the background discussions pertaining to the special character of Ps 22 and the significance of the episode in the garden of Gethsemane have been completed, the discussion will then turn in part 3 to offer a critical interpretation of Jesus's cry on the cross. It will be argued that only a *theological*—not philological, psychological, or juridical—interpretation of Jesus's lament cry does justice to all the biblical materials brought to bear on the task of interpreting his dying cry.

As background material for the proposed theological interpretation of Jesus's lament cry in part 3 of this chapter, it will be helpful to briefly summarize in this introduction the main types of analyses of Jesus's cry that have been offered in the Christian tradition down the centuries.[12] The simplest interpretation follows the line of a philological analysis in which the verb "to abandon" is taken to mean a leaving in a situation of distress and suffering, a being delivered up to one's adversaries, in which

---

12. See Rossé, *Cry of* Jesus, 73–93.

case Jesus's sense of abandonment is reduced to the simple noninterven-tion of God. This view is typical of the fathers of the church.[13] When the focus shifts to the scholastic period, the basic problem becomes how to reconcile Christ's beatific vision of God with the anguish that he experi-ences on the cross due to God's nonintervention. Thomas Aquinas, for example, offered a solution on the basis of the two natures: that is to say, the incarnate Word suffers in his body and in the "inferior" part of his soul, but the "superior" part of his soul, which has to do with the redemp-tion of humanity, cannot suffer from the nonintervention of God.[14]

It was the Rhineland mystics of the fourteenth century who intro-duced something new into the scholastic formula by proposing that the abandonment be treated not merely in terms of God's nonintervention in the passion of Jesus but also as an act of God who draws away from Jesus in his hour of need. The intimate bond that unites the Son to the Father during his public ministry "seems" to be broken, so that it becomes a question of a "feeling" on the level of the psyche. In short, the Rhineland mystics applied to Jesus's cry of lament their own mystical experience of the "dark night" of the soul. The problem with this psychological analysis is that it represents a projection of the mystic's experience of the dark night onto the scriptural narrative, hence it cannot be considered to be a proper biblical exegesis of the meaning of Jesus's abandonment.

13. The fathers of the church also espoused an allegorical interpretation of Jesus's cry of abandonment; that is to say, Jesus's cry represents the cries of sinful humanity. Augustine, for example, as we saw in the previous ch. 2, says that Jesus spoke the words of abandonment for the sake of the members of his body who are sinners and who fear death. Jesus's cry is not addressed to the Father, for it is impossible that he as God could be abandoned by God. Jesus's cry is not the cry of the head but of the members of his body.

14. According to Aquinas, Christ, by virtue of his beatific vision of God, constantly experiences supernatural joy that flows to his body. This does not, however, allow Christ to suffer, to experience sorrow, or to know fear like we humans do. Aquinas overcomes this problem by proposing that Christ prevented the normal process of overflow by a special exercise (i.e., dispensation) of divine power. By the introduction of this divine dispensation, the beatific joy of Christ remains locked up in his mind and does not flow into the sense powers, which means that he is able to experience sensible pain (*Summa theologica*, III, 15.6). This is a very abstract perspective that fails to admit that Jesus the Son descended to the temporal realm of the human (sin excepted). That is, a true kenosis of the divinity is not admitted, for the divine does not truly participate in the human realm. The two natures are thought of statically as being in mere juxtaposition, so that the human nature taken up into Jesus Christ does not exist for the divinity itself but is portrayed as a passive instrument of redemption. See Novello, *Passionate Deification*, 125–37.

Nonetheless, the mystical interpretation does have value insofar as it prevents us from "reducing the sense of the abandonment of Christ to its philological content of a simple nonintervention of God,"[15] and shifts the focus to the problem of how to reconcile the indissoluble unity of Jesus with the Father and the feeling of abandonment that this same Father inflicts upon Jesus as the Son.

When we come to the Reformers, they continue the mystical interpretation of Jesus's abandonment as an act of God, but they cross a threshold that the Rhineland mystics refrained from crossing. By invoking scriptural texts that talk about how Jesus Christ was "made sin" (2 Cor 5:21) and became "a curse for us" (Gal 3:13), the Reformers proposed a juridical view of redemption according to which Jesus on the cross is subjected to the punishment that God in his wrath inflicts upon the sinner. Jesus experiences hell on the cross, he suffers the torments and pains of the damned (*poena damni*) in the place of sinners. From the standpoint of this concept of penal substitution, Jesus's abandonment on the cross is not reduced to a mere feeling, it does not have to do with a darkening of the psyche in relation to God but is now a question of "real" abandonment, of entering into a "terrible abyss" (Calvin).[16] The Reformed concept of Jesus's real abandonment by the Father has especially been boosted in recent times by Jürgen Moltmann's classic work, *The Crucified God*, which was discussed in the previous chapter 2 of this study. Moltmann's position is very clear when he writes: "The cross of the Son divides God from God to the utmost degree of enmity and distinction. The resurrection of the Son abandoned by God unites God with God in the most intimate fellowship."[17] The real abandonment of Jesus by the Father is emphatically affirmed by Moltmann, and this rather extreme line of thought is developed in conjunction with his interest in modern atheistic protest.

Apart from the questionable assertion that the cross of the Son "divides" God from God, it is also questionable whether Moltmann is justified in holding that Jesus's cry on the cross should be interpreted

15. Rossé, *Cry of Jesus*, 82.

16. The thesis that Jesus suffered real abandonment by God, and that this God-abandonment marks the defining moment in the drama of salvation, is quite diffused in contemporary theology. See, for instance: Barth, *Church Dogmatics*, IV/1; Moltmann, *Crucified God*; Jüngel, *God as the Mystery*, 361–68; Balthasar, *Mysterium Paschale*; Jenson, *Triune God*, 49; Lewis, *Between Cross and Resurrection*, 53–54, 82–83; Volf, *Exclusion and Embrace*, 9; Pannenberg, *Jesus—God and Man*, 258–64, 269–74.

17. Moltmann, *Crucified God*, 154–55.

exclusively from the standpoint of Jesus's unique situation as the Son, without having any recourse to the established tradition of biblical lament and the tradition of the suffering righteous. Is it warranted to remove Jesus's cry from the entirety of Ps 22 and therefore to ignore the total structure of the psalm and the way it unites the prayer for help (situation of affliction) and praise for help (situation of salvation) in one arc of meaning to express what is happening?[18] In this chapter, Ps 22 will be used as a hermeneutical key to undertake "to understand Jesus in terms of the psalm, that is, to view him through the form and language of this prayer."[19] The legitimacy of viewing Jesus through the lens of this lament prayer will become apparent by highlighting the congruities between Ps 22 and Jesus's words and actions in the Gospel narrative, especially Jesus's words of institution of the Eucharist at the Last Supper and his anguished prayer in the garden of Gethsemane.

Psalm 22, Jeremiah, Isaiah's Suffering Servant, and Wisdom 2–5: The Tradition of the Suffering Righteous

The majority of scholars believe Ps 22 was composed in the postexilic period, when many righteous Jews experienced suffering at the hands of adversaries but remained firm in anticipating God's help in delivering them from their affliction.[20] Brown points out that placing the psalm in a postexilic context "makes it conceivable that Jeremiah's vocalization of his complaints to God may have had an effect on the formulation of this lamentation pattern."[21] There are concrete parallels between Ps 22 and Jeremiah, not least the psalmist's reference to God having taken him from his mother's womb (Ps 22:9–10), which recalls Jer 1:5 (also 20:17–18) where the prophet is portrayed as consecrated by God before he was formed in his mother's womb. The pattern of discouragement (groaning to God for help) and confidence (God does not hide his face from the afflicted) in Ps 22 matches the tone of Jeremiah's confessions. The prophet

---

18. Johnson, for instance, argues that Moltmann is not justified in removing Jesus's cry from the genre of biblical lament. See W. Johnson, "Jesus' Cry," 91n5.

19. Mays, "Prayer and Christology," 323.

20. See R. Brown, *Death of the Messiah*, 2:1457. Brown points out that it was customary from Augustine to Aquinas to regard Ps 22 as a prophecy about the suffering Messiah. Verse 16 of the psalm—"they have pierced my hands and feet"—was readily applied to the crucified Jesus (cf. Luke 24:39, "See my hands and feet").

21. R. Brown, *Death of the Messiah*, 2:1458.

is like "a gentle lamb led to the slaughter" (Jer 11:19) by his enemies, and he utters a profound lament to God for experiencing a life of trouble and having to suffer insults on account of proclaiming the divine word, which became for him "a joy and the delight of my heart" (Jer 15:16). Jeremiah is given the reassurance that God will deliver him "out of the hand of the wicked" and redeem him "from the grasp of the ruthless" (Jer 15:21). In the meantime, however, Jeremiah is required to utter only the "precious" divine word that is given him (Jer 15:19) and to accept suffering and sorrow as accompaniments to his prophetic ministry. Jeremiah must learn, as was argued in chapter 1, to feel for himself God's intimate attachment to Israel and to experience it from within, and thereby come to acknowledge the prophetic condition as "a state of suffering in sympathy with the divine pathos" (Heschel).

The figure in Ps 22, like Jeremiah, is one who has been committed to God since his birth (vv. 10–11), one who has always relied upon God (v. 9) and thus belongs to the "lowly" ('ănāwîm). As one of the lowly, the figure in the psalm, like Jeremiah, is plagued by "trouble" (v. 11); he is scorned and despised by his enemies (vv. 6–8) for committing his cause to God and finding delight in the Lord. It is important to emphasize that "it is not his affliction that has made him a lowly one, but rather he has undergone his affliction as one of the lowly."[22] The psalmist cries to God by day and by night (v. 2) to help him, because "there is none to help" (v. 11), and he laments that God does not answer him. From the detailed description of the psalmist's laments and sufferings (vv. 11–18), moreover, God seems not only to have forsaken him but is actually involved in his demise: "You are laying me in the dust of death" (v. 15c). If God does not intervene to deliver the psalmist from his affliction, then such an attitude of nonintervention is tantamount to God putting him in the grave.[23] The psalmist feels forsaken by God, and suddenly he imagines that "God is an ally of the adversary."[24] It is incomprehensible to the psalmist that God, who brought him out of the maternal womb, is now depositing him in the tomb.

22. Mays, "Prayer and Christology," 328.

23. Ross, *Commentary on the Psalms*, 539.

24. Schaefer, *Psalms*, 55. This same conviction is found in Job 6:4; 7:20; 10:8–17; 16:7–14.

Structure of Psalm 22

With regard to the structure of the psalm, the prayer for help (vv. 1–21) moves through two cycles (vv. 1–11 and 12–21), each concluding in the petition "be not far from me" (vv. 11, 19). The first cycle consists of two laments (vv. 1–2, 6–8), each of which is followed by an assertion of confidence in God (vv. 3–5, 9–11). The second cycle also consists of two laments (vv. 12–15, 16–18), each of which describes the surrounding bestial forces (vv. 12–13, 16), followed by descriptions of the psalmist's encroaching death. The animal metaphors used to underscore the vicious and relentless persecution of the psalmist by his enemies add to the picture of his helpless state: "the strong bulls of Bashan" (v. 12); lions with mouths open wide roaring at the sight of their prey (v. 13); and a pack of predator "dogs" (v. 16) round about him. "These animal metaphors symbolize vicious threats to life. The conventional pair of lion and bull represents the epitome of power. . . . Hounds evoke the sense of helpless prey, which is how the psalmist feels."[25] By using animal metaphors, the second petition (vv. 19–21) effectively intensifies the first petition (v. 11) by threefold repetitions.[26] The psalmist vividly describes his state of physical and emotional exhaustion. He feels as if "poured out like water," all his bones "are out of joint" (v. 14a), his strength is "dried up like a potsherd" (v. 15), and his tongue sticks to the inside of his mouth as his vital fluids drain away. All of these hyperbolic descriptions underline the psalmist's loss of physical strength, while the description of his melted heart of wax (v. 14b) is intended to convey his loss of emotional strength.[27] Though not yet dead, so terrible is his state of affliction that the psalmist feels that God is laying him "in the dust of death" (v. 15b). The enemies are powerful and menacing, "but the center of this one's distress is the feeling of separation from God to the point that here God is seen as actively participating in this one's suffering."[28] The interpretation of the "you" in v. 15 as referring to God is supported by the "why have you forsaken me?" of the opening verse. The God who is so far from the afflicted one's "roaring words"[29] is now accused of laying the deeply distressed sufferer in the

---

25. Schaefer, *Psalms*, 54. Cited by Patterson, "Psalm 22," 222.

26. Mays, "Prayer and Christology," 324.

27. Heinemann, "Exposition of Psalm 22," 294–95.

28. Declaissé-Walford et al., *Book of Psalms*, 235.

29. Declaissé-Walford et al., *Book of Psalms*, 233. It is asserted that "roaring words" (v. 1b) is an exact translation of the Hebrew: "This is not groaning or complaining or whining. These words are expressed in the raspy scream of one in deep distress" (233).

dust of death. That the "you" in v. 15 refers to God is also supported by vv. 9–10: the God who "took me from the womb," the God upon whom "I was cast from my birth," is now "laying me in the dust of death."

As the distressed lamenter bears his terrible affliction, his enemies "stare and gloat" (v. 17) over him and watch for his death so they can strip his body and divide his garments among them (v. 18). The crescendo of suffering articulated in vv. 12–18, which leaves the reader in no doubt about the psalmist's feeling of total powerlessness and helplessness, leads into a renewed petition. Once again, the psalmist turns to God and cries, "Be not far off!" (v. 19a). The address "Yahweh" is used for the first time in this renewed petition (vv. 19–21). Even in this hour of extremity the psalmist can still call the Lord his sure "help" (v. 19b). Thus a lament that begins with the words "why have you forsaken me?" (v. 1a) concludes with the petition "hasten to my aid" (v. 19b); and the question "why are you so far from helping me?" (v. 1b) becomes the plea, "be not far off" (v. 19a). The psalmist is steeped in the history of the forefathers and their experiences of the Lord's saving deeds (vv. 4–5), and he remembers his own intimate experiences of God (vv. 9–11), and this knowledge of how God is leads him to turn to the Lord as his only sure help in his hour of extreme need. What is especially interesting about the renewed petition is that its last word is not another imperative like "deliver" (v. 19) and "save" (v. 20) but is a perfect tense: from the horns of the wild oxen "you have answered me" (v. 21).[30] *The psalmist is certain of his prayer being heard by God*, so the verb in the perfect tense serves to close the lament and form an abrupt transition to the concluding section of the psalm (vv. 22–31), which is filled with exuberant rejoicing and praise of God.[31] A suffering and painful situation of being surrounded by menacing enemies is now transformed into a joyful situation of being surrounded by the worshipping community (vv. 22–26). Yet the praise of God is not restricted to those lowly ones within Israel who seek the Lord but spills over into an eschatological hymn of praise that acknowledges the universal kingship

---

30. Ross, *Commentary on the Psalms*, 543. Also Reumann, "Psalm 22 at Cross," 44; and Heinemann, "Exposition of Psalm 22," 299. The form in the Masoretic Text is a perfect tense. Many translations make it an imperative ("answer me") so as to complete the petition with another parallel verb of request. The use of the imperative would make sense if the psalm concluded with a vow of praise (i.e., anticipation of offering praise to God), but the praise section is more of an actual or declarative praise for having been heard by God rather than a vow to be fulfilled.

31. See Kraus, *Psalms 1–59*, 292, 298; and Declaissé-Walford et al., *Book of Psalms*, 236.

of the Lord. "A single theme is developed: All the living (v. 27), all the dead (v. 29), and all those yet unborn (vv. 30–31) will give praise."[32]

While the pattern of discouragement and confidence in Ps 22 matches Jeremiah's confessions or soliloquies, a discernible difference is that the psalmist displays greater confidence inasmuch as he refuses to end his psalm by cursing the day he was born (cf. Jer 20:14). Instead, the praise of God features very strongly in Ps 22, as evidenced by the fact that in place of the usual vow of praise in prayers of help, this psalm concludes with a long song of praise for God's deliverance, which is composed of two sections (vv. 22–26, 27–31). In the first section the psalmist speaks in first person style in order to focus on his praise of God in the midst of "the great congregation" (v. 25).[33] Since the psalmist's cry has been "heard" by God (v. 14b; cf. vv. 3–5, 9–11), given that God has delivered the afflicted one from the clutches of death-dealing forces, this gives rise to renewed worship of the Lord in the midst of the congregation of the lowly and righteous ones. In the concluding v. 26, the afflicted become the ones who sit at the table and "eat" and are "satisfied."[34] This first section of praise moves into the second section, which is an eschatological hymn of praise that concludes the psalm in a glorious crescendo. The circle of praise widens from the "great congregation" of the lowly within Israel to include "all the families of the nations" (v. 27), who will worship before the Lord and rejoice in the knowledge that "dominion belongs to the Lord" (v. 28).[35] The figure whom the psalmist addresses as "my God" (22:1)—what it means to say "my God" is clear from vv. 3–5 and vv. 9–12, which express utter faith and confidence in God—receives not only the praises of Israel as enthroned in the Jerusalem temple but the praises of all peoples of the earth who are expected to turn to the Lord in thanksgiving because God has acted to deliver this afflicted one from the forces of death. The psalmist can reasonably be cast as a Jeremiah-like figure, with the notable exception that he envisages his petition as answered by God

---

32. Clifford, *Psalms 1–72*, 129.

33. The language suggests that what is in view is the service of the *todah*; that is, a person whose prayer for deliverance has been answered by God goes to the sanctuary and gives praise and thanks to the Lord for the salvation experienced.

34. The theme here is much like the Beatitudes where Jesus teaches that the kingdom of God belongs to the poor and those who are hungry now shall be satisfied (Luke 6:20–21; Matt 5:6).

35. For a treatment of the two sections of praise in Ps 22, see Mays, "Prayer and Christology," 327–29.

in an act of deliverance from evil forces round about him, hence there is no room in the psalm for cursing the day the psalmist was born. Nor, it should be noted, does the psalmist curse his enemies. The thrust of the message in Ps 22 is that *God does not hide his face from the afflicted one but hears his cry for help* (v. 24) and delivers him from the terrible trouble that encircles him.

When Ps 22 is examined in the context of other prayers for help, it becomes apparent that there is an "intensity and comprehensiveness"[36] in the composition of the psalm that is simply not found in other prayers of this type. While the theme of deliverance from suffering and the eschatological vision of the servants of the Lord dwelling secure in the restored land are found separately elsewhere in the Psalter, in Ps 22 they are intimately combined: "No other psalm connects deliverance from suffering to an eschatological outlook comparable to this."[37] The full-scale prayer for help (situation of affliction) and the full-scale song of praise (situation of salvation) into which it leads come together in such a unified whole that the two situations "must be comprehended in one arc of meaning to express what is happening."[38] The figure in the psalm, moreover, cannot be identified as just any afflicted righteous one; rather, the lowly and humble figure described in the psalm "shares in the corporate vocation of Israel and the messianic role of David."[39] The expectation that "posterity" (v. 30) will serve the Lord, that all the ends of the earth shall turn to the Lord because they will "remember" (v. 27) the event of salvation of this afflicted one, indicates that the psalmist has no ordinary suffering righteous one in his sights. Of all the psalms about the suffering just, Ps 22 "must be given a special place for its extraordinary messianic richness . . . the intensity and completeness of its religious and messianic feeling

36. Mays, "Prayer and Christology," 324.

37. Lyons, "Psalm 22," 644. Psalms 69 and 102, it should be noted, do share the same argument structure as Ps 22 (i.e., description of an individual's suffering, thanksgiving for deliverance, and universal acknowledgement of the Lord), and there are many lexical parallels between the three psalms. See Driver, *Studies in the Psalms*, 156; and Marttila, *Collective Reinterpretation in Psalms*, 133. Psalm 22 is unique, though, in the way it brings together many motifs in its comprehensive eschatological outlook: meal imagery (v. 26) that suggests an eschatological banquet (cf. Isa 25:6); universal acknowledgment of the Lord by both the living and the dead (vv. 27–29); and proclamation of the Lord's salvation to a people yet unborn (vv. 30–31).

38. Mays, "Prayer and Christology," 324.

39. Mays, "Prayer and Christology," 329; also Schaefer, *Psalms*, 57.

must put it among the greatest things written to foretell the coming of Christ."[40]

The universal perspective in the closing verses of the psalm, which recalls the Abrahamic covenant, is reminiscent of many texts in Jewish Scripture that speak of the earth's final blessing. For instance, Isaiah prophesies: "And you will say in that day: Give thanks to the Lord, call upon his name; make known his deeds among the nations, proclaim that his name is exalted. Sing praises to the Lord, for he has done gloriously; let this be known in all the earth" (Isa 12:4–5). The end of Ps 22 reflects this eschatological and universal perspective in which God's salvation is proclaimed throughout the coming generations "to a people yet unborn" (v. 30). In this envisaged future time of salvation, the words of the Lord uttered through Isaiah will be fully realized: "But my deliverance will be forever, and my salvation to all generations" (Isa 51:8). *The final words of the psalm have this fully realized salvation of the Lord in view*: "For he has done it" (v. 31). The first section of the psalm is a long prayer for help (vv. 1–21), and from the long song of praise that forms the second part (vv. 22–31) it is evident that "trial has been swallowed up in triumph."[41] It is worth drawing attention to the fact that in the triumphant cry of Jesus recorded in John's Gospel—"It is finished" (John 19:30)—can be heard an echo of the closing words of Ps 22: "For he has done it."[42]

Psalm 22 and Isaiah's Suffering Servant Song

It has long been recognized that there are lexical and thematic similarities between Ps 22 and Isa 40–55, especially in relation to the Suffering Servant Songs.[43] Of particular note is the mistreatment expressed in Ps 22:6–8 which is comparable to that in Isa 50:6 and 53:3.[44] Special mention should also be made of the suffering servant pierced for our transgressions (Isa 53:5), which may be compared with the piercing of the hands and feet of the figure in Ps 22 (v. 16). There are, though, many

40. Durrwell, *Resurrection*, 3.

41. Patterson, "Psalm 22," 226.

42. Patterson, "Psalm 22," 229; Heinemann, "Exposition of Psalm 22," 308.

43. See, for instance: Briggs and Briggs, *Critical and Exegetical Commentary*, 1:190; Driver, *Studies in the Psalms*, 171, 180; Stuhlmueller, *Psalms 1–72*, 147; Mays, *Psalms*, 113; Marttila, *Collective Reinterpretation in Psalms*, 133–35; and Lyons, "Psalm 22."

44. R. Brown, *Death of the Messiah*, 2:1458. Brown points out that it has often been suggested that the suffering servant in Isaiah was patterned on Jeremiah.

more lexical parallels,[45] as well as several significant thematic parallels, chief among which are the following: (1) a righteous figure suffers and is despised by others (Ps 22:6–8, 11–18; Isa 49:7; 53:3, 7); (2) the suffering figure is vindicated by God (Ps 22: 21b–26; Isa 49:8; 50:7–9; 52:13; 53:10–12); (3) the whole earth acknowledges Israel's God (Ps 22:27–29; Isa 42:10–13; 45:22–24; 49:6–7; 51:5), who rules as king over the nations (Ps 22:28; Isa 52:7); (4) God's act of salvation is proclaimed to posterity (Ps 22:30–31; Isa 48:20; 52:10).[46] When the locutions in Ps 22 are considered by themselves, they do not provide strong evidence of literary dependence on Isa 40–55, but the presence of shared themes and a common outlook makes some kind of relationship plausible. The unusually long song of praise in Ps 22 underscores the righteous sufferer's confidence with regard to personal vindication by the Lord. Of special interest is how the praise of God is not limited to the faithful congregation within Israel (vv. 22–26) but shifts to a global and eschatological outlook (vv. 27–31): all the families of the nations will acknowledge the Lord (v. 27); universal dominion belongs to the Lord who rules over the nations (v. 28); both the living and the dead will acknowledge the Lord (v. 29); and the proclamation to posterity of the Lord's deliverance of this righteous afflicted one. "No other psalm connects deliverance from suffering to an eschatological outlook comparable to this."[47] To the Jewish mind, God deals with the nations through the corporate entity of the people of God, and God deals with the nation of Israel through the Davidic king, the Messiah, as well as, one must add, the unidentified suffering servant of the "songs" in Deutero-Isaiah. Psalm 22, then, as already asserted above, cannot be the prayer of just any suffering righteous Jew.

There are also some significant differences between Ps 22 and the Suffering Servant Songs, which should not be ignored when seeking to

45. Significant locutions include the following: Ps 22:1–2//Isa 49:8; Ps 22:6//Isa 49:7; 53:3; Ps 22:8//Isa 53:10; Ps 22:9–10//Isa 49:1, 5; Ps 22:11//Isa 49:8; Ps 22:15//Isa 53:12; Ps 22:18//Isa 53:12; Ps 22:21//Isa 49:8; Ps 22:22//Isa 52:15; Ps 22:23//Isa 53:10; Ps 22:24//Isa 49:7; 53:3, 4, 7; Ps 22:27, 29//Isa 49:7; Ps 22:30//Isa 52:15; 53:8, 10. See Lyons, "Psalm 22," 642.

46. Lyons, "Psalm 22," 643.

47. Lyons, "Psalm 22," 644. Psalm 22 does, it should be noted, exhibit quite extensive lexical parallels with Pss 69 and 102, which leads Lyons to conclude that all three psalms are in some way the products of a social movement reflected in Isa 54; 56–66. Lyons's argument is that the lexical parallels between Ps 22 and Isa 40–55 should be considered in light of a larger set of parallels with Isa 54; 56–66, in which a righteous community—the "servants"—will suffer and be vindicated like the individual servant.

shed light on the relationship between Ps 22 and Isa 40–55. The most significant differences are as follows.[48] (1) In Ps 22 the lamenter feels forsaken by God into the hands of evildoers, yet the thrust of the psalmist's cry is to express utter abandonment *to* God who alone can save him from the hostile forces that encircle him. In Isa 52:13—53:12, in contrast, there is no reference to being forsaken by God.[49] By citing the psalm, then, Jesus intends to affirm that he endures dreadful suffering at the hands of his enemies as an act of complete and utter abandonment *to* the Father, who alone can save him from death. (2) In Ps 22 the psalmist's suffering is not portrayed as part of God's plan, whereas in Isa 52:13—53:12 the servant's suffering is explicitly attributed to God's design; "Yet it was the will of the Lord to bruise him; he has put him to grief" (53:10). Yet while the psalmist's suffering is not by God's design, the psalmist does see God as involved in his demise: "You are laying me in the dust of death" (v. 15c). This means that if God does not intervene to deliver the psalmist from his affliction, it would be tantamount to God putting him in the grave. What is also relevant here is the understanding that the psalmist, like Jeremiah and Isaiah's suffering servant, suffers precisely because of his righteousness and fidelity to the Lord, upon whom he was cast from birth. In the Gospel story, moreover, Jesus in his passion predictions (Mark 8:31; 9:31; 10:33–34) repeatedly spells out to his disciples that the suffering, rejection, and killing of the Son of Man *are* by divine plan. Therefore, while the suffering of the righteous one in Ps 22 is not explicitly attributed to God's design, it is implicitly implied by the afflicted one's fidelity to the Lord, and Jesus prior to his Jerusalem ministry has already explicitly indicated to his disciples that his anticipated passion is by divine design. (3) In Ps 22 the suffering of the righteous one is not described as "sin-bearing" whereas in Isa 53 the servant's suffering is described in this manner (vv. 5, 6, 8, 10, 12). From the vantage point of the episode in the garden of Gethsemane, though, as will be discussed below, Jesus expresses dread at having to face the hour and drink the cup so as to accomplish his messianic mission. In Gethsemane it is clear that Jesus consciously goes to his cross as the sin-bearer, as the one who gives his life as a "ransom" (Mark 10:45) for many. (4) Finally, in Ps 22 the psalmist feels close to death (v. 15) but does not suffer death (vv. 21b, 24), whereas in Isa 53 the suffering servant does suffer death (vv. 8, 9, 12). Again, though, from

48. Cf. Lyons, "Psalm 22," 647.

49. In Isa 49:14 there is a reference to God-forsakenness, but it is Zion that feels forsaken.

the perspective of the episode in Gethsemane, which goes hand in glove with the Gospel narration of the words of institution of the Eucharist at the Last Supper, it is abundantly clear that Jesus knows that a violent death awaits him, and he regards the shedding of his blood as necessary for the inauguration of the "new covenant" that the prophets of Israel had spoken about.

Given the foregoing differences, some scholars, such as Lyons, contend that Ps 22 was composed not simply with reference to Isaiah's Suffering Servant Songs but also with reference to Trito-Isaiah (56–66) where a transition takes place from an individual suffering servant of the Lord to a community of righteous sufferers—the "servants."[50] The servants are those who "seek" God (65:9–10), who respond to the Lord's prophetic word and are mocked and persecuted by the godless (57:1; 66:5), and look forward to the "inheritance" (64:9) that God will give them, which includes vindication from their enemies, possession of the land, and the eschatological blessings of the "new heavens and a new earth" (65:17–25; 66:22). There are strong grounds for the proposition that Isa 56–66 draws upon and extends earlier passages in Isa 40–55, so that what is in view is a community created by the Lord's righteous servant, a community of servants who suffer righteously like him and anticipate vindication like him.[51] As James Mays writes about the first hymn of praise in Ps 22 (vv. 22–26), "The language of the hymn reflects a group who without separating themselves from the national society in a social way are thinking and speaking about themselves and their relation to God in a way that is beginning to redefine what it means to be Israel."[52] There are many examples in the New Testament, it is significant to observe, where Jesus is depicted as the righteous suffering servant of Isa 40–55 (e.g., Mark 10:45; Luke 2:30–32; 3:22; 22:37; Acts 26:23), and his followers identify themselves as servants of the Servant, the ones who are called to suffer like Jesus (Acts 9:16; Phil 1:29; Col 1:24; 1 Pet 2:19–25; 4:12–14) in carrying out his mission in the world (Acts 1:8; 13:47; Rom 10:14–15; 2 Cor 5:18–6:2).[53] By citing Ps 22, then, Jesus may well have had in mind

---

50. Lyons, "Psalm 22," 648–52. After Isa 53, the figure of the individual suffering servant of the Lord disappears and is replaced by a community called the "servants" (54:17; 56:6; 65:8; 9, 13–15; 66:14).

51. Beuken, for instance, maintains that the theme of the "servants" is the major theme of Trito-Isaiah. See Beuken, "Main Theme," 67–68.

52. Mays, "Prayer and Christology," 328.

53. Lyons, "Psalm 22," 655. See also Betz, "Jesus and Isaiah 53."

that his followers, nourished by the celebration of the Eucharist that he instituted, will have to be prepared to endure suffering as his ongoing embodiment in the world, so that the life of the Crucified One might be manifested in their mortal flesh (cf. 2 Cor 4:7–11).

Jesus Intended the Whole of Psalm 22

With regard to determining whether the first line of Ps 22 cited in Mark 15:34 and Matt 27:46 would have implied the remainder of the psalm, a variety of approaches could be employed to collectively show the plausibility of an affirmative finding.[54] First, light can be shed on the question by examining the use of "incipits" as a literary device before, during, and after the first century CE; second, evidence can be gathered from an examination of the liturgical use of the psalms in the temple, synagogue, and Qumran communities of the first century CE; and third, an investigation of the use of Ps 22 as an intertext in roughly contemporary texts around the time of Jesus will serve to highlight any parallels between these texts and Mark's use of Ps 22. With respect to the first approach, it has often been held that the first lines of psalms, or incipits, sometimes functioned as titles, that is, they served to indicate that the entirety of the psalm was implied. In the Scriptures we find that it is sometimes customary to name a book by the first word(s) of the book. The books of Genesis and Exodus are prime examples of this practice. Within the book of Exodus, furthermore, it is worth highlighting how the title to Miriam's song (Exod 15:21) is the incipit of the Song of Moses sung immediately before (Exod 15:1).[55] With regard to the psalms, William Albright has provided a helpful discussion on the use of incipits, especially in Ps 68.[56] He maintains that since this psalm is made up of some thirty incipits of ancient hymns, it functioned originally as a type of catalogue of ancient lyric poems or hymns. After discussing Albright's argument, Holly Carey turns to discuss two strands of evidence from the Qumran documents that provide evidence of incipit use in the first century CE,[57] then she

---

54. See Carey, *Jesus' Cry from Cross*, 106–25.

55. Carey, *Jesus' Cry from Cross*, 108.

56. Albright, "Catalog."

57. Carey, *Jesus' Cry from Cross*, 109. Qumran scrolls 4Q365 6a.ii.1–7 and 4Q174 are taken as evidence of the practice of incipits.

proceeds to give examples in the Mishnah of the use of incipits.[58] The evidence for the employment of incipits both before and after the time of Jesus lends support to the view that Jesus employed the same method of incipits when citing the first verse of Ps 22.

Another helpful source of evidence comes from the liturgical use of psalms in the temple and synagogue, as well as in the Qumran community.[59] While the main focus of scholars has been on the practice of psalmody and prayer in the synagogue,[60] the issue of worship in the temple before its destruction in 70 CE, and in the Qumran community, is also significant inasmuch as they constitute two other arenas in which worship with the psalms was practiced. In the context of the synagogue, the evidence we have indicates that prayers and psalms were chanted during the service. "This involved the reciting of a portion of the psalm by the leader of the service, which was followed by the rest of the congregation either repeating after him or proceeding to recite the remaining part of the psalm."[61] The practice of chanting implies the knowledge of the whole psalm by the assembly of worshippers.

With regard to the third approach, there are a number of writings that are roughly contemporary to the time of Jesus and Mark's Gospel (100 BCE–100 CE) that make use of Ps 22 to vividly portray the experiences of their protagonists. These include the Wisdom of Solomon (2–5), Odes of Solomon, Joseph and Aseneth, and the Hodayot of Qumran.[62] Here we shall refer only to Wis 2–5, since we have already had occasion to mention this piece of wisdom writing in chapter 1 of this study. The author of the Wisdom of Solomon paints a picture of an exemplary righteous sufferer, which has been created from the vocabulary and themes of Isaiah's fourth Servant Song (52:13—53:12).[63] Vocabulary and themes borrowed from the fourth Servant Song include the following: (1) in Wisdom of Solomon the "righteous one" (Wis 2:12; Isa 53:11) is referred to as the "servant of the Lord" (Wis 2:13; Isa 52:13); (2) the righteous one is despised, rejected, and oppressed (Wis 2:12, 19; Isa 53:3, 7–8),

---

58. Carey, *Jesus' Cry from Cross*, 109–10. The examples from the Mishnah are taken from Tamid 7.4. The Mishnah appeared as relatively fixed around 200 CE. See Neusner, *Mishnah*, xi.

59. Carey, *Jesus' Cry from Cross*, 111–15.

60. See, for instance, McKinnon, "On Question of Psalmody."

61. Carey, *Jesus' Cry from Cross*, 114.

62. Carey, *Jesus' Cry from Cross*, 115–24.

63. See Suggs, "Wisdom 2:10—5," 28–31; Lyons, "Psalm 22," 654–55.

yet displays gentleness and patience in his affliction and suffering (Wis 2:19; Isa 53:7); (3) the righteous one is condemned to death (Wis 2:20; Isa 53:8–9, 12); (4) those hostile to the righteous one are characterized by sin and lawlessness (Wis 2:12; Isa 53:5) and "going astray" (Wis 5:6; Isa 53:6); (5) the righteous one will be vindicated (Wis 5:1; Isa 52:13; 53:12) and many will be "amazed" (Wis 5:2; Isa 52:14) at "seeing" him (Wis 5:2; Isa 52:15).

Wisdom of Solomon alludes not only to the suffering servant of the Lord in Isaiah but also to Ps 22.[64] In Ps 22:6 the psalmist complains, "I am despised by the people," and in Wis 4:18 the wicked have "contempt" for the righteous one. In Ps 22:6 the psalmist laments, "I am scorned by men," and in Wis 5:4 the wicked have made the righteous a term of "reproach." In Ps 22:8 the enemies mock the afflicted one by saying, "Let the Lord help him," and in Wis 2:18 the enemies of the righteous one mock him by saying if he is God's son then "God will help him." After deliverance is accomplished, the psalmist exclaims that the hearts of the afflicted who seek the Lord shall "live forever" (Ps 22:26), and in Wis 5:15 we read that the righteous "live forever." Finally, the conviction in Ps 22:28 that "dominion belongs to the Lord, and he rules over the nations," parallels the statement in Wis 3:8 that the righteous will "judge nations, rule over peoples." There is strong evidence, to conclude, that Wisdom of Solomon constructs a picture of the exemplary righteous one by drawing on vocabulary and themes borrowed from Isaiah's Suffering Servant Songs and Ps 22.[65]

The validity of the assertion that Ps 22 should be treated in its entirety when treating Jesus's cry on the cross is also indicated by the fact that a significant number of the features of the psalmist's experience appear in the Gospel narratives, especially in Mark and Matthew. The strongest parallels are as follows:[66] v. 1a, "My God, my God, why have you forsaken me?" is quoted in Mark 15:34 and Matt 27:46; v. 6b, "scorned by men, and despised by the people," is alluded to in the mockery of Jesus in Mark 15:29 and Matt 27:39; v. 7a, "All who see me mock at me," is probably alluded to in Luke 23:35a; v. 7b, "they make mouths at me, they wag their heads," appears in Mark 15:29 and Matt 27:39; v. 8, "He has

64. See Carey, *Jesus' Cry from Cross*, 116–17.

65. Lyons, "Psalm 22," 655.

66. See R. Brown, *Death of the Messiah*, 2:1460–61. Brown lists twelve allusions to Ps 22 that scholars have detected in the Gospel passion narratives, but I have restricted the listings to the stronger and more plausible allusions.

committed his cause to the Lord; let him deliver him, let him rescue him, for he delights in him!" is echoed in Mark 15:30, Matt 27:40, 43, and Luke 23:39b; v. 16c, "they have pierced my hands and feet," is echoed in Luke 24:39; and v. 18, "they divide my garments among them, and for my raiment they cast lots," lies behind the division of Jesus's clothes in all four Gospels, and appears verbatim as a fulfillment citation in John 19:24. While it would be pushing the argument too far to maintain that the Synoptic passion narratives were structured on Ps 22,[67] nevertheless it can reasonably be said that the experiences of the one who prays in Ps 22 are incorporated into the Synoptic narration of Jesus's passion. In her study of the intertextual relationship between Ps 22 and Mark's Gospel, Holly Carey argues that using the term "*the* Righteous Sufferer" is entirely appropriate when referring to the Marcan Jesus.[68] The paradigm of persecution (crucifixion) and vindication (resurrection) manifested in the Marcan passion-resurrection predictions fits well into the righteous sufferer tradition, although the righteous sufferer functions more as a motif rather than as a title.[69] It is significant that at the climactic moment of Jesus's death, Mark's use of the motif corresponds closely to the experience of the Righteous Sufferer in Ps 22, except that Jesus is not rescued from impending death.

It is time to sum up the findings of the discussion in this section. (1) On the basis of the many lexical parallels and thematic similarities that exist between Ps 22 and Jeremiah, Isa 40–66, and Wis 2–5, there can be little doubt that the motif of the righteous sufferer was very much "in the air"[70] during the Second Temple Period, which includes the time of Jesus. (2) Jesus would have been well versed in the use of the psalms in the liturgical setting of the local synagogue and Jerusalem temple. Hence when Jesus utters the first verse of Ps 22 on the cross, we should not think that he merely intended to express his very real anguish and sense of being forsaken by God, and nothing more.[71] By uttering the first line of the psalm, Jesus would have intended the remainder of the psalm. (3) It has been shown that Ps 22 features an "intensity and

---

67. R. Brown, *Death of the Messiah*, 2:1462.

68. Carey, *Jesus' Cry from Cross*, 126–38; emphasis original.

69. Carey, *Jesus' Cry from Cross*, 130.

70. Carey, *Jesus' Cry from Cross*, 97. The first part of ch. 5 of Carey's study seeks to show the widespread tradition of the righteous sufferer in the first century CE.

71. R. Brown, for example, comes to this conclusion in his analysis of the meaning of Jesus's dying cry (*Death of the Messiah*, 2:1051).

comprehensiveness" in its composition that is not found in other prayers of this type. It describes in hyperbolic detail the suffering of the righteous one; it proclaims unwavering confidence in God who hears the cry of his afflicted servant; it overflows with praise and thanksgiving for God's act of deliverance; and it envisions a comprehensive eschatological outlook that includes meal imagery (cf. the banquet in Isa 25:6), the universal acknowledgment of the Lord by both the living and the dead, and the proclamation of the Lord's salvation to a people yet unborn. (4) What is especially highlighted in Ps 22 is that God hears the cry of the afflicted one (v. 24) and answers according to God's own perfect wisdom.[72] The psalm is not just about suffering, it also proclaims a definitive triumph— trial is swallowed up in victory—which will be universally proclaimed to generations yet unborn.

Jesus certainly fits the mold of one who has displayed unwavering fidelity to the way of the Lord and has always relied upon God (Ps 22:9–10), which culminates in the suffering of his passion as the Just One who is mocked, scorned, and despised by his enemies (Ps 22:6–8) who encircle him like a pack of dogs (Ps 22:16). At the most extreme moment of suffering the figure in Ps 22 petitions God, "O Lord, be not far off. O thou my help, hasten to my aid" (v. 19). The lament that begins with the words "Why have you forsaken me?" concludes with the petition "hasten to my aid," and we can well believe that Jesus likewise would have petitioned the Father to come to his help, especially given the fact that his personal identity as the Son is established in relation to the God whom he addressed as Father. In Ps 22 deliverance from terrible affliction does come—"You have answered me"—but Jesus's predicament is different in that his fate is in keeping with the picture painted by Isaiah's fourth Servant Song and Wis 2:10–20, where the Righteous One is not spared death. The Lord's response to Jesus's petition comes in the eschatological act of raising him from the dead, in the power of the Spirit (cf. Rom 1:4).

Did Jesus expect to be vindicated by God once he had entered the realm of the dead, thereby bringing about the conquest of the powers of death in his own person? The remainder of this chapter will seek to offer a response to this fundamental question. An important backdrop for interpreting Jesus's citation of Ps 22 on the cross, which the next section will examine, is the narration of the episode in the garden of Gethsemane. Jesus's pleadings with the Father in Gethsemane are especially important

---

72. Heinemann, "Exposition of Psalm 22," 305, 308.

because they illustrate that Jesus's view of his impending death is consistent with Isa 52:13—53:12 and Wis 2:10-20. What is lacking in the picture painted by Ps 22 is complemented by the anguished scene in the garden of Gethsemane. Jesus's prayer to the Father in Gethsemane is significant not only because it forms a line of thematic continuity with Jesus's words of institution of the Eucharist at the Last Supper and his repeated passion predictions communicated to his disciples, but also because it brings to a climactic point Jesus's perfect obedience to the Father, which springs from his unfathomable love of the Father.

Jesus's Prayer in the Garden of Gethsemane: United with the Father in Unfathomable Love

A key Gospel text that forms a preparatory framework for any critical discussion of the crucifixion of Jesus is the narration of the episode in the garden of Gethsemane. In Gethsemane Jesus is portrayed as being in a highly troubled and distressed state as he contemplates what awaits him, which leads him to pray that the hour might pass from him (Mark 14:35) and that the cup be removed from him (Mark 14:36).[73] While it is clear from all the Gospels that Jesus's obedience to the Father characterizes his entire life and messianic mission, Gethsemane marks a crucial transition point for the enactment of Jesus's obedience to the Father. The transition in the story, as Hans Frei has explained, is from a certain liberty of action and scope of movement that Jesus had enjoyed as a figure of authority and power, to a situation of powerlessness and helplessness which Jesus enters into freely when he gives himself over to the religious and political authorities.[74] The transition from power to helplessness is clearly in focus

---

73. Jesus's request that the cup be removed from him should be thought of as an interior, not exterior, temptation of Jesus. In the past, Jesus's temptation in the garden of Gethsemane was traditionally regarded as an "exterior" temptation. Since it was asserted that Christ was born free of original sin, was imbued with sanctifying grace, possessed all the gifts of the Holy Spirit, and possessed all the virtues perfectly, he was not able to experience the *fomes peccati* or any "interior" temptation. This position was typical of the scholastic period. Aquinas, for instance, allowed only exterior temptations in Christ—the notion of *propassion* is used to assert that Christ's superior reason quickly overrides any non-congenial passion that he experiences—in order to ensure that the work of redemption in Christ is not obstructed in any way. For a discussion of this issue, see Novello, *Passionate Deification*, 125-37.

74. Frei, *Identity of Jesus Christ*, 102-15. Frei argues that in the final events of Jesus's life, what happens to the close interaction between Jesus and God is that Jesus's action

in the words uttered by the chief priests and the scribes: "He saved others; he cannot save himself" (Mark 15:31; cf. Ps 22:7–8; Wis 2:18–20). These words suggest that if Jesus had not given up the power to save himself, he could not have saved others, in which case we are to see in the transition from power to helplessness the actual realization of Jesus's saving power. It is fitting here to also appeal to the writer of the Letter to the Hebrews who, in speaking about Jesus's prayers and supplications to God when facing his impending death, asserts that Jesus actually "learned obedience" (Heb 5:8) at this point of his public ministry. For all his sovereignty, Jesus the Messiah is depicted in Gethsemane as truly tested in his fidelity to the Father as he is given over into the hands of his enemies.[75] Karl Barth expresses Jesus's testing situation in Gethsemane in the following words: "It is now shown where the victory which Jesus won in the temptation in the wilderness leads [cf. Luke 4:13], that the end will involve the death of the victor."[76] Hans Urs von Balthasar reinforces this perspective when he maintains that the coming of Jesus's "hour" represents a line of demarcation between the active life of Jesus in his mission to Israel and his "being given up" by Jews and gentiles, by his disciples, and finally by the Father as well.[77] Jesus is not a mere passive victim, though, since the transition marked by Gethsemane hinges on his perfect obedience in carrying out the will of his Father.

In Mark's Gospel there are three passion predictions (8:31; 9:31; 10:33–34) that spell out the suffering, rejection, and killing of the Son of Man, which are *by divine plan*. It therefore strikes the reader as odd that Jesus should petition God that the hour might pass from him. The oddness stems from "misunderstanding the relationship between prayer and the divine will."[78] We saw in chapter 1 that in the biblical outlook it is not

---

is superseded by God's action. At the climactic point of the divine action, namely, the resurrection, God alone is active, and it is Jesus alone who is manifested.

75. The testing of faith shows that Jesus has a genuine human will, which is in constant interaction with the divine will. The two natures must not be thought of statically as juxtaposed to one another but dynamically as interacting with one another, so that each nature advances through the other in the process of salvation taking place in the person of Jesus the Messiah.

76. Barth, *Church Dogmatics*, IV/1:264.

77. Balthasar, *Action*, 237. The Son's "hour" is especially prominent in the Gospel of John (2:4; 7:30; 8:20; 12:23, 27; 13:1; 16:32; 17:1), where it refers to the completion of the Son's mission, that is, the hour of his passion and glorification (John 12:23 and 17:1 refer to the Son's death as his "glorification").

78. R. Brown, *Death of the Messiah*, 1:166.

irreverent to ask God to reconsider an intended action. For instance, in the Sinai wilderness Moses often pleads for divine justice, such as when the people make for themselves gods of gold (Exod 32:31–32). Moses intercedes for the people and pleads with God to turn from the divine wrath and forgive them for their transgression. Every time Moses is faced with a crisis and honestly petitions God to rethink an intended divine action, it is Moses who is portrayed as prevailing in the dialogue. Moses also dares to express displeasure with God and complains that the burden placed on him is "too heavy" (Num 11:15).[79] In such instances, the prayer raised to God is not one of rebellion but of confidence. "God will listen and will grant the request if it is reconcilable with overall Providence."[80] In the episode in Gethsemane, Jesus prays to God in a deeply troubled and distressed state, and he is confident that the Father hears his prayer and will consider his petition, since "all things are possible to you" (Mark 14:36). The issue here is whether Jesus's petition is reconcilable with the divine plan that has been spelled out in the three passion predictions. A few verses after Jesus's prayer it becomes evident that God does not grant the petition, for Jesus says to the disciples Peter and James and John, "The hour has come; behold the Son of Man is given over into the hands of sinners" (Mark 14:41). The "hour" therefore symbolizes God's action or initiative in giving Jesus over into the hands of sinners, who will put him to death.[81]

But are we dealing here only with the hour of Jesus's destiny and impending death, or is "the hour" in Mark 14:35 used eschatologically? In the only previous use of "the hour" in Mark, the term is clearly eschatological since it designates *the* appointed time of the coming of the kingdom of God: "But of that day or the hour no one knows, not even

---

79. In addition to Moses's pleadings for divine justice, Abraham similarly raises questions to God. Abraham's pleadings concern the divine intention to destroy the wicked city of Sodom (Gen 18:16–33). God heeds Abraham's prayer and decides to spare the righteous Lot. Joshua also boldly questions the divine character: "Why have you brought this people over the Jordan at all, to give us into the hands of the Amorites, to destroy us?" (Josh 7:7). Finally, it is also worth noting how Hezekiah weeps bitterly and prays to God concerning his impending death (2 Kgs 20:1–6), and God grants him his request and spares him from death.

80. R. Brown, *Death of the Messiah*, 1:167.

81. Stanley, *Jesus in Gethsemane*, 109, 135; also R. Brown, *Death of the Messiah*, 1:168. God, it should be noted, is not the only one who "gives over" Jesus. Jesus is also given over by Judas, the chief priests, and Pilate, and even by himself when his petition to God is not granted.

the angels in heaven, nor the Son, but only the Father" (13:32). In his predictions of the suffering and death of the Son of Man by divine plan, Jesus relates the destiny of the Son of Man to the coming of the kingdom, which suggests that "the hour" in Mark 14:35 is eschatological. This perspective is reinforced by the persistent theme of Jesus encountering the opposition of Satan, of unclean spirits, and of demons while proclaiming the kingdom of God.[82] Of special importance is Mark 3:22–27 where Jesus speaks of a kingdom of Satan and the conquest of that kingdom: "But no one can enter a strong man's house and plunder his goods, unless he first binds the strong man; then indeed he may plunder his house" (3:27). The death of the Son of Man is required to bind Satan and conquer his household, which is an eschatological event of salvation. The "hour" that Jesus prays might pass from him refers not simply to his being given over into the hands of sinners but also implies that it is through his unjust and violent death that the kingdom of Satan will be conquered and the kingdom of God will reign throughout Israel and the world. The death of Jesus is not just a historical ordeal for him but also an eschatological-apocalyptic event that pertains to the cosmic struggle of good over evil.[83] It is therefore not plausible to hold that "Jesus sees his death as the death of his cause."[84] Far from being the death of his cause, *Jesus sees his death as the accomplishment of his mission*, as the triumph of the kingdom of God over the reign of sin and evil in the world.

In Mark, Jesus's indirect request that the hour might pass from him leads immediately into his direct words in the next verse: "Remove this cup from me" (14:36). The hour in the previous verse therefore signifies the hour when the cup is to be drunk by Jesus. In Jewish Scripture, especially in the writings of the prophets, "the cup" refers to God's wrath or judgment against evildoers (Isa 51:17; Jer 25:15–18; Ezek 23:32–34).[85] In the book of Revelation, an apocalyptic cup of wrath is also envisaged (14:10; 16:19).[86] Is Jesus, then, being asked to drink the cup of God's wrath

---

82. Mark 1:13, 23, 32, 39; 4:14; 5:8; 6:7, 13; 7:25, etc.

83. R. Brown, *Death of the Messiah*, 1:168.

84. Sobrino, *Christology at the Crossroads*, 94.

85. For a discussion of the cup of God's wrath against sin in Scripture, see Balthasar, *Action*, 338–51. Since God is gracious, he must be able to show anger as well. But God's anger is not an irrational emotion, as it normally is in human beings; rather, God directs his anger according to his good pleasure.

86. When Jesus speaks of a kingdom of Satan and the conquest of that kingdom (e.g., Mark 3:22–27), he espouses the cosmic dualism typical of the apocalyptic genre.

against sin? There are two earlier texts in Mark's Gospel that shed light on what the cup signifies. The first narrative concerns the disciples James and John who desire to sit one to the right and one to the left of Jesus "in his glory" (10:37). In response to the disciples' request, Jesus poses the question: "Are you able to drink the cup that I drink, or to be baptized with the baptism with which I am baptized?" (10:38–39). It is clear in this passage that the cup and baptism are symbols of the redemptive character of Jesus's anticipated suffering and death, which is envisaged as a great trial. The saying of Jesus with which the passage concludes leaves the matter beyond all doubt: "For indeed the Son of Man has come to serve, not to be served, and to give his life as a ransom for many" (10:45). The sacrificial offering of his life as a "ransom" for sinners (cf. Isa 53:10), which highlights Jesus's life of total service to others, points to the ominous sense of the cup as found in the writings of the great prophets of Israel.[87] "It is not therefore simply a 'bitter cup of suffering' but a symbol of the wrath and judgment of God."[88] Jesus's life of pure and complete service is revealed in his willingness to vicariously take upon himself the divine judgment upon sinful humanity, so that God's coming salvation might make all things new.

The second reference to the cup prior to Gethsemane is found in Mark's version of the words of eucharistic institution at the Last Supper: "And he took a cup, and when he had given thanks he gave it to them, and they all drank of it. And he said to them, 'This is my blood of the

---

This cosmic dualism (evil without) is closely interconnected with an anthropological-ethical dualism (evil within) that highlights the individual's wilful rebellion against God. This ethical dualism is implicit in the basic structure of Judaism: "I have set before you life and death, blessing and curse; therefore choose life, that you and your descendants may live" (Deut 30:19); "Behold, I set before you the way of life and the way of death" (Jer 21:8); "In the path of righteousness is life, but the way of error leads to death" (Prov 12:28). Cosmic dualism and ethical dualism function within the framework of an eschatological dualism that is integral to the apocalyptic understanding of history: it is a dualism on the temporal plane, which concerns the final and definitive replacement of "this age" by "the age to come," when God will establish "a new heaven and a new earth" (Isa 65:17; Rev 21:1). For a treatment of Jewish apocalyptic under the three rubrics of cosmic, ethical, and eschatological dualism, see Otzen, *Judaism in Antiquity*, 83–97, 171–218. For a perspective on the nature of evil in the apocalyptic writings, see Novello, "Nature of Evil."

87. The metaphor of ransom provided the dominant interpretative category for making sense of Christ's death for the first thousand years of Christianity. See Lombardo, *Father's Will*, 181–239.

88. Schnackenburg, *Gospel*, 2:54.

covenant, which is poured out for many'" (14:23–24). The cup is Jesus's own life-blood, his saving blood that will be shed for the forging of the new covenant, which involves "a totally new relationship with God on the part of redeemed humanity."[89] At the Last Supper, the cup of wine symbolizes Jesus's life of total service, which culminates in the sacrificial shedding of his blood "as a ransom for many" (Mark 10:45). The historicity of Jesus's institution of the Eucharist alone suffices to establish the claim that "Jesus expected a violent death, and that *he saw his death as advancing his objectives.*"[90] In Mark's Gospel, then, Jesus is depicted as accomplishing his mission by being the covenant inaugurator who must drink the cup of God's judgment against sin. Jesus, though, must not be thought of as the object of God's wrath, for he as the beloved Son is without sin; his passion is the consequence of his faithful proclamation of his Father's benevolent kingdom in word and deed. On the synthetic or dynamistic view of God's wrath as his consent to the working out of human sin into its inevitable consequences—as discussed in chapter 1 of this study—Jesus's drinking of the cup is to be understood in the sense that he consents to bear in his person the consequences of the people's sin and rebellion, of which the cross is the consummate sign.[91] The drinking of the cup does not simply refer to the historical ordeal of Jesus's suffering unto death but has a decidedly eschatological thrust in that his death will take place "in the apocalyptic context of the great struggle of last times when God's kingdom overcomes evil."[92]

---

89. Stanley, *Jesus in Gethsemane*, 138.

90. Lombardo, *Father's Will*, 130. The whole of ch. 6 of Lombardo's study seeks to establish the claim that Jesus expected his death to advance his objectives. The inspiration for Lombardo's argument comes from McKnight, *Jesus and His Death*, 79–84.

91. It must be borne in mind that there is no divine anger against sin for anger's sake. God's wrath is instrumental; that is, it is intended to bring about repentance, to turn the people's hearts back to God. God's wrath is an aspect of the divine pathos, that is, one of the modes of God's responsiveness to humankind.

92. R. Brown, *Death of the Messiah*, 1:170. Scholars have appealed to the "great tribulation" (see Dan 7:9–14; also Rev 1:7, 13; 7:14; 14:14) as a penetrating insight into how Jesus saw his impending death. See Schweitzer, *Mystery of the Kingdom*, 315–54; Allison, *End of the Ages*, 115–41; Wright, *Jesus and the Victory*, 576–92. Other scholars, such as C. H. Dodd and T. W. Manson, look to the Suffering Servant Songs of Isaiah for insight into Jesus's mission and understanding of his impending death. But Stuhlmacher maintains that both Isa 52:13—53:12 and Dan 7:9–14 are behind Jesus's mission ("Vicariously Giving His Life"). For a discussion of these various perspectives, see McKnight, *Jesus and His Death*, 86–88.

As with the hour, the cup that Jesus requests be removed from him has both a historical and an eschatological meaning. In response to James and John, Jesus asks, "Are you able to drink the cup that I drink?" and now in Gethsemane Jesus is asking the Father to remove the cup from him. This may present as a difficult problem to resolve, but Jesus's direct request to the Father simply adds to the picture of him as deeply sorrowful and greatly distraught by the prospect of what lies ahead. In Gethsemane we see the man Jesus as we have never seen him before. He pleads with the Father that the cup be removed from him because he is overcome by powerful passions that render him emotionally vulnerable. His heart is at breaking point as he renounces the liberty of action that he had enjoyed as a figure of power and authority and now enters a situation of powerlessness. Yet he manages to steel himself for the mammoth struggle that lies ahead in his ultimate enactment of obedience to the Father, which will bring his benevolent mission of proclaiming the kingdom of God to completion. What comes into focus in Gethsemane is the genuine humanity of Jesus the Son, as his obedience to the Father is put to an ultimate test. His messianic mission of wondrous sayings, authoritative teachings, power over demons, and miraculous deeds sheds light on the divinity of his sonship, but we should not think of his divinity as overriding his real and genuine humanity.[93] We are required to think in terms of the two natures constantly and mutually interacting with each other, and advancing through one another in the accomplishment of Jesus's mission. It is helpful on this point to adopt Karl Barth's perspective and conceive of Jesus's humanity as mediating his divinity, so that what

---

93. The Chalcedonian definition of the two natures in the person of Christ has often given rise to deviations in the direction of monophysitism, which suffers from an inadequately developed idea of kenosis. With monophysitism, the Word made flesh never really leaves the domain of divine being, hence the humiliation of the Word in entering the human temporal realm is not properly recognized. The human nature is seen as passive in relation the divine nature, and this passivity makes of human nature a mere means or instrument of redemption. Sergius Bulgakov, for example, is especially critical of the failure of patristic thought to develop a consistent and adequate idea of kenosis, hence the mutuality of the life of the two natures, their interaction and mutual reception, is negated (*Lamb of God*, 247–61). In modern Russian Orthodox theology, the idea has developed that the divine kenosis is not confined to the incarnation of the Son of God in the person of Jesus of Nazareth but is something eternal in the life of the triune God. This implies that the divine kenosis is involved with the very act of creation and the whole divine economy of salvation. Representatives of this movement include Sergius Bulgakov, Vladimir Soloviev, M. M. Tareev, and Vladimir Lossky. Hans Urs von Balthasar is a Catholic representative of this theological movement.

takes place in his person is the history of the humiliation of the Son of God and the exaltation of the Son of Man.[94]

The testing of Jesus's resolve and obedience to the Father in Gethsemane bears a strong family resemblance to the tested faith of Jeremiah and fits perfectly well into the tradition of the righteous sufferer portrayed in Ps 22, Isaiah's Suffering Servant Songs, and Wis 2:10–5. We saw in chapter 1 how for Jeremiah the words of the Lord became "a joy and the delight" (Jer 15:16) of his heart, but as he took up his prophetic mission the emotions of joy and delight gave way to suffering emotions and profound laments at having to stand alone before a wicked people to endure their insults and barbs: "Why is my pain unceasing, my wound incurable, refusing to be healed" (Jer 15:18); "Why did I come forth from the womb to see toil and sorrow, and spend my days in shame?" (Jer 20:18). In carrying out his prophetic vocation, Jeremiah suffers greatly at the hands of a sinful people, and he calls upon God to relieve his pain. The faith of the prophet is clearly tested by God, who regards pain and sorrow as integral to the privilege of representing God before a rebellious people. Jeremiah must learn that his suffering is in sympathy with the divine pathos, that is, the suffering of the prophet mirrors the suffering of God before the people.

When we come to the Gospels, especially Luke's Gospel, Jesus is portrayed as standing in the line of Israel's prophets. When some Pharisees warn Jesus not to journey towards Jerusalem because Herod wants to kill him, Jesus replies: "For it cannot be that a prophet should perish away from Jerusalem. O Jerusalem, Jerusalem, killing the prophets and stoning those who are sent to you! . . . Behold, your house is forsaken" (Luke 13:33–35; cf. 19:41–44; 21:20–24; 23:27–31). As Jesus approaches the holy city and it comes into view, he is overcome by strong emotions that cause him to weep profusely (Luke 19:41–44). What causes Jesus to weep so bitterly is not merely the awareness of his own impending fate in Jerusalem but the impending destruction of the holy city of Jerusalem,

94. The early Barth, like Emil Brunner, viewed revelation as occurring through the medium of God himself—"God reveals himself through himself"—while the later Barth adopted the perspective that Christ's human nature per se is the medium of revelation and it mediates the divine nature to us. See McIntyre, *Shape of Christology*, 157–61; Barth, *Church Dogmatics*, IV/2:98. To Barth's mind, the recognition of the divine in the human implies that there can be no evading the child in the crib at Bethlehem, Jesus's growing in wisdom and understanding, his being tempted in the wilderness, his constant need to pray to the Father, the episode in the garden of Gethsemane, and his genuine suffering in helplessness on the cross.

which is deeply cherished by Jesus as the place associated with the destiny of Israel, and the center of the fully redeemed world to come. Jerusalem has special meaning because of God's history of covenant lodged there. Isaiah spoke of his weeping bitter tears at the prospect of "the destruction of the daughter of my people" (Isa 22:4), and Jeremiah is overcome by grief and dismay for "the wound of the daughter of my people" (Jer 8:21).[95] Jesus stands in this prophetic tradition of weeping in anticipation of the desolation that will overtake the people of God—*in the person of Jesus is embodied the mourning of God for his anguished people.* Jesus's own fate is intimately linked with the fate of Jerusalem, hence the coming of the holy city into view draws from Jesus a prophetic announcement of impending doom (i.e., divine judgment). The people's rejection of Jesus and the failure to recognize in his person God's special visitation of his people, will bring the destruction of Jerusalem.

While Jesus can justifiably be viewed as a prophet whose state of suffering is in sympathy with the divine pathos, at the same time it is important to appreciate that Jesus is not merely a prophet. A prophet is a messenger of God, someone who suffers by virtue of proclaiming the word of God to a wayward people and warning them to repent so as to avert the calamity of divine judgment. Jesus certainly proclaims the word of God, but he proclaims it in such a way that the kingdom of God is being fulfilled in his very own person: "The time is fulfilled, and the kingdom of God is at hand; repent, and believe in the gospel" (Mark 1:15). The people are called to repentance in response to the kingdom being made manifest in the person of Jesus. The good news of the blessings of the kingdom in the here and now—i.e., forgiveness of sins, power over demons, miraculous deeds, wondrous sayings, and authoritative teaching—is intended to stir the hearts and minds of the people and move them towards repentance. In carrying out his mission, moreover, Jesus is portrayed in the Gospels not just as an ideal covenant partner, as the prophets before him were; instead, his mission is accomplished as the *inaugurator of the covenant* (cf. Jer 31:31–34; Ezek 36:24–28), which is a role assigned or reserved to God. Once we appreciate this dual role

95. The link with Jeremiah and Isaiah is bolstered by Luke's account of the cleansing of the temple (Luke 19:45–46), which immediately follows the account of Jesus's bitter weeping over Jerusalem. Jesus appeals to Scripture, quoting Isa 56:7 ("My house shall be a house of prayer") and Jer 7:11 ("a den of robbers"), thereby making it clear that Jerusalem's judgment has already begun in his action of driving out those who use the temple as a marketplace and not for worship of the Lord of the covenant.

of Jesus as both ideal covenant partner and covenant inaugurator, the relationship between his emotions and the covenant becomes more complex by virtue of his emotions tending in both a human and a divine direction.[96] As the Son in whom the "fullness of divinity dwells bodily" (Col 2:9), his ultimate rejection by his own people—which is movingly expressed by his bitter weeping over the fate of Jerusalem—is felt more deeply than the prophets before him. The prophets suffered in sympathy with the divine pathos, but Jesus the Son suffers as the unique embodiment of God's pathos in history, and it is precisely through his suffering and horrible death that the new covenant which the prophets spoke about is established. As the inaugurator of the new covenant, Jesus fulfills the special role of the suffering servant of the Lord (Isa 52:13—53:12). He as the Just One makes himself "an offering for sin" (Isa 53:10) and "makes many to be accounted righteous" (Isa 53:11); he is the one who gives his life as "a ransom for many" (Mark 10:45).

In light of Jesus's congenial and suffering emotions being more complex and more intense than any ordinary human being on account of the fullness of both humanity and divinity dwelling in his person, we can appreciate the episode in Gethsemane where Jesus pleads with the Father that the cup be removed from him. The extreme anguish is due not merely to Jesus's acute awareness of the horror of his impending death but his having to renounce the power and authority he had previously exercised as he is given over into the hands of malefactors. Precisely because he is the Son, Jesus is deeply distressed by the prospect of drinking the cup, of having divine judgment taken out of his hands while his enemies prepare to execute their ungodly judgment upon him. Yet despite his state of distress, Jesus's prayer in Gethsemane concludes by confirming his obedience to the Father: "Yet not what I will, but what you will" (Mark 14:36). The emphasis in the Gospel account of Gethsemane, then, is not intended to fall on Jesus's pleading to the Father that the cup be removed from him. Rather, the crux of the episode in the garden is Jesus the Son's determination to be perfectly obedient to the Father as *a decisive manifestation of his unity with the Father in unfathomable love.* This ineffable unity with the Father had already been on display during the course of Jesus's active ministry to Israel—e.g., Matt 3:17, 11:25-27, 17:5; Mark 9:7; Luke 10:21-22; John 10:30, 14:31, 17:1-26—but now, reduced to a state of powerlessness and helplessness in Gethsemane, it

---

96. See Novello, *Passionate Deification*, 168–82.

is shown what the perfection of obedience to the Father entails in order to advance and accomplish his mission as the Son. Love is the first and chief of Jesus's emotions, from which springs his compassion for his own, as well as his obedience to the Father:[97] "I do as the Father has commanded me, so that the world may know that I love the Father" (John 14:31). Jesus's mission is to make known the Father's benevolent love for his people, who are like sheep without a shepherd.

While it is important when reflecting upon Jesus's prayer in Gethsemane to acknowledge Jesus's oneness and unity with the Father— ineffable love of the Father is the source of Jesus's obedience to the Father—it is equally as important not to lose sight of Jesus's very real agony and deep anguish precipitated by his acute awareness that he is about to be given over into the hands of sinners and taste the bitterness of the cup; that is, the cup of the new covenant in his blood which will be "poured out for many for the forgiveness of sins" (Matt 26:27–28; Mark 14:24). The shedding of Jesus's blood on Calvary is presented in the passion narrative as the content or purpose of his perfect obedience to the Father enacted in Gethsemane. It is worthwhile listening to Barth's understanding of Gethsemane, so as to highlight Jesus's real anguish and dread at having to drink the cup:

> It was not a matter of His suffering and dying in itself and as such, but of the dreadful thing that He saw coming upon Him in and with His suffering and dying. He saw it clearly and correctly. It was the coming of the night "in which no man can work" (John 9:4), in which *the good will of God will be indistinguishably one with the evil will of men and the world and Satan*. It was a matter of the triumph of God being concealed under that of His adversary, of that which is not, of that which supremely is not. It was a matter of God Himself obviously making a tryst with death and about to keep it. It was a matter of the divine judgment being taken out of the hands of Jesus and placed in those of His supremely unrighteous judges and executed by them upon Him. . . . Jesus saw this cup. He tasted its bitterness. He had not made any mistake. He had not been needlessly afraid. There was every reason to ask that it might pass from Him.[98]

In Gethsemane, Jesus becomes acutely aware of the coincidence or siding of God's good will with the evil will of humankind, so that from this

---

97. See Novello, *Passionate Deification*, 204–210.

98. Barth, *Church Dogmatics*, IV/1:271; emphasis added.

moment onward Jesus is consumed by the darkness of being forsaken by God and delivered into the hands of his enemies. In the prophetic texts, divine judgment is not presented so much as the breach of a legal contract as the breakdown of an intimate relationship.[99] God patiently bears the sins of a rebellious people, God chooses the road of suffering for the people, yet the divine patience eventually comes to an end and judgment falls on the people: "The Lord could no longer bear your evil doings and the abominations which you committed; therefore your land has become a desolation" (Jer 44:22). Images of withdrawal, forsaking, hiddenness, or giving the people up are typically employed when speaking of divine judgment. The failure of the people to respond to God's repeated efforts to heal the covenant relationship builds to the point of God allowing destructive forces to have their way with the people. When the Lord withdraws and hides his face from the people, they are given over to forces of destruction and death, and this constitutes divine judgment on them. The divine intention is never to give up on them but to exercise compassion in the midst of their calamity, mercifully redeem them, and offer them new life in the land as the people of God. Divine judgment is always directed towards redemptive purposes and covenant goals that make possible a new future for Israel and the world.

In the citation above, Barth asserts that what Jesus dreaded in Gethsemane, what he saw coming upon him, was the dark hour in which "the good will of God will be indistinguishably one with the evil will of men and the world and Satan." This is precisely the view of divine judgment that we find in the prophetic writings. The will of God is always a good will towards the people, but when God forsakes them and gives them over to forces of destruction and death, the good will of God coincides with "the evil will of men and the world and Satan." In Gethsemane what causes Jesus the Son to experience such awful dread is his acute awareness of what the accomplishment of his mission entails; namely, the vicarious bearing of the cup of divine judgment upon sinners in a final act of perfect obedience to the Father. This implies that we must view Jesus as dying not only at the hands of evildoers but also at the hands of his Father who gives him over into the hands of his enemies and therefore forsakes him. This forsaking of Jesus, though, does not mean that the Father is angry and indignant towards him, for Jesus is the "beloved Son" (Matt 3:17; 12:18; 17:5; Mark 9:7; Luke 9:35) who is without sin; his entire

---

99. This was discussed in ch. 1 of this study.

life and mission is defined by his obedience to the Father as a manifesta-tion of his ineffable love of the Father.[100]

To conclude, what takes place in the narration of the episode in the garden of Gethsemane is most important for a discussion of Jesus's cry on the cross because it is "the key to all that is about to happen, a warning to read all that follows in this light."[101] Gethsemane marks a transition point in Jesus's mission from a figure of power and authority to a fig-ure of powerlessness and helplessness as he is "given over" by his Father into the hands of his enemies. Jesus is not only given over by his Father, though, but is also given over by himself in order that "the scriptures of the prophets might be fulfilled" (Matt 26:56). Ineffable love of the Father is the springboard of Jesus's obedience to the Father, which is put to the ultimate test in Gethsemane. Jesus's reference to the hour and the cup indicates that he views his impending death as an eschatological event—the apocalyptic great trial—that concerns the final victory of good over evil (cf. Luke 4:13). When we come to consider Jesus's cry on the cross, his final words must not be separated from Ps 22's context of prayer, which is of a piece with his prayer in Gethsemane, as Donald Senior explains in his study of the passion in Mark's Gospel:

> The words of Psalm 22 now serve as the final words of Jesus in the Gospel. Within the context of the suffering Just One theol-ogy and of Mark's Gospel as a whole, there can be no question that these words are an expression of *faith*, not despair or bit-terness. The opening line of the Psalm should not be separated from its context of prayer. These words are, in effect, the final version of the prayer in Gethsemane where, also in a "lament," Jesus affirmed his unbroken trust in his Father while feeling the full horror of approaching death (cf. Mark 14:32–42).[102]

100. While I have cited Barth favorably with regard to his view of Gethsemane, I do not follow him when he contends that Jesus on the cross suffers "real" abandonment by God; that is, Jesus suffers "hell" in the place of sinners. Notwithstanding the fact that Barth speaks of God's holy love, not God's wrath, as the cause of Jesus's passion, I do not believe that the unity of the Son and the Father in unfathomable love, which is on display in Gethsemane, allows us to conceive of the cross in terms of a real abandon-ment or "separation" of the Son from the Father. This will be discussed further below.

101. Rossé, *Cry of Jesus*, 63. Rossé, rightly in my view, argues that behind the dis-tressing events that are narrated, there unfolds another story hidden from the eyes of flesh; namely, the story of love between the Son and the Father, which culminates in Jesus's cry on the cross. The cry must be interpreted in the light of Jesus's words in the garden of Gethsemane.

102. Senior, *Passion of Jesus*, 123–24.

By willingly and faithfully accepting the horror of his impending death like a lamb led to the slaughter, Jesus manifests what it means to be the Son who proclaims the Father's covenant of grace.[103] While the emphasis in the Gethsemane scene falls on Jesus's determination to be perfectly obedient to the Father as a manifestation of his unity with the Father in unfathomable love, at the same time the narrative leaves the reader in no doubt concerning Jesus's extreme anguish, deep sorrow, and real dread as the hour approaches. Jesus's trust in God is not broken, but in Gethsemane Jesus feels the fierce assault of his impending death. Holy love of the Father, "through the eternal Spirit" (Heb 9:14), is what enables Jesus to embrace the mammoth struggle that lies ahead, which is required to bring his messianic mission to completion.

Jesus's Cry on Calvary: A Composite Theological Interpretation

Against this important backdrop of Jesus's prayer in the garden of Gethsemane, we can now proceed to undertake a critical discussion of Jesus's cry on the cross. The earliest Christians had to address not only the problem of preaching a Messiah who had experienced death but the much bigger problem posed by the cross, which was a form of death reserved for hardened criminals, rebellious slaves, and rebels against Roman rule. "A crucified Messiah, son of God or God, must have seemed a contradiction in terms to anyone, Jew, Greek, Roman or barbarian, asked to believe such a claim, and it will certainly have been thought offensive and foolish."[104] Paul sums up the situation succinctly when he writes that to preach a crucified Messiah is "a stumbling block to Jews and folly to Gentiles" (1 Cor 1:23). The earliest Christians simply could not present their gospel message to the Jewish world without first attempting to resolve the scandal of a crucified Messiah.

To address this key problem, recourse was made to the Jewish wisdom motif of the just one who suffers despite fidelity to God's will

---

103. It is not plausible to maintain, as Leander Keck does, that Jesus's death involves not only a crisis in our understanding of God but also in Jesus's understanding of God. See Keck, *Future for Historical Jesus*, 229–31.

104. Hengel, *Crucifixion in Ancient World*, 10. Hengel asserts that crucifixion is a specific expression of the sadistic cruelty and inhumanity dormant within us all, and which, in our time, finds expression in "the call for the death penalty, for popular justice and for harsher treatment of criminals" (*Crucifixion in Ancient World*, 87).

and who feels abandoned by God to adversity. This wisdom tradition is evident in the psalms of lament and in the book of Job. Job complains to God that he suffers as an innocent man, and he boldly calls into question the justice of God. The lengthy divine speeches in response to Job's lament have the effect of silencing Job, who is humbled before God. Job comes to acknowledge that suffering has a mysterious dimension, and if accepted with humility the righteous lamenter is able to experience personal intimacy with God: "Now my eye sees you" (Job 42:5). In the psalms of lament this theme of suffering despite fidelity to God is given abundant expression. Unlike Job, though, the psalms of lament express trust and confidence in God to deliver the afflicted from their distress, and they characteristically end with a pledge or vow of praise and thanksgiving for God's anticipated act of deliverance. The basic structure of the lament psalm witnesses to a robust form of faith, where lament functions to keep hope alive. The cry lifted up to God is motivated by a deep confidence that God is characterized by pathos; that is, God is involved with his people, is affected by the cries of the afflicted, and will act to deliver them from their suffering.

The motif of the suffering righteous underwent a significant development, however, which is apparent in Jeremiah's confessions (11–20), Deutero-Isaiah's Suffering Servant Songs (42:1–7; 49:1–7; 50:4–9; 52:13–53:12), Ps 22, and the book of Wisdom (2:10–20). In these particular texts the just one is persecuted not *despite* the fact that they are upright and righteous but precisely *because* they bear faithful witness to the living Lord.[105] While the sufferings are still seen as putting the faith of the righteous to the test so that they may be proved to be worthy of God—cf. Wis 3:5; Jer 15:19–21; Ps. 22:4–5; Isa 49:4, 50:8, 53:12—the *primary emphasis falls on depicting the suffering endured as proof of their justice.* The persecution of the righteous by the godless on the grounds of the just lives they lead in committing their cause to God, becomes the sign of divine election. The text of Wis 2:10–20, which purports to be the scornful talk of the impious and godless (cf. Ps 22:6–8; Isa 50:6, 52:14, 53:3), was one of the primary sources for the Gospel narration of the passion of Jesus, as he is cast in the role of the one who is unjustly put to a shameful death

---

105. This understanding is still in evidence in contemporary Judaism. It is movingly narrated, for example, by Zvi Kolitz in his story entitled *Yossel Rakover's Appeal to God*, the historical background of which is the Warsaw ghetto uprising of April 1943. In Kolitz's story, to suffer as the people of God is at the very heart of what it means to be a Jew. For a presentation of this story, see Van Beeck, *Loving the Torah*, 14–26.

for having irritated the powers that be by his radical proclamation of the kingdom of God. As he hangs on the cross, Jesus's faith in God is put to a decisive test by his scornful rejectors. The renunciation on Jesus's part of any kind of self-justification before his enemies (cf. Mark 15:29–30; Matt 27:39), and the acceptance of his unjust suffering unto death without the expectation of any saving act by God as demanded by those who mock and taunt him (cf. Mark 15:31–32; Matt 27:41–43; Luke 23:35–38), is thoroughly consistent with the motif of the persecuted just one depicted in the book of Wisdom (cf. 2:18–20), as well as Isaiah's Suffering Servant Songs (cf. Isa 50:6; 53:3, 7). In Ps 22, by contrast, the suffering righteous one does not actually die, nevertheless his state of affliction is so terrible that he feels that God is laying him "in the dust of death" (v. 15b). As the psalmist loses his physical and emotional strength, he feels that death is encroaching, which leads his enemies to "stare and gloat" (v. 17) over him and to cast lots to "divide his garments among them" (v. 18). This depiction of the psalmist's state of affliction certainly mirrors the Gospel narration of those who mock and taunt Jesus as he hangs on the cross.

Where Ps 22 is especially effective, more so than in the book of Wisdom and the Suffering Servant Songs, is in the depiction of the *terrible trouble* that encircles the lamenter. The powerful animal metaphors (vv. 12–13, 16) vividly express the extreme suffering of the psalmist at the hands of his enemies. The conventional pair of lion and bull represents the epitome of power, while hounds evoke the sense of helpless prey, which is how the psalmist feels. What is more, the psalmist vividly describes his state of physical and emotional exhaustion: he feels as if "poured out like water"; all his bones "are out of joint" (v. 14a); his strength is "dried up like a potsherd" (v. 15); and his tongue sticks to the inside of his mouth as his vital fluids drain away. All of these hyperbolic descriptions underline the psalmist's loss of physical strength, while the description of his melted heart of wax (v. 14b) is intended to convey his loss of emotional strength. These palpable descriptions of the surrounding bestial forces of cruelty and wickedness are supremely suited to describing how Jesus would feel hanging on the cross with death encroaching. As Jesus bears his affliction, his enemies "stare and gloat" (Ps 22:17) over him and watch for his death so they can strip his body and "divide his garments among them" (Ps 22:18). It is certainly plausible to contend that when Jesus uttered the first verse of Ps 22 on the cross, which would have implied the remainder of the psalm, part of the reason he appealed to this particular psalm was to convey the depth of his suffering at the hands of his enemies. The crescendo of suffering articulated in Ps 22:12–18 leaves the reader in no doubt about the righteous sufferer's state of total powerlessness and help-lessness as forces of wickedness encircle him, and stare and gloat over him, and cast lots to divide his garments among them. Psalm 22's vivid description of the terrible suffering of the righteous one who was cast upon God from his birth, is especially well suited to conveying Jesus's state of utter humiliation on the cross, which he as the Son bears out of unity with the Father in unfathomable love.

Psalm 22, unlike the book of Wisdom and Isaiah's Suffering Servant Songs, does envisage a divine act of deliverance as the righteous sufferer approaches death, but this does not mean that by citing the psalm on the cross Jesus expects God to spare him death. On the contrary, it is already clear from the episode in Gethsemane that by entering into a state of powerlessness and helplessness as he is given over into the hands of his enemies, Jesus does not expect any act of deliverance by his Father, since his anguished plea that the hour might pass from him is not granted (see also Matt 26:53). In order to accomplish his mission as the Son, Jesus performs a final act of obedience to his Father and commits himself to drinking the cup of the covenant in his blood: "He was oppressed, and he was afflicted, yet he opened not his mouth; like a lamb that is led to the slaughter, and like a sheep that before its shearers is dumb, so he opened not his mouth" (Isa 53:7). By accepting a shameful and cruel death at the hands of sinners, Jesus's suffering becomes the proof both of his divine election and the integrity of his justice:[106] "Yet he bore the sin of many, and made intercession for the transgressors" (Isa 53:12).

By virtue of standing *for* God the Father, Jesus the Messiah stands *against* evil forces that thwart the reign of God in the world. As the "Holy and Righteous One" (Acts 3:14) who proclaims the kingdom of his heavenly Father in word and deed, Jesus's mission necessarily involves suffering as he is confronted by people with hearts of stone, legalistic attitudes, hardness of understanding, and wicked intentions. This view is consistent with the prophetic literature of Israel, where God's suffer-ing before the people—i.e., Israel's forsaking of God—is embodied in the life of the prophet who suffers in sympathy with the divine pathos. The prophet's lament springs from his proclaiming of the word of God to a stubborn and rebellious people, which means that the prophet's mourn-ing is not a word of the people to God but a word of *God* to the people.

---

106. See Van Beeck, *Loving the Torah*, 62–65.

The prophet's lament to God, then, is inseparable from God's grieving and sorrow due to Israel's forsaking of God (cf. Isa 1:4). The prophet suffers as the embodiment of God's sorrow before the people. What is more, when the prophet Jeremiah persists with his complaints once he has been rebuked by God (Jer 15:19), God henceforth falls silent to the prayers of Jeremiah who continues to suffer in his prophetic office. The silence of God takes on special significance, though, inasmuch as we are required to appreciate that the prophet's suffering mirrors the divine suffering on account of Israel's forsaking of God. When God falls silent to Jeremiah's prayers, this should not be taken to mean that God is absent and removed from the prophet's suffering. On the contrary, God's silence should be interpreted in positive terms; namely, God is present in his silence and identifies with the suffering of the prophet.

Jesus certainly views himself as standing in the line of the prophets of Israel (Matt 23:37; Luke 13:33) and as suffering in sympathy with the divine pathos. His suffering, though, is greater than the prophets before him and greater still than the Lord's suffering servant (Isa 52:13—53:12) in whom suffering is raised to a new key. This is because the man Jesus is the personal embodiment or incarnation of the divine Son: "the fullness of deity dwells bodily in him" (Col 2:9). His humanity is no ordinary humanity, for it is the humanity of the eternal Word and hence a divine humanity. The unity of divinity and humanity in the one person of Jesus Christ means that his divinity is expressed through his humanity, which is to say that the two natures constantly address one another and advance through each other in his person. As the divine Son who condescends to the historical realm and participates in adamic flesh, we can appreciate the reality of Jesus's anguish in the garden of Gethsemane and his extreme agony on the cross. Yet his cry of God-forsakenness should not be regarded as a merely human lament in the tradition of the suffering righteous, for it is the cry of the incarnate Son whose humanity mediates and attests to his divinity. This means that *in the person of the incarnate Son, God has internalized the divine suffering due to the people's rebellion and hardness of heart in an unsurpassable fashion.* As a human lament in the tradition of the suffering righteous, Jesus's cry indicates that his suffering endured at the hands of his enemies is proof of his justice, the sign of divine election. But Jesus's lament is also divine, for his suffering on the cross is the definitive Word of *God* to the people; his crucified body is the unique embodiment of God's suffering before a rebellious people. In Jesus's drinking of the cup, we are led to understand that God has internalized the history of Israel's forsaking of him as Lord in an extraordinary fashion in the crucified Son. As Jesus hangs on the cross and is mocked and taunted by his scornful malefactors, divinity and humanity are joined together in an ultimate agony, with the intention of bringing to fullness the covenant of grace that proffers new life to Israel and the world.

Psalm 22 is superior to the book of Wisdom (2:10–20) and Isaiah's Suffering Servant Song (52:13—53:12) when it comes to depicting the terrible trouble that encircles the afflicted one, but another distinctive feature of the psalm is the lamenter's *confidence that God has heard his petition* and comes to his help. This confidence is expressed in the second petition (vv. 19–21) where the last word is in the perfect tense—"you have answered me" (v. 21). The psalmist wholly trusts that God does not hide his face from the righteous afflicted one (v. 24). Psalm 22 is not just about the terrible suffering of the righteous one at the hands of evildoers but proclaims with confidence God's response to the plea for help; that is, the emphasis is on a definitive triumph over the forces of sin and evil, which will be universally proclaimed to the living and the dead, as well as to generations yet unborn. Even in his hour of extreme suffering, the psalmist still refers to the Lord as his sure help. A lament that begins with the words "Why have you forsaken me?" (v. 1a) concludes with the petition "hasten to my aid" (v. 19b), and the question "Why art thou so far from helping me" (v. 1b) becomes the petition "be not far off" (v. 19a). Jesus, like the psalmist, has committed his life to the way of the Lord and has always relied totally upon God the Father (Ps 22:9–10). His utter commitment to proclaiming his Father's kingdom to Israel culminates in his state of suffering as the Just One who is mocked, scorned, and despised by his enemies (Ps 22:6–8) who surround him like a pack of dogs (Ps 22:16). At the most extreme moment of suffering, the figure in Ps 22 petitions God, "O Lord, be not far off. O thou my help, hasten to my aid," and it is indeed most reasonable to maintain that by citing the opening verse of Ps 22 on the cross, Jesus is petitioning the Father to come to his help.

In the prior episode in the garden of Gethsemane, where Jesus is in a state of heightened anguish, we see him petitioning the Father that the "hour" might pass from him and the "cup" be removed from him. Jesus in Gethsemane turns to the Father to deliver him from the terrifying ordeal that awaits him, so it is hardly surprising that in his hour of extreme agony on the cross Jesus should once again petition the Father to hasten to his aid. Of course, we know that in the Gethsemane narrative Jesus's petition is not granted and that the emphasis falls on depicting Jesus as determined to be perfectly obedient to the Father as a decisive manifestation of his unity with the Father in unfathomable love. Yet it is precisely because of this ineffable unity with the Father that *Jesus's cry should be interpreted as an expression of faith and unbroken trust in his Father as his only sure help.* The essential message of Ps 22 is that God does not hide his face but hears the cry of the afflicted one (v. 24) and responds to deliver his servant from forces of evil that encircle him. The cry of the psalmist is directed not *against* God, it is not a cry of abandonment *by* God but a cry of total abandonment *to* God who alone can save the suffering righteous one. Jesus's cry, likewise, is not directed against the Father but to the Father, who is the saving God of Israel, who alone can save him from the clutches of evil forces. It is simply not convincing to maintain, as Moltmann does, that Jesus cried out to God in despair and died as one rejected by the Father, so that Jesus's cry indicates a "rift" or "divide" in the very life of God.

The psalmist is steeped in the history of the forefathers's experiences of the Lord's saving deeds (vv. 4–5), and he remembers his own intimate experiences of God (vv. 9–11), and this knowledge of the nature of God, of how God actually is, leads the afflicted one to turn to the Lord as his only sure help in his hour of extreme need. Jesus, as the Messiah, is most certainly steeped in the history of God's saving deeds towards the people, and as the incarnate Son who is in the bosom of the Father, he most certainly has intimate knowledge of how God actually is, all of which would lead him in his hour of most extreme suffering to turn to the Father as his only sure help. It is clear from the Gospels that Jesus's identity is a relational identity, that is, his divinity as the Son emerges in his modus of being related to the Father in unfathomable love, which in essence means that Jesus has committed the totality of his life to the just cause of the Father. It therefore follows that Jesus has none other than the Father to turn to as he hangs on the cross and is mocked and taunted by his enemies. As in Ps 22, Jesus expects vindication and deliverance by the Lord, but his situation of affliction differs from the psalmist in that it reflects the picture painted by Isaiah's fourth Servant Song, as well as Wis 2:10–20, where the suffering righteous one is not spared death. Jesus's prayer to the Father in Gethsemane, together with the words of institution of the Eucharist at the Last Supper, indicate most clearly that the objectives of Jesus's mission will be accomplished by the shedding of his blood of the new covenant. Jesus expects God's response to his lament to come in the form of his being raised from the dead, which sounds the death knell to the kingdom of Satan. This expectation on the part of Jesus is already very much in evidence during the course of his Galilean ministry when he begins to instruct his disciples that he will be rejected by his own and put to death but "after three days rise again" (Mark 8:31; 9:9, 31; 10:34; cf. Hos 6:2; Dan 12:2). As the Holy and Just One, his death is no ordinary death but an apocalyptic event that completes his messianic mission. Yet since Jesus expects the Father's response to his lament cry to come in the divine act of raising him from the dead, his resurrection emerges as *the* eschatological event. His death, in other words, is to be seen as *a glorifying death*: "But we see Jesus . . . crowned with glory and honor because of the suffering of death" (Heb 2:9).[107] The blessings of the new covenant in his blood are seen as conquering the powers of death—the kingdom of Satan—and as offering resurrection life to the people: "And I, when I am lifted up from the earth, will draw all men to myself" (John 12:32). Talk of Jesus's confidence in his petition being heard by the Father (Easter Sunday) must not allow us, though, to detract from the reality of his extreme suffering on the cross (Good Friday) and his descent into the grave (Holy Saturday).[108] For what is in view prior to the unspeakable joy of Easter Sunday is the manner in which God, in the person of the incarnate Son, has internalized the human situation of sin and death, so as to bestow upon humanity the transforming power of the new covenant of grace that brings unspeakable joy and new life to the world.

At this point it will be worthwhile to elaborate on the manner in which the essential message of Ps 22—i.e., God hears the cry of the suffering righteous one and does *not* hide his face from him—can be asserted while holding to the view that Jesus on the cross drinks the cup of God's

---

107. The Catholic biblical scholar F. X. Durrwell cites Heb 2:9 to make the case that the mystery of the incarnation reaches its zenith with Christ's glorifying death (Durrwell, *Eucharist Presence of Christ*, 18). As a glorifying death, as a passing from this world of sin and death to the Father, Jesus's resurrection refers to the plenitude of salvation. Durrwell protested against a "truncated" theology of redemption, where the resurrection of Jesus was not redemptive at all. See Durrwell, *Holy Spirit of God*, 41; and Hunt, *Trinity and Paschal Mystery*, 14–15.

108. Barth, following Reformed thought, asserts that Jesus on the cross suffers hell in the place of sinners, but Balthasar in his theology of Holy Saturday contends that Jesus suffers hell in his "going to the dead," which is the most extreme point of his kenosis as the Son.

judgment against sin. In the writings of the prophets, the language of judgment commonly uses images of forsaking or giving the people up to the consequences of their own actions: God "surrenders" his people to the working out of sin into its inevitable consequences. In the case of Jesus, then, he is forsaken in the sense that the Father gives him over into the hands of evildoers (cf. Rom 8:32) and thereby surrenders him to the working out of the sin of the world into its gruesome consequences; namely, Jesus's suffering of the cross, which is the consummate sign of the world's estrangement from God. It is in this fashion that Jesus the Son has vicariously borne the divine judgment against sin. We should also appreciate, however, that since it is the will of the Father to hand over the Son into the custody of evildoers, Jesus dies not only at the hands of his enemies but also at the hands of the Father. This means that the abandonment of the Son should not be treated as simply the nonintervention of God but is by divine design and hence an act of God for the sake of the salvation of the world—this is already made clear by Jesus's passion predictions in the Gospel story. The cross as an act of God should not be interpreted, however, as *God*-abandonment.[109] The scene in Gethsemane reveals Jesus's perfect obedience to the Father as a decisive manifestation of unity with the Father in unfathomable love. It is this union in love, "through the eternal Spirit" (Heb 9:14), that enables Jesus to obey the Father and surrender himself into the hands of his enemies, and this same union in love is what motivates the Father to surrender himself to evildoers in the one whom he hands over to them. In the very act in which the Son abandons himself to the Father, the Father gives himself entirely to the world in the handing over of his beloved Son, so that talk of the Son's abandonment should not be taken to mean that the Father withdraws his presence from the Son.[110] It is worth listening to how Joseph Moingt positively states the Father's silence on Calvary:

109. W. Johnson, "Jesus' Cry." The author refutes the thesis of God-abandonment that has risen to the level of an axiom in certain theological circles.

110. Asserting that God is present when Jesus cries out on the cross gives us confidence that our own cries to God are joined to Jesus's cry and therefore redeemed. This basic point is argued by W. Johnson ("Jesus' Cry," 90). It is worth noting that Terence Fretheim, in his study of suffering in the writings of the Old Testament, explains that the biblical texts speak of differing intensifications of God's presence and that the notion of God's "absence" is regarded not as the withdrawal of the divine presence altogether but as a loss of intensification of God's presence (*Suffering of God*, 65). In this view, while God is present on Calvary, Jesus experiences a loss of intensification of the Father's presence. The heightened intensification of the Father's presence that

When interrogated in the light of Easter, the scandalous silence of God on Calvary becomes revelation. God manifests himself by disappearing in the death of Christ. He manifests himself as the interiority of this event of death . . . as the exchange of relationships and of gifts that constitute them, the one and the other, in their being of Father and Son. The Father reveals himself on the cross not despite his silence and his non-intervention, *but positively, by contrast, in this silence and by the very fact of abandoning his Son.* He intervenes insofar as he abstains from intervening, and this abstention is a decisive and definitive act.[111]

In the very act of forsaking his Son on the cross, the Father also abandons or surrenders himself in the one whom he delivers up to a sinful and cruel world. Jesus's cry should not, therefore, be taken to mean that the Father has withdrawn from the Son, for the Father remains the "interiority" of the event. What the cross manifests is the extreme communion of the Son with the Father, which is hidden or concealed under its opposite of abandonment. In the reciprocal forsakenness of Father and Son is made manifest the "highest union possible in love."[112] The silence of the Father on the cross is not the absence of God but rather a "self-concealing presence," which in effect has never left the Son in his affliction.[113] In this perspective we can understand why the dying Jesus would utter the opening verse of Ps 22 to express his utter abandonment *to* the Father, in

---

was evident in Jesus's authoritative proclaiming of God's kingdom to his own is now reduced in Jesus's passion to a state of powerlessness in which God reveals himself by disappearing in the death of his Son, which is a glorifying death.

111. Moingt, "Montre-nous le Père," 324; emphasis added.

112. Balthasar, *Last Act*, 263. Balthasar, though, subscribes to the God-abandonment thesis. He thinks of the Son's passion in terms of "real" abandonment and thus "separation" of Son and Father—Christ was "made sin." At the same time, though, the extreme abandonment manifests the "highest union possible in love." Balthasar repudiates the view, based on Ps 22, that Jesus had an expectation of glorification; instead, he stresses that the will of the Father is loved for its own sake, which is to say that Jesus does not look to anything beyond the sacrificial death he is about to suffer (*Mysterium Paschale*, 106). A narrow perspective is in view, which is not strongly supported, I would contend, by a systematic drawing together of the biblical writings.

113. Samuel Terrien asserts that because the complaint to God in the first section of Ps 22 is transmuted suddenly into a canticle of triumph, the "self-concealing presence" has, in effect, never left the lamenter in despair (*Psalms*, 235). The author explains that the traditional expression *Deus absconditus*, "the hidden God" (with a passive participle), is a misleading translation, for the Hebrew verb indicates an active-reflexive sense, that is, "a God who conceals himself" (Isa 45:15a). This self-concealing God is "God of Israel, Savior!" (Isa 45:15b).

the confidence that the Father hears his cry and will come to his aid and glorify him as the Holy and Just One.[114] Jesus trusts and expects that his great apocalyptic trial will end in glorious triumph, which leads us into the following discussion of the remaining distinctive feature of Ps 22.

Another distinctive feature of Ps 22, as highlighted earlier, is that the second petition (vv. 19–21) ends with a verb in the perfect tense: "you have answered me from the horns of the wild oxen" (v. 21b). The verb in the perfect tense expresses confidence that God does not hide his face from the afflicted one, but it also serves to close the lament and form a transition to the comprehensive concluding section on the praise of God (vv. 22–31). By virtue of God's response to the psalmist's petition to hasten to his aid and deliver him from terrible trouble, the first part of the concluding section (vv. 22–26) expresses the psalmist's reinvigorated praise of God in the midst of "the great congregation" (v. 25). A feature of this renewed praise of God is the psalmist's use of meal imagery—the afflicted ones "shall eat and be satisfied" (v. 26)—which calls to mind the text of Isa 25:6 (cf. Rev 19:9) where the atmosphere of glad rejoicing at the coming of God's salvation is described in terms of a banquet feast.[115] The prophet has in view the day on which the Lord "will swallow up death forever, and . . . will wipe away tears from all faces" (Isa 25:8). This use of meal imagery in Ps 22:26 and Isa 25:6 assumes special significance in light of Jesus's words of institution of the Eucharist at the Last Supper: "Jesus took bread . . . and said, 'Take, eat; this is my body.' And he took a cup, and when he had given thanks, he gave it to them saying, 'Drink of it, all of you; for this is my blood of the covenant, which is poured out for many for the forgiveness of sins'" (Matt 26:26–28). With these extraordinary words, which point to his redemptive death on Calvary, Jesus is saying that those who eat his body and drink his blood will receive the gift of salvation and rejoice in his Father's kingdom of life, love, and freedom. At the Last Supper, Jesus clearly envisages his impending death as the new Exodus event, which will liberate the people from the slavery of sin and death, thereby bringing about renewed praise of God in the midst of "the

---

114. In both Mark and Matthew, the first result of the death of Jesus is the tearing open of the veil of the temple. For the temple itself this is a sign of judgment, but at the same time it signifies an "opening" in that God no longer resides in the "holy of holies" but is now present in the crucified body of Jesus (cf. Heb 10:19–20). If the crucified Jesus opens up access to God, then this bolsters the view that God is not absent on the cross but is a self-concealing presence.

115. See Lyons, "Psalm 22," 644n11.

great congregation." By means of partaking in the eucharistic meal in the memory of Jesus, his disciples offer thanksgiving to God for the gift of the Son, and they anticipate the banquet feast spoken of by the prophet Isaiah. The meal imagery used in Ps 22:26 certainly has a strong affinity with the meal imagery of the Last Supper.

The conquest of the powers of death by the redemptive death of Jesus, though, is an eschatological event of salvation that cannot be restricted to the faithful within Israel. The shedding of Jesus's blood of the new covenant is to be seen as the fulfillment of the Abrahamic covenant: "And by you all the families of the earth shall bless themselves" (Gen 12:3). In Ps 22 the praise of God in the midst of the congregation overflows into a second section of praise of God (vv. 27–31) which has a thoroughly universal outlook. The circle of praise widens to include "all the families of the nations" (v. 27) who shall acknowledge the dominion of the Lord (v. 28). What is surprising about this universal sweep of praise of God is that it is not envisaged as limited to the living but includes the dead (v. 29),[116] as well as the generations of people yet unborn (v. 31). The figure whom the psalmist addresses as "my God" (22:1) receives not only the praises of Israel but the praises of all peoples of the earth—the living, the dead, and the coming generations—who will turn to the Lord in praise and thanksgiving because God has acted decisively to deliver the afflicted one from the terrible trouble that is laying him in the dust of death. This markedly universal and all-embracing perspective of the psalm is congruent with the thrust of the Gospel story, where Jesus predicts his passion and informs his disciples repeatedly that he will be condemned to death, but in three days he will rise from the dead. In John's Gospel, the universal significance of his rising from the dead is spelt out in the words "And I, when I am lifted up from the earth, will draw all men to myself" (John 12:32).

The comprehensive section on the praise of God in Ps 22 is another very plausible reason why Jesus would elect to cite the opening verse of this psalm as he hangs on the cross and is about to breathe his last. The theme of praise of God is at the heart of Jesus's entire life and mission. As a Jew raised in a humble and pious Jewish family, Jesus is fully immersed

---

116. That the dead shall also acknowledge the universal dominion of the Lord is a departure from the view expressed in other psalms, such as Pss 88:3–6, 10–12; 115:17. On the other hand, Ps 139:7–12 acknowledges the presence of the Lord's spirit even in Sheol, and Pss 42:5, 11 and 43:5 speak of a cast down and disquieted soul that hopes to praise God again.

in the Scriptures and his entire life and mission to Israel is lived within the framework of the covenant. The great Shema sets out the fundamental disposition of Jewish life: "The Lord our God is one Lord; and you shall love the Lord your God with all your heart, and with all your soul, and with all your might" (Deut 6:4–5). To be a servant of the Lord is to love the Lord with all one's heart, and this wholehearted love of the Lord is the foundation of obedience to Torah, which brings joy and delight to the Jewish soul. Love of the Lord is synonymous with praise of God, and this basic dynamic of Jewish existence is apparent in Jesus's life from a young age (cf. Luke 2:41–51). Jesus's obedience to the Father is synonymous with his profound love of the Father, and his mission of proclaiming the Father's benevolent kingdom to his own is synonymous with his praising of God. Everything Jesus says and does is directed towards the praise and glory of the Father with whom he is united in unfathomable love (cf. Matt 11:27; Luke 10:22; John 3:35; 5:20; 17:25); he as the Son is filled with ineffable joy (cf. Luke 10:21) in proclaiming the abundant blessings of his Father's kingdom.

Jesus's authoritative proclamation of the kingdom of God, the Gospels make plain, is initially received by the people with much astonishment and amazement (cf. Mark 1:21–45), but it does not take long for the Jewish religious leaders to take issue with Jesus's ministry and accuse him of serious blasphemy. Early in Mark's Gospel, for example, in response to Jesus forgiving people their sins and claiming to be lord of the Sabbath, we read that the Pharisees held counsel with the Herodians against Jesus, "how to destroy him" (3:6). Problems also soon emerge, however, in regard to Jesus's own disciples who also are without understanding (Mark 8:17). This motif of the disciples' hardness of heart is put into sharp relief when Jesus asks his disciples "Who do you say I am?" (Mark 8:29). This question that Jesus puts to his disciples marks a turning point in the Gospel story as Jesus shifts his focus to the prediction of his passion. Jesus teaches his disciples that he will be rejected by the Jewish leaders, suffer many things, and be put to death, but after three days he will rise again (Mark 8:31). Peter cannot accept Jesus's passion prediction and actually rebukes Jesus, which shows that the disciples simply do not understand what Jesus is saying to them. This is forcefully conveyed by Jesus's strong rebuke directed at Peter: "Get behind me, Satan! For you are not on the side of God, but of men" (Mark 8:33). Despite the fact that the disciples of Jesus are on the "inside" (cf. Mark 4:11), they display a spiritual obtuseness and struggle to accept his status as Messiah in terms of his passion prediction, which shows that even they share the kind of messianic expectations (cf. Luke 24:21) held by the Pharisees. As Jesus seeks to advance his messianic mission, then, his identity as the Son is forged in an atmosphere of increasing hostility, rejection, loneliness, and isolation, which is in keeping with the troubled life of the prophets who went before him (cf. Luke 13:33–35).

The way of obedience to the Father is for Jesus the Son a way of righteous suffering that carries him forward all the way to the Last Supper, to Gethsemane, and to Calvary. As the Gospel story unfolds and reaches its climactic point, it becomes apparent why the lament speech form, such as we find in Ps 22, perfectly describes the mission of the Son and offers insight into the meaning and purpose of his suffering and death. Suffering on account of fidelity to the cause of God is endured in the conviction that the righteous sufferer will be vindicated by the Lord and God's coming salvation will make all things new. Lament never stands alone but is intimately intertwined with the expectation of renewed thanksgiving and praise of God. It is not until Jesus is presented as the one forsaken by God on the cross that his identity as the Son becomes complete. The one forsaken by God is the Son of God! It certainly makes a lot of sense to maintain that by citing Ps 22 on the cross, Jesus intends to communicate his expectation that the new era of divine blessings associated with the new covenant in his blood will give rise to Israel's renewed praise of God "in the great congregation" (Ps 22:22–26). But since Jesus envisages the fall of the kingdom of Satan on account of the sacrificial shedding of his blood, God's coming salvation cannot be limited to Israel but takes on a universal and eschatological outlook, such as we find in Ps 22:27–31. God the Father will receive not only the praises of Israel but the praises of "all the families of the nations" for the sending of the Son into the world. The "new covenant" in the blood of Jesus finally brings to fulfillment the Abrahamic, Noachic, Mosaic, and Davidic covenants of grace: "For behold, I create new heavens and a new earth . . . be glad and rejoice forever in that which I create" (Isa 65:17–18). By citing Ps 22, it is certainly intelligible to maintain that Jesus views his torturous and violent death as necessary for defeating evil and redeeming Israel and the world, and thus as precipitating exalted praises of God who will be universally enthroned in the "new Jerusalem" (Rev 21:2). In this new order of creation, God will dwell with his people, and he will wipe away every tear from their eyes, and death shall be no more (Rev 21:3–4).

In conclusion, since Jesus would have been well versed in the use of the psalms in the liturgical setting of the synagogue and temple, and the Gospel story of his messianic mission clearly reflects the plight of the suffering servant of the Lord, it follows that when he utters the first verse of Ps 22 on the cross, we should not think that he intends to merely express his real agony of being forsaken by God into the hands of evildoers, and nothing more. By uttering the first line of the psalm, Jesus intends the totality of the psalm, which, it has been shown, is quite distinct from other lament psalms and the tradition of the righteous sufferer in three notable ways: it depicts the terrible suffering of the righteous one at the hands of his enemies, who have pierced his hands and feet and cast lots for his raiment; it expresses trust with regard to God's reception of the petition and God's act of deliverance; and it concludes with renewed thanksgiving and praise of God, which is not limited to the faithful within Israel but is universal and eschatological in its vision and scope. By appealing to Ps 22 as his last words, Jesus intends to convey his conviction that the Father does not hide his face from his righteous Son in the throes of terrible affliction, and all peoples will bow down to the Father when the crucified Jesus is raised up from the dead, which will sound the death knell for the powers of sin and death in this world: the afflicted "shall eat and be satisfied" (Ps 22:26; cf. Isa 25:6) and their hearts will "live forever" (Ps 22:26; cf. Jer 31:33; Ezek 36:26). When the three distinctive sections of Ps 22 are taken collectively as forming one arc of meaning, it becomes apparent why it is reasonable to hold that a connection should be drawn not only between the prayers of Jesus and Ps 22, "but as well between the person of Jesus and the person portrayed in the self-description of the psalm."[117] The intent of Ps 22 "came to supreme expression in Jesus,"[118] who cited the opening verse of the psalm to express not merely his real agony of being handed over by the Father into the custody of evildoers but "to emphasize the prophetic connection between Himself and the psalm."[119]

On the basis of the argument developed hitherto, it should now be clear that the long song of praise that concludes Ps 22 does not allow us to gloss over or tame Jesus's lament cry by turning it solely into a cry of trust in God, and certainty about being vindicated by God, who alone is

---

117. Mays, "Prayer and Christology," 322–23.

118. Reumann, "Psalm 22 at Cross," 58.

119. Heinemann, "Exposition of Psalm 22," 289.

sovereign judge of the world.[120] Jesus's cry on the cross marks the culminating point of the Gospel story's presentation of Jesus's increasing isolation, loneliness, and rejection in carrying out his mission to Israel: he is abandoned by the Jewish people at large, by the Jewish religious authorities, by his very own disciples, and now he is forsaken by God to terrible adversity at the hands of his enemies. We should, then, fully appreciate the immediate sense of abandonment conveyed by the opening words of Ps 22 on Jesus's lips and not downplay it by turning his lament into a cry of trust in God and future praise of God. At the same time, though, it is also unwarranted to interpret Jesus's lament as a cry of despair, as the cry of a desperate person who sees his messianic claims crumbling before him as he is reduced to abject misery. By virtue of the way in which the various sections of Ps 22 fit closely together to form a unity of meaning—which reflects the Gospel story of Jesus's total commitment to the cause of God in the face of mounting opposition—we are required to uphold a *composite perspective* in which Jesus's agony of being forsaken by God into the hands of malefactors is inextricably entwined with the enactment of his perfect obedience to the Father in advancing his messianic mission and bringing it to completion. Jesus surrenders or abandons himself fully to the will of the Father, and the Father abandons himself in giving up the Son to a sinful world, hence it is important to appreciate that the Father remains the interiority of the event of the cross. This means that Jesus's lament should not be interpreted as a cry of *God*-abandonment. While the reader is left with a palpable sense of Jesus's utter rejection by his own and his terrible affliction on the cross, this psychological aspect of his passion is not the primary focus of the Gospel narrative, just as the affliction of the righteous one is not the primary focus in Ps 22. Instead, the emphasis falls, as is apparent from the episode in Gethsemane, on Jesus's perfect obedience to the Father as a decisive manifestation of personal unity with the Father in unfathomable love.[121] The mystery of the person

120. The view of the scholastic period, where the problem was how to reconcile the beatific vision of Christ with his suffering on the cross, tended to undermine his genuine lament. Aquinas, for example, offered a solution on the basis of the two natures of Christ: the incarnate Word suffers in his body and in the "inferior" part of his soul, but the "superior" part of his soul, which has to do with the redemption of humanity, cannot suffer from God's nonintervention (see *Summa theologica*, I, 47.3, 50.2).

121. This interpretation of Gethsemane is reinforced by Ps 22, where the righteous one who has been committed to the way of the Lord since his birth continues to rely upon God in his most extreme hour when his enemies are laying him in the dust of the earth. It is unity with God that causes the lamenter's suffering, and this unwavering

of Jesus lies in his being inextricably united with the God whom he called Father, which the Christian tradition has articulated in terms of Jesus's "consubstantiality" with the Father as to divinity. The divinity of Jesus, as the Gospels make plain, should be thought of in terms of his modus of being related to the Father in unfathomable love. On the understanding that the inner quality of Jesus's unity with the Father is his complete and unconditional self-surrender—i.e., kenosis—or abandonment to the Father, his identity as the Son is essentially a responsive identity, which, moreover, takes place in the Spirit who rests upon Jesus as the Anointed One.[122]

Jesus's dying cry is not merely a human lament in the tradition of the suffering righteous but the cry of the embodied Son of God whose humanity mediates and attests to his divinity. We are required to understand that Jesus's lament cry not only expresses his experience of being forsaken by God into the hands of his enemies but also brings into focus the history of Israel's forsaking of God. The latter is the cause of God's grieving and sorrow, of God's internalizing of the people's sin and rebellion, which reaches its zenith with the crucified body of Jesus. On the cross, Jesus becomes a once-and-for-all "offering for sin" (Isa 53:10) that inaugurates the new covenant, which is efficacious not only for the sins of Israel but for the whole world. And at the same time the cross illuminates God's suffering in relation to the world, as well as other forms of the divine pathos such as mercy and compassion, which know no bounds in bringing about the fullness of the covenant of grace: "Behold, I make all things new" (Rev 21:5; Isa 43:19). While the cup that only Jesus can drink does refer to God's judgment upon sin, the discussion in this chapter has consistently refuted a forensic or juridical interpretation of Jesus's cry on the cross.[123] The various sections of this chapter collectively point to a

---

commitment to the cause of God in the face of persecution, violence, and death becomes a sign of divine election and proof of the lamenter's justice.

122. The incarnation of the Logos should not be treated in terms of two inert natures but in terms of the one historical man, Jesus, who is wholly God in human form. As God in human form, Jesus's humanity mediates and attests to his divine power and authority, so that no dualistic modes of thought are allowed to drive a wedge between the divine and the the human. This way of thinking avoids any metaphysical abstractions that detract from the concrete event of Jesus Christ. When the divinity of Jesus is conceived as an inner core of his person, all his knowledge and actions appear as the unfolding of a predetermined divine program and thus, humanly speaking, irrelevant. The pitfall of docetism is perhaps the most entrenched of all heresies.

123. By invoking texts such as 2 Cor 5:21 and Gal 3:13, the Reformers proposed

theological interpretation—i.e., an interpretation of Jesus's cry in its rev-
elational reality and its salvific value for us—which can be formulated as
follows: *Jesus, the Just One, who suffers at the hands of his scornful enemies
in perfect self-abandonment to the Father in unfathomable love, drinks the
cup of God's judgment upon a rebellious people in order to accomplish his
messianic mission (i.e., God's forsaking of Jesus to the consequences of the
people's sin), and at the same time Jesus completely assumes the history
of the people's forsaking of God (i.e., God's internalizing or bearing of the
people's sin and rebellion), of which his crucified body is the consummate
sign; yet in this coming together of human and divine suffering in the ultimate agony, Jesus trusts that the Father does not hide his face but hears his
cry and will save him out of death and raise him up in glory, so as to bring
good out of evil and establish the new heavens and new earth that will
resound with unspeakable joy and exalted praise of the living God.*

According to this proposed theological interpretation, Jesus's cry
takes on a complex character since it contains both human and divine
dimensions, in keeping with the view that Jesus's humanity mediates and
attests to his divinity.[124] There is clearly a divine aspect to Jesus's cry simply

---

a juridical view of redemption according to which Christ suffered the punishment
of hell in our place and appeased the wrath of God against the sinner. Barth and
Balthasar, while still adopting the notion of substitution, have distanced themselves
from this traditional penal substitution theory, for they wish to stress that God's love,
not wrath, is the cause of the passion of Christ. The term *punishment* is still used by
Barth and Balthasar, but it is used to express Jesus's suffering endured as the "second
death." See Lauber, *Barth on the Descent.* While the view that God's love is the cause of
Jesus's passion is a welcome one, I do not go along with Barth and Balthasar when they
interpret Jesus's passion as *God*-abandonment.

124. The proposed theological interpretation, it should be noted, contains elements
of both the philological and psychological interpretations of Jesus's cry, which were
briefly mentioned in the introduction to this chapter. With respect to the philological
interpretation, I agree that Jesus is left in a situation of distress, that he is delivered up
to his enemies. I part company, though, with this philological interpretation when I
hold that Jesus's abandonment does not simply refer to the Father's nonintervention
but is an *act of God.* The latter is affirmed by the psychological interpretation of the
Rhineland mystics, but unlike them I do not interpret the act of God as the Father
drawing away from Jesus in his hour of need. Instead, I argue that God's nonintervention is to be understood positively, that the Father remains the interiority of the event,
that he identifies with the Son, who is his self-donation to the world. Jesus does not
"feel" the Father's presence as he did when he proclaimed the kingdom of God with
authority, but the bond between the Son and Father is not broken. I oppose the juridical view of the Reformers, who contend that Jesus experienced hell on the cross, that
is, his abandonment by God is not a mere "feeling" but a "real" abandonment, suffered
as separation from the Father. For if Jesus is without sin, if he is perfectly obedient to

by virtue of his divine identity as the Son of the Father, who forsakes him, although it must be borne in mind that the Father in forsaking the Son also abandons himself in giving up his beloved Son to a world estranged from God. But as the incarnate Son who inaugurates the new covenant in his blood, Jesus's lament also incorporates the divine dimension of God's bearing or internalizing of the history of the people's forsaking of him as Lord. What comes into view here is that God suffers "for us," that is, God, in the person of Christ, bears our sin and is not exacting as to matters of judgment. These divine aspects of Jesus's cry are inseparable, though, from the human dimension of his lament in accordance with the tradition of the suffering righteous. The latter serves to emphasize that the incarnate Son knows intimately the situation of suffering humanity *from within*, which is to say that God suffers in solidarity "with us." Insofar as Jesus's cry is human, we can confidently say that the Son participates in the concrete reality of our adamic flesh; and insofar as Jesus's cry is divine, we can assuredly say that the living God is personally engaged with our present situation, is not overwhelmed by suffering, but has an infinite capacity to internalize suffering so as to transform this grief-stricken world into the unutterable joy of the new creation.

What does the proposed theological interpretation of Jesus's cry have to say about the thesis of *God*-abandonment that many today subscribe to? One of the interesting things about the God-abandonment interpretation is that it is usually based on the premise that the Son and the Father are intimately united in love. Rossé, for example, claims that Jesus on the cross experiences separation from God or the loss of God, yet at the same time Rossé stresses that the event proceeds from the Son's perfect unity with the Father: "It is fidelity to the Father and not rebellion that carries Christ far from God, far also from the felt experience and the support of love, even if precisely this love is the exegesis of the event: *the extreme abandonment manifests the extreme communion of the Son with the Father.*"[125] Balthasar holds the same view, for he maintains that in the abandonment of the Son by the Father, the Son is in absolute unity with

---

the Father, how can his cry be that of the damned? Is not hell the absolute refusal of love? It is fidelity and unity with the Father, not rebellion, that carries Jesus all the way to the cross. That Jesus was "made sin" does not mean he became a sinner and suffered separation from God; it means that he has assumed in his person the world's forsaking of God, so that the world might be reconciled to God and enjoy the fellowship of communion with God, which makes all things new.

125. Rossé, *Cry of Jesus*, 116; emphasis added.

the Father, which is "the highest union possible in love."[126] Both Rossé and Balthasar expressly say that Jesus's abandonment by God "paradoxically" expresses his perfect unity with God. The problem with paradoxical language, though, is that it often proves to be somewhat self-contradictory. If Jesus is in perfect unity with the Father in unfathomable love, which is affirmed as the exegesis of the event of the cross, how can his dying cry be interpreted as extreme abandonment or extreme separation from God? In the view that the Father is present on the cross in his silence and nonintervention, from which we are to understand that the Father also abandons himself in surrendering his beloved Son into the custody of sinners, how can this dynamic of self-sacrificing love be interpreted as Jesus's loss of God? The cross, to be sure, does speak of separation, but not Jesus's separation from the Father; rather, it speaks in the strongest possible terms of the separation or estrangement of the world from God. What Jesus's cry reveals is the manner in which the world's estrangement from God has been overcome by the perfect unity of the Father and the Son in their self-sacrificial love for one another, in their Spirit of inalienable communion. On the cross, the Father is not absent in his silence but surrenders himself to a sinful world in the Son whom he delivers into the hands of evildoers, for the sake of the redemption of Israel and the world. The Father, in other words, is the inner reality of Jesus's terrible suffering, hence the Father is with Jesus and for Jesus in his cry, which spells the accomplishment of his messianic mission. For *the crucified Jesus unites sinful humanity with himself in the very act of total self-abandonment that unites him perfectly with the Father.* Jesus therefore "represents" us sinners before the Father, and, conversely, Jesus represents the Father before the world, hence the Crucified One is the Mediator between God and the world.

The proposed theological interpretation of Jesus's lament cry not merely highlights his consubstantiality with the Father as to divinity but also underlines his solidarity with the concrete human condition, which is what the Christian tradition means when it affirms that Jesus is "consubstantial" with us as to humanity. In the crowning act of perfect obedience to the Father in suffering a humiliating and torturous death on a cross, the forsaken Jesus has identified himself fully with adamic flesh (sin excepted) in order that sinful humanity might be "reconciled to God" (Rom 5:10) and "raised up" (John 6:40; 12:32) to glorious union

126. Balthasar, *Last Act*, 263.

with God as its final end. This interpretation lends its support to much contemporary rethinking of satisfaction theories of atonement insofar as the Son was not stricken by God's thirst for retributive justice but by the violence of a sinful humanity that refuses to accept the kingdom of God as proclaimed by the Son.[127] Jesus's solidarity with adamic flesh does imply, though, as this chapter has consistently maintained, that the Son has borne God's judgment against sin, but not in the sense of appeasing an angry God who demands retributive justice.[128] Rather, following the "synthetic" or "dynamistic" view of divine judgment found in the prophetic texts, the cup that Jesus alone can drink refers to the Father's forsaking of him in handing him over into the custody of his enemies; that is, Jesus suffers the working out of the people's sin and rebellion into its inevitable consequences as the Father forsakes him. But by invoking Ps 22 on the cross, Jesus conveys his firm belief that God does not hide his face from the righteous afflicted one (v. 24), hence he expects that his apocalyptic trial will end in glorious triumph, to the everlasting praise of the Father.

We saw in the introduction to this chapter that Moltmann claims that Jesus's cry on the cross should not be interpreted from the vantage point of Ps 22, but from the standpoint of the uniqueness of Jesus's situation as the Son of the Father. The "my God" invoked by Jesus on the cross is not simply the God of the Old Testament but the God whom Jesus addresses as Abba, the God with whom he is conscious of having a unique filial relationship. The cry must therefore be interpreted in a distinctly theological manner as the "I" of the Son, that is, as something that happens between Jesus and his Father, and between the Father and Jesus, for the sake of a godless world. Moltmann is right to stress that there is not only a religious (blasphemer) and political (rebel) aspect to Jesus's death, but also a distinctly theological dimension at play here. Problems arise, however, when Moltmann contends that the passion of the Son "divides" God from God, insofar as the Father imposes his will upon the acquiescing Son, and then this conflict of wills is resolved by the resurrection of

---

127. See Jersak and Hardin, *Stricken by God?*; Heim, *Saved from Sacrifice*; Sanders, *Atonement and Violence*.

128. René Girard and his followers argue that the language of sacrifice should be dropped, but such language must continue to be used because it serves to effectively convey the costly self-giving of Jesus Christ for the sake of a sinful humanity. See O'Collins, *Jesus Our Redeemer*, 159.

the crucified which "unites" God with God.[129] Moltmann stands in a long line of Western theologians who contend that God is *for us* only by being *against Jesus*; Jesus breathes his last forsaken by all around him, but he is especially forsaken by God. Counter to Moltmann's argument, this chapter has argued that the Father does not impose his will upon the acquiescing Son; rather, Jesus's perfect obedience indicates his ineffable unity with and profound love of the Father, who, in his silence on Calvary, remains the interiority of the event as he identifies with his crucified Son. Also problematic in Moltmann's writings, though, is the contention that the uniqueness of Jesus as the Son means that we cannot interpret Jesus's cry in terms of Ps 22. But why should the acknowledgment of Jesus's uniqueness as the Son prohibit us from reflecting upon his person and work from the vantage point of Jewish traditions and expectations? Since Jesus was raised in a thoroughly Jewish world in which the Scriptures provided the fundamental orientation to his life, is it not completely plausible to hold that the tradition of the righteous sufferer, which was very much in the air in the time of Jesus, would have shaped and formed Jesus's self-understanding and messianic mission? Is not the God whom Jesus the Son addresses as Abba the God of Israel, the God of the Scriptures that he knew so intimately? Is it not therefore perfectly reasonable to assume that Jesus was well familiar with the lament speech form, especially Ps 22, which has an "intensity and comprehensiveness" not found in other prayers of this type?

The meaning of the personal address "my God" with which Ps 22 begins is clearly revealed by vv. 3–5 and vv. 9–11. The God who has forsaken the psalmist is the God in whom the psalmist has confidence and trust, the God upon whom he was cast from birth, the God whom he petitions "Be not far from me, for trouble is near" (v. 11). The "my God" uttered by Jesus on the cross can be interpreted in exactly the same way as the psalmist: Jesus in his mission as the Son has always displayed total dependence and complete trust in his Father; from his very conception, Jesus the Son is destined and sent forth by the Father to proclaim the kingdom of God (cf. Luke 1:32–33); and now that his enemies have

129. Moltmann, *Crucified God*, 152; and his *Trinity and the Kingdom*, 80–83. Moltmann also speaks of a conformity of wills between the Son and the Father, but, as David Lauber has pointed out, it is questionable whether this is consistent with his contention that in the Son's passion the relationship actually breaks off (*Barth on the Descent*, 119–20). Paul Fiddes is also critical of Moltmann for placing too much stress upon "God against God" so that the Son appears as one who suffers with us while the Father appears as the one who inflicts the suffering (*Creative Suffering*, 196–97).

"pierced his hands and feet" (Ps 22:16) he petitions the Father "Be not far from me." The previous section on Gethsemane is helpful here in confirming that on Jesus's lips "my God" refers to his Father with whom he is united in unfathomable love as he endures the scorn and mocking by the people and the shame and agony of dying by crucifixion. Like the figure in Ps 22, Jesus belongs to the "lowly," to those who depend utterly and totally on God. As the Son, Jesus endures his affliction out of perfect obedience to the Father, which stems from his profound love of the Father, and he is confident on the basis of his ineffable oneness with the Father that his cry for help will be "heard" (Ps 22:24). God's response is expected in the form of Jesus being raised from the realm of the dead, which represents an apocalyptic-eschatological event of salvation.[130] This expectation on Jesus's part is consistent with the cup of the covenant in his blood, which implies that the powers of sin and death—the wages of sin is death—in the world will be conquered by his redemptive death, through which comes the ineffable grace of forgiveness of sins and the acquisition of a "new heart" with which to love the Lord above all else (cf. Jer 31:33; Ezek 36:26; Isa 43:19).[131]

Jesus's participation in adamic flesh, moreover, should not be reduced to his solidarity with sinners but should be broadened to include *his solidarity with all the suffering just and with the manifold infirmities and afflictions of humanity.* Jesus suffers not only "because" of sin and "for" sinners but "with" the afflicted, with all those who mourn, who suffer loneliness, who suffer rejection and persecution, who suffer grief and sorrow, who sigh and lament, and who suffer death. While the suffering emotions of Jesus come into sharpest relief in his passion, we should not lose sight of the fact that Jesus also exhibits an array of disturbing and suffering emotions during the course of his messianic mission: he is angered by obstacles to the proclamation of his Father's kingdom of grace (Mark 3:1–6; 10:13–16; Matt 9:27–31); he is angered by corrupt worship

130. Jesus's resurrection from the dead should not be seen merely as God's vindication of the Son as the Just One. Instead, since we are dealing with an eschatological event in which Christ's humanity attains to a glorified state, his resurrection should be thought of as the furthering of nature. Nature is not a closed and defined system but an open and indeterminate system. See Novello, "God's Action."

131. The acquisition of a "new heart" implies that the grace of salvation involves the conversion of our emotions. To put on Christ is to fix our gaze on the paschal mystery of Christ as the new object of our congenial emotions (love, joy, and compassion), disturbing emotions (anger, indignation, and sighing), and suffering emotions (grief, dread, sorrow, and lament). See Novello, *Passionate Deification*, 233–52.

and legalistic attitudes to Jewish faith (John 2:13–17; Mark 3:1–6); he sighs at the physical infirmities that afflict his people (Mark 7:31–37); he sighs at the testing of the Pharisees (Mark 8:11–13); he sighs at the spiritual obtuseness of his disciples (Mark 6:52; 8:17, 27–33); he suffers increasing loneliness, isolation, and rejection as he seeks to advance his messianic mission (Mark 8:31; 9:30–32; 10:33–34); he weeps bitterly on his approach to Jerusalem as he contemplates the destruction of the holy city on account of the people's rejection of his mission (Luke 19:28–44); and he is deeply grieved and troubled by the death of his beloved friend Lazarus (John 11:35). These suffering emotions of Jesus bring to light the divine Son's genuine condescension to the human plane, his making himself vulnerable before his own people and before the world. The theological interpretation of Jesus's lament cry proposed as a conclusion to this pivotal chapter does complete justice to the notion of the real participation of the divine in the human existential realm, for the sake of realizing the fullness of the covenant of grace. That is, the participation of the human in the divine: "You shall be holy, for I the Lord your God am holy" (Lev 19:2; 1 Pet 1:16).

What Jesus's cry of lament on the cross announces with special force is the intimate connection that exists between human lament and divine lament. The theological category of divine pathos portrays God as personally engaged with and exhibiting ultimate concern for humanity and the world. God is not removed from or unaffected by the suffering of his people, but rather is a participant in human suffering and works from within the historical context of his people to bring about final salvation for Israel and the world. The sufferings of the Messiah underscore the view that God is in solidarity with the wretchedness, brokenness, and limits of the human condition, as well as with all the suffering innocent who are tortured and put to death by human cruelty and violence. Jesus, the Just One, who is perfectly united with the Father in unfathomable love, dies not a gentle death like Socrates and his cup of hemlock or a peaceful passing at the end of a lengthy and full life but a torturous and utterly humiliating death on a cross. There is no question that the word of the cross "caused offence, but in this very offence it revealed itself as the center of the gospel," as God's new response to the troublesome "Why, Lord?" and "How long, Lord?" questions that are characteristic of the lament speech form.[132] What transpired at the Last

132. Hengel, *Crucifixion in Ancient World*, 89.

Supper, in Gethsemane, and on Calvary, reveals God's astonishing yes to a fragmented and afflicted humanity groaning for its redemption and salvation, which, however, does not remove the suffering or explain it away but rather inserts it into the incomprehensible mystery of God, who alone is able to end suffering, deliver justice, and create new life out of death.[133] "Believing, by the Spirit's power, that God is present in the person of Jesus Christ when he cries out, we have confidence that our own cries are joined to Jesus' cry and redeemed."[134] Because God is present, not absent, as the interiority of the event of Jesus's crucifixion, given that God is "for" the crucified and "with" Jesus in his cry, we can confidently say that God is "for" us and "with" us in our own cries. This joining of our own cries to Jesus's cry implies that suffering is integral to the process of our deification in his person, and poignantly reveals how God is always at work in the midst of our troubled and afflicted world, transforming grief (lament) into joy (praise of God).

133. Ultimately the fullness of salvation in the crucified and risen Christ can come only in the event of our death as a dying into the saving death of Christ. For a comprehensive treatment of this thesis on death as salvific event, see Novello, *Death as Transformation*. Despite some notable and successful human efforts to alleviate human suffering and to establish a more just world, as long as history continues to run its course the ugly reality of sin and evil will remain with us, and physical suffering, as well as psychological, moral, and spiritual suffering, will also remain an integral aspect of the human landscape. Try as we may, suffering in its manifold forms will not be eliminated, and the advancement of the common good will never reach the ideal anticipated by the Enlightenment. While God is not the direct cause of evil and suffering, God does choose to bear ultimate responsibility for the human predicament in this world, as revealed by the death and resurrection of Jesus the Messiah.

134. W. Johnson, "Jesus' Cry," 90.

4

IMPLICATIONS OF LAMENT
FOR SYSTEMATIC THEOLOGY

I N THE PREVIOUS CHAPTER it was shown that the essential message of
Ps 22 is that God does not hide his face from the righteous afflicted
one but hears his cry and comes to his aid to deliver him from affliction.
In the case of Jesus, his cry on the cross reveals his total abandonment
to the Father in a defining act of unfathomable unity with the Father
in love, hence he expects the Father to come to his help by raising him
from the dead, which will sound the death knell for the forces of sin and
evil in the world. Jesus's resurrection from the dead is *the* eschatological-
apocalyptic event, but this does not mean that lament has now fallen
silent, that it has no place in Christian life and can be left behind. Instead,
as Oswald Bayer emphatically maintains, "it becomes louder and more
sharp,"[1] as evidenced in the New Testament call *maranatha*: "Our Lord,
come!" (1 Cor 16:22; Rev 22:20). Lament and petition always give rise to
the *maranatha*, to the calling on God to end all our distress and trouble,
and fulfill our longing to share in the glory of the risen Christ, who is the
new creation in person. To confess the risen Christ as the new creation,
though, means that the calling on God to transform grief into everlasting joy cannot be restricted to the personal afflictions of the individual
but includes the tragedies of world history and the distress of natural

1. Bayer, "Toward Theology of Lament," 212. In light of the event of Easter, Bayer
talks of a "Christology of answered lament," an "anthropology of answered lament,"
and an "eschatology of answered lament."

history. There are many dimensions of distress experienced in the world, and as Christians walk by faith, not by sight, in the risen Christ, they must attend to the path that they are travelling along, which can all too easily erode trust and hope in God. Bayer is correct when he says that too often Christian theology quickly reaches a happy ending without taking seriously the uncertainties, ambiguities, and afflictions suffered along the way. "Yet when the precarious temporality of the way often interrupted is considered seriously, it decisively shapes the layout and structure of a systematic theology."[2] Matthias Wüthrich is in full agreement with Bayer when he writes that "a closer systematic theological analysis of lament could bring to light its transformative potential for all aspects of dogmatics."[3]

In this chapter we shall give a selective account of some of the consequences of the findings of this study for systematic theology. Before proceeding to discuss some of the implications for systematic theology, the first section will offer a comprehensive definition of Christian lament and will list five major functions of lament in the life of faith. We shall then proceed to discuss a number of selected topics. The discussion will not be exhaustive, for there are many other topics that normally fall within the ambit of systematic theology that will not be discussed. However, the selected topics will serve to indicate lines of thought that impact upon all aspects of systematic theology. For instance, the theological interpretation of Jesus's cry proposed in chapter 3 supports an interpersonal model of the immanent Trinity as self-emptying sacrificial love for the "other"—the Other of the Son and the other of creation—which takes issue with Moltmann's extreme theology of creation. According to the latter, God in creating the world "withdraws" to make room for the creation, so that the created world is thought of as a God-forsaken space. It therefore follows that Jesus on the cross *must* suffer *God*-abandonment, that is, *real* abandonment, not merely a "felt" absence of God. The Father abandons the Son to utter darkness and despair in his hour of greatest need, so as to overcome the God-forsakenness of the created world. This rather dark picture of creation and redemption is closely tied to the view that God's being consists in three individual centers of consciousness.

In contrast to Moltmann's thought, an interpersonal model of the Trinity, which views fatherhood and sonhood in terms of the dynamic

2. Bayer, "Toward Theology of Lament," 216.

3. Wüthrich, "Lament for Naught," 73.

of eternal kenosis or self-emptying love, affirms the cross of the Son as the revelation of God as self-sacrificial love; that is, the self-renouncing humility of the Lamb of God, "foreordained before the foundation of the world" (1 Pet 1:20). In such a perspective, God does not "withdraw" to make room for the creation. Instead, since the Father lives not in himself but in proceeding out of himself in the begetting of the "other" of the Son, and the Son as the begotten other lives not in himself but in self-emptying receptivity and thanksgiving to the Father for the gift of divinity, then the Father's letting go of his divinity in the begetting of the Son provides not only the "space" for the other of the Son but also the other of creation. The creation cannot be a God-forsaken place in this perspective, because the Trinity is the place of creation. The Spirit, as the fruit of the eternal act of self-sacrificing love between the Father and the Son, is the principle of God's self-communication to the created world and therefore the *presence* of God in our midst. The Spirit is present in the world prior to the event of the Son being made flesh, but it is only with the death of the Son, as a passover from this world to the Father, which takes place "through the Spirit" (Heb 9:14), that the eternal begetting of the Son is fully "accomplished" within creation (see below). This means, given the eternal begetting of the Son by the Father takes place in the Spirit, that the death of Jesus emerges as the fullness of the Spirit within creation. This understanding precludes the possibility of conceiving of Jesus's redemptive suffering as *God*-abandonment. Jesus, by citing Ps 22 on the cross, intends to situate himself in the tradition of the righteous servants who have committed their cause to God and whom God will *not* abandon. The Father does not abandon Jesus on the cross but fully identifies with the Son in his passion; this is the sacrifice and sorrow of the Father, his supreme gift to the world loved by him. And this climactic event of Jesus's passion takes place in the indissoluble unity of their Spirit of self-sacrificing love, which on Calvary is revealed in its fullness within creation.

A second related topic arising out of this particular perspective is the doctrine of divine providence. It is difficult to see why people would trust the kind of God Moltmann describes. Trust in God is based on the conviction that God knows our situation in this afflicted world, has ultimate concern for the world, is not overwhelmed by the suffering of his creation, hears the prayers of his people, and is able to transform grief (lament) into unutterable joy (praise of God). If we follow Moltmann and say that Jesus died in God-abandonment, that he died as one rejected by his God and his Father, then what would keep God from abandoning any others subjected to unjust suffering and a violent death? Moltmann, given his engagement with protest atheism, is keen to make us understand that in abandoning Jesus, God was subjecting himself, in the person of the Son, to abandonment, thereby overcoming the God-forsakenness of the world. Yet this position does not allay concerns about the God-abandonment thesis. "The question is whether, as such, divine 'abandonment' of the other—in this case Jesus—is a godly strategy under any circumstances."[4] Moltmann does say that God is suffering along with our suffering world in the crucified Jesus. But God's presence in this world rings somewhat hollow if God abandoned Jesus to darkness and despair on the cross, and, moreover, we have to await the eschatological renewal of all things before God's true power is made manifest. Contrary to Moltmann, this study has argued that God is for us not because God is against Jesus but because God is "for" the crucified and "with" Jesus in his unjust suffering at the hands of evildoers. It is because God hears Jesus's cry that we can be assured that God hears our cries, too, and in the power of the Spirit of the risen Christ we are enabled to persevere in the pilgrim life of faith as an ongoing embodiment of Christ in the world, which is summed up in the Eucharist. By participating in the Eucharist, which incorporates lament into praise and thanksgiving, the followers of Christ give witness to an ongoing transformation of grief into joy, which is the work of God's grace in Christ. The following section outlining the various functions of the lament speech form elaborates on this process of ongoing transformation in the Spirit of the crucified and risen Christ.

A Definition of Christian Lament and Its Multifaceted Functions

In light of the discussions in the previous chapters of this study, and given the undeniable and enduring reality of suffering and evil in this world in its whole depth, a complex definition of Christian lament is called for, which can be stated thus:

Lament is a pleading with God for help through the modality of affective attachment to the crucified Christ whose dying cry was heard by God, which holds God accountable to the covenant promises and thus invokes the eschatological salvation that is desired, so that a dialogical-reciprocal

4. W. Johnson, "Jesus' Cry," 85.

relationship with the living God arises out of the depths, in which the faithful come to know God as "for" them and "with" them in their afflictions, hence they are able to persevere in the life of faith as an ongoing embodiment of Christ in the world, which is a journey of ongoing transformation of grief into joy, the hoped-for end of which is the glory of resurrection life and ecstatic praise of God in a new creation. It will be useful to unpack this comprehensive definition by highlighting the various interrelated functions of lament, which are listed as follows:

1. The first function of lament is that it invites us to abandon the conception of the divine-human relationship as a monologue and embrace in its place a dialogical understanding of the covenant relationship, which reconfigures the distribution of power between the parties, inasmuch as the petitionary party is truly heard and taken seriously by God who becomes engaged in the human predicament.

2. To affirm lament as truly heard and taken seriously by God is to recognize the theological category of the divine pathos, according to which God is affected by what happens in history, displays ultimate concern for humanity and the world, and is therefore engaged with his creation. Lament repudiates the notion of God as detached and uninvolved in history, and affirms the God of the covenant, who is the God of Jesus Christ, as a truly "living" God who suffers "for" us and "with" us.

3. Lament is unthinkable without trust and confidence in God to hear the cries of the faithful and come to their help, which means that lament keeps hope alive as the faithful persevere in their journey towards the eagerly awaited glory of resurrection life as the fullness of salvation in the Lord Jesus Christ.

4. When the lament cries of the faithful as the body of Christ are joined to Jesus's lament cry as the head, God is encountered in the midst of suffering (guilty or innocent) and the faithful come to accept their suffering as integral to the process of deification, that is, to their ongoing embodiment of Christ in an unredeemed world.

5. By articulating that which is lamentable, the lament (grief) invokes the salvation (joy) that is desired. Lament is not the opposite of praise but a form of praise (doxology) that holds God accountable to the divine promises, hence it is an essential component of a Christian theodicy.

These specific functions of the lament speech form are indicative of the ways in which the lament prayer is necessary to support the life of faith in an unredeemed world that is "groaning" (Rom 8:22) for its salvation. The lament speech form offers the faithful an indispensable voice to express the reality of terrible suffering and evil in this world and to address our pain and suffering to God as the initiator of the covenant and the guarantor of the promises of the covenant. As the creator of embodied life, God redeems and saves embodied existence by God's own embodiment in the person of Jesus Christ, which underscores the pathos of God and the inalienable relevance and pertinence of humanity and the world to the living God. The human lament addressed to God receives its definitive response in the event of Jesus Christ, who is the unsurpassable self-communication of God in history. As such, Christ's humanity mediates and attests to the divine pathos that reaches out to a sinful and suffering humanity so as to bring final salvation to the whole of creation. From the standpoint of the messianic mission of Christ, which culminates in his lament cry on Calvary, we can affirm the legitimacy of the Hebrew Bible's view of God as suffering "because" of the people's rebellion, and "for" the people in that God bears their sin, and "with" the people when calamity strikes them. The divine aspect of Jesus's cry as the Son of God reveals how God bears the history of the people's sin and rebellion in the crucified body of the Son—God suffers "for us"—while the human aspect of Jesus's cry as the Son of Man reveals that God truly participates in the concrete reality of adamic flesh and suffers in solidarity "with us." The human and divine aspects of Jesus's cry are inseparable, just as the human and divine natures united in his one person are inseparable. In order to properly uphold the mystery of the incarnation, we must not divide or separate the two natures, as if Christ does certain things according to his divinity (e.g., his miracles) and experiences other things according to his humanity (e.g., his suffering). The mystery of the incarnation requires us to affirm that Christ is not two persons but one person, which is to say that he does everything as the *God-man*. What the Chalcedonian definition intends to uphold is the *mutuality* of the life of the two natures united in the one person of Christ; the natures mutually interact without division or separation, and without confusion or change.[5] The life and suffering of the prophet, which was discussed earlier in chapter 1, already points

---

5. This point is strongly argued by Bulgakov, *Lamb of God*, 247–61. Bulgakov is determined to dispel all forms of docetism and monophystism that have plagued Christological thinking in the past.

to the mutuality of divinity and humanity, which receives its definitive expression in the event of Jesus Christ.

Prayers of lament are often regarded as an acknowledgment of God's absence, yet on the basis of the findings of this study it would be more correct to speak of the self-concealing of God in lamentable situations that shake the foundations of faith. The silence of God on Calvary does not mean that God is absent; rather, God is present in his silence and remains the interior reality of Christ's passion. The resurrection of Christ confirms that God hears his cry on the cross, and is for him and with him, hence we know that God is with us and for us in testing times, because our own cries are joined to Jesus's cry, thus we continue to believe in the promises of God expressed in the idea of covenant.[6] When the followers of Christ cry to God out of the depths, God's nearness is no longer "felt" as when God is effortlessly praised for all things bright and beautiful, yet the faithful trust that God hears their cry and is present in their suffering, so that lament becomes a form of praise that invokes the salvation that is deeply desired. Once we appreciate that the lament speech form holds God accountable to the covenant promises that receive their ultimate expression and final formulation in the paschal mystery of Christ, then lament takes on an essential role in Christian theodicy.

Theodicy as Divine Theodicy: God's Self-Justification in Jesus Christ

The majority view on theodicy in the Hebrew Bible, which is clearly represented by Job's friends, regards God as just and human suffering as justified since it is the result of human sin, hence the proper response to suffering is repentance. According to the principle of individual reward and retribution, "there can be no victim, for all individuals receive their just deserts."[7] Job is blamed by his friends for his troubles, and not a few religious people today—and many nonreligious people—continue

---

6. The covenant is summed up in God's pronouncement, "I will be your God, and you will be my people." The covenant refers to a relationship between God and humanity as fulfilled in Jesus Christ. At the center of Barth's doctrine of creation is the assertion that the covenant is both the ground and goal of creation: creation is the external basis of the covenant, and covenant is the internal basis of creation. "Covenant is not a question of a static relationship in eternity, but a historical relationship in which God freely loves his creation" (Gabriel, *Barth's Doctrine of Creation*, 100).

7. Crenshaw, *Defending God*, 118.

to adhere to this principle of reward and retribution.[8] When faced by personal illness or tragic accident, the instinctive reaction of many is to ask themselves, What have I done to deserve this? There is a tendency to connect personal disaster with guilt.[9] The book of Job exposes the shortcomings of the principle of reward and retribution and introduces a mysterious dimension to suffering. Job strongly defies his friends and maintains his innocence, and ultimately comes to accept that there are things too profound and wonderful for him to understand. The proper attitude to innocent suffering, unpredictability in life, and randomness in this world, is to display humility and trust in the inscrutable wisdom of God: "True wisdom cannot be found in the land of the living."[10] It is by acknowledging his inability to bring the proud low and tread down the wicked, and by accepting limits to human knowledge, that Job enters into a new relationship of personal communion with God as ineffable mystery.[11] Leibniz boldly asserted that "God has chosen the best of all possible worlds," which was not meant to be taken in a brashly optimistic or ideal sense. This famous proposition does not mean that this world is a perfect world, but it does imply that this world is worthwhile and will bring forth appropriate results. There are many kinds of evil in this world, but Leibniz argues that if we could see the world-process as a whole, it would be the best possible. The fact that most people are not full-fledged malcontents or utopians but live, in spite of their complaints, *as if* this world has value and is worthy of hope, gives us some insight into Leibniz's fundamental assumption. "There is perhaps an echo here of the Almighty's challenge

8. The principle that individuals get what they deserve has quite a strong foundation in human experience: those who seek to avoid unnecessary risk, to live a cautious lifestyle that does not expose them to the consequences of lawlessness, debauchery, and dangerous pursuits, are able to live good lives with a modicum of peace, while those who live on the edge often come to a bad end. Nevertheless, as Crenshaw rightly points out, "the world has so much randomness that no individual can ever count on reaping the benefits of a noble life" (*Defending God*, 120).

9. Even when justice is deferred to a future existence—belief in life beyond the grave—the principle that God punishes evildoers and rewards the righteous continues to exert its influence. This eschatological perspective is apparent in biblical texts such as Dan 12:1–3, 2 Macc 7:1–42, and Wis 3:7. For a discussion of this eschatological perspective, see Crenshaw, *Defending God*, 149–63.

10. Crenshaw, *Defending God*, 166.

11. Chapter 28 of the book of Job especially highlights the limits of human knowledge. The book of Ecclesiastes, like the book of Job, also portrays the deity as not subject to rational calculation and challenges the principle of reward and retribution in light of so much unpredictability, randomness, and absurdity in this life.

to Job, to take over the running of the universe and make a better job of it."[12] Once it is accepted that human reason is not able to fathom the unfathomable, it follows that it cannot convict the Almighty of being unjust, and theodicy is ultimately rendered insoluble.[13]

What the discussion in chapter 1 of this study has demonstrated is that the majority view of suffering as justified because it is the result of sin—i.e., God is exonerated by incriminating humankind—is not the only perspective on theodicy in the Hebrew Bible. The lament speech form represents an alternative minority perspective in which complaints or protests to God become the proper response to suffering. The faithful in the grip of suffering do not remain silent before God or continue to offer hollow words of praise or thanksgiving but dare to open their grieving hearts to God in cries of lament. The monologue of the majority view gives way to honest dialogue in the minority view, thereby bringing about a shift in the balance of power between the parties. God is still the powerful and sovereign party, but God is now portrayed as hearing the cries of the afflicted and as being personally present to the suffering faithful. The lamenter is not concerned to offer a theodicy in any formal sense but is wanting to express the *reality* of suffering and goes head-to-head with God in seeking viable answers to the "Why?" and "How long?" questions that characterize the life of faith, as well as human life in general. An important gain in this counter-tradition of the lament speech form, it was argued, is the maintenance of the divine-human dialogue. By virtue of the prayers of protest, the status of the human being is lifted to a new level, for to pray is to become personally engaged with God, to become a partner with God in the temporal process, which is marked by manifold trials, tribulations, and sufferings. In the lament psalms there is still praise of God but only after the complaints have moved from petition

12. Macquarrie, *In Search of Deity*, 124.

13. The idea that the human mind cannot fully fathom the divine is already to be found in the book of Deuteronomy, where Moses addresses Israel concerning the words of the covenant: "The secret things belong to the Lord our God; but the things that are revealed belong to us and to our children forever, that we may do all the words of this law" (Deut 29:29). According to this text, Israel has not been granted full disclosure of the divine reality. There are "secret things" that belong to God, and Israel's task is to carry out the revealed divine will by keeping Torah in the land. Suffering will undoubtedly test the fidelity of the people, and with the book of Job the notion of "disinterested righteousness" is introduced to expose the shortcomings of the principle of reward and retribution.

to praise of God, implying that the Lord has heard the petition and has responded to remove the source of suffering and pain.

Notwithstanding the genuine dialogue with God which is opened up by the practice of lament, in the end the lamenter usually does not receive satisfactory answers from God concerning their suffering. Abraham, Moses, and Joshua, it was shown, are exceptions, for in their pleadings for divine justice, in their standing head-to-head with God and insisting that they be taken seriously, they actually prevail at times. But the other biblical figures that were discussed are presented in quite a different light. Job does not get satisfactory answers from God but is silenced by God's questions; he acknowledges his lack of knowledge and power, he admits that he is of small account and comes to accept suffering as having a mysterious dimension. The crux of the book of Job is that it is precisely *in* his suffering that Job comes to experience intimate communion with God—"now my eye sees you"—by virtue of which he is granted the power of intercession for his friends. Jeremiah's experience of wrestling with affliction and suffering is more dramatic still than Job's, since it is intimately connected with his prophetic proclamation of the word of God to a rebellious people. Jeremiah laments the lack of divine action toward healing his suffering, so much so that he boldly raises the specter of a divine deception: "Wilt thou be to me like a deceitful brook, like waters that fail?" (15:18). The divine response to the claim of deception comes as a divine rebuke; Jeremiah must purge himself of "worthless" talk and utter only the "precious" divine word that is given him. The prophet is required to understand that to be a mouthpiece of God is a cherished privilege, even if it involves suffering, pain, and sorrow. Jeremiah is given the reassurance that God will deliver him "out of the hand of the wicked" and redeem him "from the grasp of the ruthless" (15:21), but in the meantime he must bear his affliction and anguish in proclaiming the unpopular word of God to the people. With Jeremiah we encounter the notion of the righteous one who suffers precisely *because* of fidelity to keeping Torah. While Jeremiah's suffering is not depicted as vicarious, it is possible to discern a rudimentary framework for the principle of substitution, which is fully developed in Isaiah's suffering servant of the Lord. According to the principle of substitution, which represents something quite new, the undeserved suffering of the righteous one makes atonement for the sins of many (Isa 52:13—53:12).[14]

14. In a way, this idea of suffering as atonement is not really radically new, for it can be seen as arising out of Israel's sacrificial cult, where the sacrificial animal symbolizes

The prophet Habakkuk, like Jeremiah, also laments that divine justice seems slow in coming, and he, too, is given the reassurance that it will come, "it will not lie" (2:3). The righteous are to "wait" (2:3) for divine justice, they are to "live" (2:4) by God's faithfulness and the assurance of God's coming salvation, when the wicked will be crushed. God does not respond to the "why" question put to him, and to the "how long" question Habakkuk is told that he will have to wait expectantly and run assuredly towards the ultimate deliverance. The prophet comes to accept his life as an eschatological existence towards a divinely appointed time. In both Jeremiah and Habakkuk, *theodicy is essentially eschatological in character*, for their laments are directed towards a future good that will justify all the suffering and travail that has occurred on the way to attaining it. The lament speech form, in other words, emerges as the mode by which hope is born anew out of a situation of anguish and suffering. Since hope is directed towards an expectant future action of God that will overcome the forces of evil and chaos in the world, the question of theodicy cannot be content to look to the past to seek an explanation of evil in its origins but must look towards the coming future of God's benevolent reign of salvation (cf. Jer 31:31–34; Hab 3:18).

The foregoing statements are concerned with human laments addressed to God, but when the divine lament materials are integrated into the discussion a much fuller perspective on the issue of theodicy in the Hebrew Bible emerges. The fuller picture revolves around the important theological category of the divine pathos, which serves to radically underscore the genuine reciprocity of the divine-human relationship. In relation to historical happenings in time and space, God is not a detached and unmoved onlooker but is personally engaged and emotionally involved with his people, for whom he displays ultimate concern.[15] The

---

the people's sins. Moreover, the idea of many benefiting from the sacrifices of a few is already contained within the doctrine of election: the purpose of the divine election of Abraham is the blessing of many (the nations) through the few (Israel). The covenanted people are called into being for the sole purpose of being a light to the nations.

15. In classical theism, by contrast, as represented for example by Thomas Aquinas, God is pure act; in God there is neither passivity nor potency. God affects the world but is not affected by it (divine impassibility). The divine pathos, on the other hand, serves to qualify God's transcendence by recognizing God's immanence and vulnerability in opening up his heart to the world. Abraham Heschel states the biblical view of the relationship between God's transcendence and immanence especially well when he writes that "God remains transcendent in His immanence, and related in His transcendence" (*Prophets*, 486). According to Heschel, the significance of the divine pathos in all its forms (love, grief, joy, mercy, wrath) is that it reveals "the extreme

divine pathos effectively emphasizes the presence of God in the midst of the people and how God internalizes the lamentable state of the covenant relationship. The dismal state of the people is felt deeply by God, who is moved to bring about their redemption and return them to the land and create a new heart in them, so that they might be a holy people and a light to the nations. By virtue of the divine pathos the world enters into the divine self with the power not only to wound—God suffers "because" of Israel's sinfulness and God suffers "for" the people's rebellion—but also to redeem and heal the broken state of the relationship by the exercise of the pathos of love and compassion for his cherished people—God suffers "with" the afflicted people.

The theological category of the divine pathos reveals God as transcendent Subject, as personally engaged with Israel and the world, as having ultimate concern for his creation—God is not removed and detached from suffering but is a participant in suffering and works in a hidden manner to bring about salvation for Israel and the world. By virtue of the divine pathos, the question of theodicy is deeply bound up with the notion of the possibility of God. "Suffering will always have a dimension of mystery, as the Book of Job assures us, but a great deal of light is nevertheless cast by the affirmation that God suffers with humanity."[16] Just as God gave birth to Israel at the beginning of its life (Deut 32:18), God initiates a new action in order to birth Israel anew. Here the *birthing of a new creation is inseparable from the suffering of God*, which has its earthly parallel in the suffering of the prophet and the suffering servant of the Lord as depicted in the book of Isaiah (52:13—53:12) and the book of Wisdom (2:10–20). Both the Lord and his faithful servant enter deeply into Israel's dismal state of affairs, so that the death-dealing forces of sin may be conquered and transformed from within, and a new creation may burst forth out of the shared suffering of the human and the divine.

In this particular perspective where the suffering of God's earthly servant is reflective of the suffering of God, both the "existential" view of evil as utterly malevolent and the "instrumental" view of evil as divinely permitted because God works to bring a future good out of it, are at play and closely intertwined.[17] This gives theodicy a strongly eschatological

pertinence of man to God, His world-directness, attentiveness, and concern" (*Prophets*, 483). God is not one-sidedly transcendent, separate from and over or above the world, for a God of sheer power without pathos would hardly command our worship.

16. Fiddes, *Creative Suffering*, 31.

17. Hick, *Evil and God*, 388–400. The existential view of evil as truly evil is a

character. It is important to stress that God, unlike the human, is not overwhelmed by suffering—God remains transcendent in his immanence and related in his transcendence (cf. Isa 12:6; 55:8–9)—nor does God directly cause suffering. The theological category of the divine pathos forbids the thought that God inflicts suffering on his people. When divine judgment comes, we saw in chapter 1 that it tends to be conceived not in legalistic or forensic terms as just punishment for the people's sin, but rather as God's withdrawing from the people and hiding his face from them so that the consequences of the people's rebellion are allowed to play themselves out in history. In other words, God works judgment through the existing moral order, which is why in Jeremiah, for example, God says concerning a wicked people: "I will pour out *their* wickedness upon them" (Jer 14:16).[18] The effects of the people's wickedness are portrayed as intrinsic to the evil deeds committed. Divine retribution, then, "is not a new action which comes upon the person concerned from somewhere else; it is rather the last ripple of the act itself which attaches to its agent almost as something material. Hebrew in fact does not even have a word for punishment."[19] God does not create evil and suffering, and the people's responsibility and culpability is not denied, yet the emphasis in the biblical texts examined in chapter 1 is placed on God's steadfast love and saving purposes. *God chooses to bear ultimate responsibility for granting freedom to Israel and the world,*[20] which necessitates divine grieving, suffering, and lament. The granting of freedom to Israel and the world necessarily implies a disjunction between God and humanity, for which God chooses to bear ultimate responsibility via a process of divine suffering. "Any theodicy which includes God's ultimate responsibility for the predicament of the world must affirm the suffering of God."[21] In the book of Isaiah, God recalls the Noachic promise in order to emphasize that his "steadfast love" will not depart from sinful Israel, and his "covenant of peace" shall not be removed (54:9–10). It is no coincidence that the latter text follows the Suffering Servant Song of Isa 53, for the reader is

---

dualistic and philosophical conception of evil (Augustinian type of theodicy), while the instrumental view of evil as serving God's sovereign and ultimate good for creation is a monistic and theological conception of evil (Irenaean type of theodicy).

18. Fretheim, "Character of God," 308. See also Miller, *Sin and Judgment*; Koch, "Doctrine of Retribution"; and Tucker, "Sin and Judgment."

19. Von Rad, *Old Testament Theology*, 1:385.

20. Hick, *Evil and God*, 317.

21. Fiddes, *Creative Suffering*, 35.

required to understand that the grieving of God becomes embodied in the world in the person of the suffering servant of the Lord. This genuine reciprocity of relationship between the divine and the human, which is highlighted by the life of the prophet,[22] is integral to fathoming the event of the passion of Christ, when divinity and humanity are together cruci-fied in the ultimate agony.

The analysis of Jesus's cry of lament offered in the previous chapter 3 certainly bolsters the view that the question of theodicy is ineluctably bound up with the divine pathos. The unity of divinity and humanity in the one person of Jesus Christ means that on the cross humanity and divinity are united in the ultimate agony as they encounter and address each other in a unique revelatory and salvific event, so as to bring to fruition the final salvation of Israel and the world. The theological inter-pretation of Jesus's cry proposed in chapter 3 builds on the perspective of the prophetic life as a state of suffering in sympathy with the divine pathos, although this perspective is raised to a higher and unsurpassable level in that Jesus's humanity is the humanity of God. As such, Jesus's cry is not a purely human lament in the tradition of the suffering just but also assumes a divine dimension since Jesus is the Son of God who is forsaken by the Father into the hands of evildoers. The cry of Jesus concretely reveals the truth about the divine character, about how God in the person of the Son participates in adamic flesh (God suffers with us) and graciously bears the sin of the world (God suffers for us), so that we sinners might participate in the life of God and enjoy the fullness of the covenant relationship. "If there is no capacity in God to embrace our suffering and to make it God's own, then the biblical witness to God's intimate care and concern for our salvation is vitiated."[23]

To speak about the human and the divine in this way is to con-solidate the view that theodicy is essentially eschatological in character, since both human and divine suffering are directed towards the future good of "a new heaven and a new earth" (Rev 21:1), which is proleptically

22. The suffering of the prophet, it should be kept in mind, is not portrayed as vicarious in the sense that the prophet's life becomes a sin offering, although the prophetic texts do provide a conceptual framework that is conducive to the line of development that is found with the figure of the suffering servant of the Lord, whose death is regarded as an offering for sin that "makes many to be accounted righteous" (Isa 53:11; also Wis 2:10–20).

23. W. Johnson, "Jesus' Cry," 87. The idea of a suffering God is often criticized for incapacitating God and/or portraying God as mutable. The discussion below will offer a credible framework for conceptualizing the idea of a suffering God.

anticipated in the person of the risen Lord Jesus Christ. Theodicy cannot be content to look to the past for an explanation of evil and suffering in its origins but must look to the future, "expecting a triumphant resolution in the eventual perfect fulfillment of God's good purpose."[24] All too often theology has sought to exonerate God for the existence of sin, evil, and suffering by incriminating humankind,[25] but the theological category of the divine pathos, which receives ultimate legitimacy in the event of Jesus Christ, compels us to give serious attention to the incrimination of God for allowing forces of sin and evil to menace his creation.[26] The idea of the protological goodness of creation has been used to exonerate God of all culpability for the dark side of creation, but the findings of this study support the view that this traditional idea should be abandoned. We have to say that evil is well and truly malevolent (against the shallow modernist doctrine of progress), yet in the end it will be conquered and made to serve God's eschatological purpose for the creation (against the nihilistic deconstructive analyses of postmodernity). On the basis of the new covenant forged by the paschal mystery of Christ, we have to take an eschatological perspective of God's good purpose for creation as a whole. The opening chapter of the Bible does talk of the goodness of creation: "And God saw everything that he had made, and behold, it was very good" (Gen 1:31). But in the context of making, good is always good in relation to some purpose. The declaration by God that creation is "very good" can only mean "that creation is good for that which God intends it."[27] The goodness of creation, in other words, is not an ethical or objective judgment that the human being exercises; rather, the Genesis text is saying that creation is good in the eyes of God who views all things

24. Hick, *Evil and God*, 376.

25. Ever since Augustine, attempts to articulate the relationship between God and evil have always been attempts to exonerate God and incriminate humankind.

26. Barth's approach to the theodicy question is notable in that his thought does not fit into Augustinian-influenced attempts to exonerate God. With his notion of "nothingness" (*das Nichtige*) Barth does not seek to exonerate God or to uphold the ontological depotentiation of evil. Instead, he asserts that God takes nothingness seriously, for it is an entire system of elements that includes the forms of sin, evil, death, the devil, demons, and chaos. Nothingness is the "reality" that opposes and resists God (Barth, *Church Dogmatics*, III/3:289–305). Barth repudiates the anthropological reduction of evil and takes the concrete history of Jesus Christ as both the noetic and ontic basis for the discussion of nothingness. See Wüthrich, "Lament for Naught," 65–70.

27. Westermann, *Creation*, 61.

from the standpoint of the divine purpose for the whole course of history. The divine verdict "very good" does not apply simply to any given time: "It is true, rather, of the whole course of history in which God is present with his creatures in incursions of love that will finally lead it through the hazards and sufferings of finitude to participation in his glory."[28] It is God's abiding presence through "incursions of love" that is constitutive of the goodness of creation.

There is no greater incursion of love in human history than the extraordinary event of the crucifixion of Jesus Christ, the incarnate Word of God, in whose person humanity and divinity are united in an ultimate agony, so as to transform the present situation of affliction and death into the joy of the new creation. Because God proves and manifests his justice in the event of Jesus Christ, it is not possible to justify God before the tribunal of modern reason. With regard to the question of theodicy we can speak only of a divine theodicy based on the reality of the divine pathos manifested in the event of Jesus Christ. That is to say, we can speak only of God's *self-justification* in the crucified Christ, in whom the many kinds of evil and suffering in this world have been transformed into the ineffable joy and glory of resurrection life. From the standpoint of the event of the incarnation of the Son which culminates in his paschal mystery, we are compelled to say that God does indeed suffer, yet this assertion must be qualified by adding that no suffering overwhelms God but is absorbed and transformed in the divine being. It is important to properly conceive of the relationship between divine passibility and impassibility, which is well expressed by John Macquarrie when he writes:

> There may be many ways in which the suffering of God differs from the suffering of human beings, but there is one fairly obvious difference. Whereas the suffering of a human being can overwhelm and eventually destroy the person concerned, this cannot happen in the case of God. He can accept the world's pain, and does in fact accept it because he is immanent in the world-process, but he is never overwhelmed by it. *He has an infinite capacity for absorbing suffering, and even for transforming it.* . . . Without his passibility, his sharing in our affliction, there could be no bond of sympathy between him and us. Without his impassibility, his power to absorb and overcome and transform, there could be no final faith in God and we would have to join those pessimistic atheists who tell us that the cosmos is

28. Pannenberg, *Systematic Theology*, 3:645.

fundamentally absurd and meaningless, so that it would have
been better if this sorry scheme of things had never come into
existence.[29]

Macquarrie makes the valid point that any affirmation of God's passibility before this world, if it is to avoid incapacitating God and eroding faith
and hope, must also acknowledge God's impassibility. A God who merely
suffered along with his creatures would hardly deserve the name "God,"
yet a God of sheer power without pathos would hardly command our
worship either. In order for any God to be adored as God, he would have
to be one who shares in our afflictions and yet one who can rise above
the affliction. On the basis of the sustained arguments presented in this
study, we may believe that God in relation to his creation does suffer,
but because he is God, no suffering overwhelms him but is absorbed
and transformed in the divine being. The citation above reflects a very
similar position held by Abraham Heschel who regards the divine pathos
as a theological category and stresses that God, unlike humankind, is not
overwhelmed by suffering, for God remains transcendent (God's otherness from the world) in his immanence (God's indwelling of the world).
In the Bible, the transcendence of the living God is portrayed as God's
presence among his people as the Holy One. This is to say that God's
transcendence is manifested by the *way in which* God's being is present;
namely, steadfast in love, merciful and compassionate, patient and slow
to anger, long-suffering yet not overwhelmed by suffering, committed
to justice, unwavering in his redemptive purposes, and displaying ultimate concern for Israel and the world. It is by virtue of the living God's
pathos that the world enters into God's being, so as to heal and transform
humanity and the creation as a whole and finally realize God's good purpose for all that is. The paschal mystery of Christ reveals definitively how
God absorbs or internalizes the manifold sufferings (innocent and guilty)
of this world, with a view to transforming grief into the joy of a glorious
new creation.

The theodicy of God's self-justification in the event of Jesus Christ,
central to which is the understanding that the birthing of a new creation
is inseparable from the suffering of God, is the only Christian response
that can be given to the type of atheism that is morally motivated. Protest
atheism arises out of a sense of outrage that God should have contrived
a world in which there is so much injustice, suffering, and evil. This type

---

29. Macquarrie, *In Search of Deity*, 180–81; emphasis added.

of atheism is commonly represented by the character Ivan Karamazov in Dostoyevsky's novel *The Brothers Karamazov*. Ivan wishes to have no part in a world that permits the senseless suffering of children, and he anticipates the thinking of Albert Camus, who wrote that the only proper response to this world is what he called "metaphysical rebellion."[30] In the cases of both Ivan Karamazov and Albert Camus, though, it is the god of classical theism who is indicted. That is, a distinctly "monarchical" god who is one-sidedly transcendent, separate from and above the world, and whose impassibility contrasts with the sufferings of the temporal world. But if we were able to make the case for a god who is passible and shares our sufferings but has an infinite capacity to absorb and transform the many kinds of evil and afflictions that are a disturbing feature of this world, "then the moral argument for atheism would lose much of its force."[31]

From the standpoint of a divine theodicy based on the paschal mystery of Christ, "the true atheist would be not the one who does not believe in God but the one who cannot bring to God his or her suffering, doubt, and anguish, in the expectation that God will respond."[32] Jesus cried out to God on the cross, he abandoned himself totally to God, he expected that God would respond and would not hide his face, and he was "heard" (Ps 22:24; Heb 5:7) by God whose response came in the eschatological act of raising him from the dead. In the light of the crucified and risen Christ, we can assuredly say that God is affected by what happens in the temporal realm and participates in the human predicament, with a view to transforming evil and suffering from within and establishing a new creation resplendent with the glory of the divine life. While the realities of sin and evil are still very much a blemish on the landscape of this world, what has changed since the event of Christ's paschal mystery is that our cries of affliction are now joined to Jesus's cry, hence we can have confidence that God hears our cries and does not hide his face but is present with us in the Spirit of the risen Christ. Since God was for the Crucified One and with Jesus in his cry, we know through the activity of the indwelling Spirit that God is for us and with us in our own cries, taking up our suffering into the infinite capacity of divine being, so as to transform our grief (lament) into joy (praise of God). When we conceive

---

30. Macquarrie, *In Search of Deity*, 50.

31. Macquarrie, *In Search of Deity*, 50.

32. LaCugna, *God for Us*, 341.

of Christian life in the Spirit as an ongoing process of transformation of grief into joy (see next section), we are better able to keep alive the eschatological hope of sharing in the glory of Christ's resurrection, when we shall rejoice with "unutterable and exalted joy" (1 Pet 1:8).

The Apophatic Way, Life in the Spirit, and Eucharistic Lamentation

This eschatological perspective in relation to a divine theodicy gives rise to a distinctly *apophatic* or negative way of unknowing in theology, since the dynamics of the divine pathos revealed in the event of Jesus Christ remains unfathomable to the human mind: "For my thoughts are not your thoughts, neither are your ways my ways, says the Lord. . . . For as the heavens are higher than the earth, so are my ways higher than your ways and my thoughts than your thoughts" (Isa 55:8–9). In apophatic theology the one definition proper to God is the quality of incomprehensibility. This means that God no longer presents himself as an object to be perceived and fathomed by the human mind, for it is no longer a question of discursive knowledge of God but of mystical union with God. From the vantage point of the theological interpretation of Jesus's cry proposed in chapter 3, our own sufferings are ontologically joined to the redemptive suffering of the Crucified One; that is, by virtue of our own cries as the body of Christ being joined to Jesus's cry as the head, our suffering takes on a mysterious dimension and becomes the means of redemption and of entering into personal union with God. Christian life in the activity of the Spirit means, in other words, that we participate in the mystery of Christ's relationship with the Father, which reaches its unfathomable climax in the paschal mystery. This emphasis in apophatic theology on union with God implies that God can be experienced, that is, we should think of God in terms of personal presence and ultimate concern for human life, rather than in the image of an abstract idea. In the biblical story of Job's laments to God, for example, Job receives no rational explanation from God for his innocent suffering. The divine responses have the effect of silencing Job, who comes to acknowledge the inscrutable wisdom of God. Job adopts a new attitude of humble surrender to God, which enables him to experience personal union with God. In the confessions of Jeremiah, God eventually falls silent to the prophet's constant laments, so that Jeremiah comes to learn that as God's representative before a rebellious people, his state of suffering is in sympathy with the divine pathos. When we turn our attention to Jesus the Messiah, his suffering displays a similar situation to Job and Jeremiah, for Jesus is truly tested in his obedience as the Son, he abandons himself completely to the will of the Father, so that his suffering becomes the manifestation of his personal unity with the Father in unfathomable love. The emphasis in the biblical figures of Job, Jeremiah, and Jesus is placed on mystical union with God in their suffering. Jesus, though, is also distinct from Job and Jeremiah. The distinction consists in his being the incarnate Word or Son of God, who vicariously suffers the agony of crucifixion as a once and for all sin offering for the redemption of the world and who, as the Risen One, is the new creation in person, the one through whom all the covenant promises will come to fruition.

The followers of Christ, on this apophatic way of doing theology, are those who abandon themselves to the cause of God in the face of opposition, who come to accept God's inscrutable wisdom manifested in the crucified Lord, who humbly accept their suffering as mysteriously joined to the suffering of Christ, who are convinced that God hears their cries because God has heard Jesus's cry on the cross and who look to the sure hope (cf. Heb 11:1) of the fullness of salvation to come, when darkness shall give way to perpetual light, and grief to unspeakable joy. In the Christian life the lament speech form is necessary to sustain and nurture hope in the coming glory of the new creation anticipated in the person of the risen Christ, because embedded in the lament is "an appeal that arises out of trust in the God whose love is forever. Lament is the mode by which hope is reborn."[33] The constant rebirthing of hope through prayers of lament is indicative of the fact that faith and worship deal with the testing realities of this world and are shaped by "life as it comes to us."[34] Since prayers of lament are evoked by the afflictions of this life, they serve to promote a robust faith that matures through the manifold sufferings of historical existence. Saint Paul gives voice to this view of Christian faith and worship when he writes that not only is the whole of creation "groaning" for its salvation, but Christians also, who have "the first fruits of the Spirit," groan inwardly as they await the redemption of their bodies (Rom 8:18–23). The redemption of our bodies has to do with our being

---

33. Hicks, "Preaching Community Laments," 79. Hicks gives as an example the "sorrow songs" of African American liturgy, which enabled an oppressed community to persevere and endure through faith.

34. Brueggemann, *Psalms and the Life*, 67.

glorified with Christ, but for St. Paul there can be no glorification without sharing in the sufferings of Christ (Rom 8:16–17). This is made even clearer in 2 Corinthians where St. Paul uses the lovely metaphor of "this treasure in earthen vessels" (2 Cor 4:7) to describe the Christian life as a suffering with Christ on the way to the glory of the risen life.

But if Christians always carry in their bodies the death of Jesus so that the life of Jesus may be manifested in their mortal flesh, and Jesus on the cross cited Ps 22 in dealing with his suffering and bringing his mission as the Son to completion, then this would imply that lament must have its place in those who seek to imitate Christ and are placed before God by him.[35] The resurrection of Jesus, which is confessed as the Father's response to his lament cry, offers us the strongest indication as to why lament should be recognized as integral to Christian life. In the Eucharist, the Crucified One is present as the Living and Risen One; he speaks as the One who has been "heard" (Heb 5:7) by the Father, and together they send the Spirit of new life, which is the power that saves and re-creates out of the midst of suffering and death. The Eucharist, as the sacrament of the *eschaton*, incorporates lament into thanksgiving, as the Christian faithful journey towards that day when they will drink of the fruit of the vine with the glorified Jesus in his Father's kingdom (see Matt 26:29; Mark 14:25). It is therefore appropriate and desirable to talk of "eucharistic lamentation," by which is meant that the Eucharist forms the church in the memory of Christ's suffering and glorification, into which the memory of all human sufferings is gathered. To participate in the Eucharist is to give witness to "the divine compassion that stands firm in the midst of suffering, oppression, and calamity."[36] To put on Christ implies a commitment to witnessing to God's compassion in the midst of the suffering of this world. The word *solidarity*, properly understood, begins with grief, with the readiness "to share the sorrow of others . . . the voice of a solidarity which begins in grief is lament. Lament not only embraces the suffering of humanity but extends to the whole created order."[37] In the Eucharist, the bread and the wine are acknowledged as

35. Saint Paul, as was discussed in ch. 2 of this study, maintains that suffering should not be lamented, for to follow Christ and suffer in his name takes on the positive aspects of honor and "rejoicing" (Col 1:24). It is acceptable to talk of Christians as "groaning" (Rom 8:22–23) for the eschaton, but there is no room for lamenting their suffering in Christ's name.

36. Power, *Eucharistic Mystery*, 339.

37. Power and Downey, *Living the Justice*, 84.

fruits of the earth and works of human hands, hence the whole of creation gives thanks to the living God for the salvation that comes through
the body and blood of our Lord Jesus Christ. "When the things of the
earth become signs of Jesus Christ, as they do in the eucharist, the earth
itself is not transcended but shepherded and shared and loved."[38] In the
risen Christ, who is the "new creation" in person, history and nature are
no longer divorced, and by participating in the Eucharist we will hear the
divine words addressed to Moses from the burning bush: "Remove the
sandals from your feet, for the place on which you are standing is holy
ground" (Exod 3:5). Integral to the Eucharist is a commitment to "a lively
love and care for the conditions of the earth."[39]

Given the magnitude of suffering, oppression, and calamity in
our troubled world, participation in the Eucharist keeps alive the firm
Christian hope that the day shall come when God "will wipe away every
tear from our eyes, and death shall be no more, neither shall there be
mourning nor crying nor pain any more, for the former things will have
passed away" (Rev 21:4). As long as the fullness of salvation in Jesus
Christ is yet to be revealed, as long as the world remains unredeemed,
the only Christian life we know is entwined with death and the only joy is
entwined with lament. Lament is not something we experience occasionally in this life but is durative: "How long, O Lord? How long?" (Ps 13:1).
As we strain forward towards the *eschaton*, we must set our hearts upon
the deep and carry in our bodies the sufferings and death of Jesus, so that
the life of Jesus may be manifested to the world and God may be praised
as a compassionate God who is in solidarity with suffering humanity
and transforms grief into "unutterable joy" (1 Pet 1:8). Once lament is
incorporated into thanksgiving, it serves as an effective corrective to the
type of religious faith that wishes to withdraw from the present struggles
of life and lose itself in the detached, unreal world of heavenly or holy
things. The profession of Jesus as the "Holy and Righteous One" (Acts
3:14) is not possible apart from Jesus's personal involvement with the
harsh realities of Jewish life in first-century Galilee and his proclamation
of the kingdom of God to his own for whom he had compassion because
they were "harassed and helpless, like sheep without a shepherd" (Matt
9:36; cf. John 10). The holiness of the Crucified One is very much an
"involved holiness" that illuminates the divine pathos and the wondrous

38. Lathrop, *Holy Things*, 216.
39. Lathrop, *Holy Ground*, 152.

workings of divine salvation in relation to Israel and the world. Among Christians it is common to think that the victory of Easter Sunday was so complete and glorious that it effectively annihilated the darkness of Good Friday. This makes for a bad and heartless theology that stills the voice of lament by obliterating the wounds of the crucified Messiah. C. Clifton Black makes this very important point when he argues for the persistence of Christ's wounds:

> Christians should occasionally pause to marvel that God raised Jesus from death itself but did not wipe away his lacerations . . . God did not eradicate the scars of his death but, instead, vindicated this Crucified One, and no other, as the Messiah. Just there lies the most important reason for the practice of lament. Without it, whether they know it or not, Christians again deny the One whom God has both vindicated and forever verified as Christ on the cross. The wounds of the Messiah's crucifixion are the inexpungible identification by which God has embodied himself for us, for our healing, for the salvation of all. Until that day when every tear has been wiped away and death shall be no more (Rev 21:4), all of God's people—Rachel and Ann, Jesus and Paul, all of us without exception—unite their voices in lament, hopeful but without closure.[40]

This understanding of lament as essential to sustaining a hopeful Christian life, but without closure, underscores the apophatic way of unknowing in theology, as well as Christian discipleship as the ongoing embodiment of Christ in the world; that is, the view that the Spirit of God leads us out of a provisional existence and "into the *adventure of incarnation*."[41] If we are to enter into God's mystery in Christ, it is not information that we need, for our conceptual language breaks down in the presence of God.[42] What is required is a genuine and proper Christian spirituality understood as "*the activity of being led by the Spirit into Christ's relationship with the Father*."[43] Life in the Spirit means that

40. Black, "Persistence of the Wounds," 56–57.

41. McIntosh, *Mystical Theology*, 6; emphasis added.

42. In the Christian mystical traditions, knowing and loving are often held together. The ultimate form of knowledge is not conceived as an event in which certain information is imparted to the mind; rather, the mind is drawn to a new level of perception by being transformed in love. The ancient technical term for teaching that helps to lead others to a "participatory" understanding of the divine mystery is *mystagogy*. See McIntosh, *Mystical Theology*, 27–29.

43. McIntosh, *Mystical Theology*, 152; emphasis added. This is McIntosh's definition

Christ's followers are drawn ever more deeply into his own encounter with the one he called Abba, and therefore share in God's knowledge of himself, which to *us* must look like darkness. "So that our faith seems not like an increase of knowledge but, if anything, an increase in ignorance. We become more acutely aware of our inadequacy before the mystery as we are brought closer to it."[44] It is not that apophatic theology has very little to say about God, but rather the awe and wonder of the encounter with God is always more than one can say; there is always a "superabundance of meaning,"[45] which demands that we let go of the grasping for knowledge as a possession and accept our vulnerability before the "holy mystery."[46] As we are drawn up into the holy mystery of God through the activity of the Spirit, we are exposed to the profound questioning at the very heart of the Christian struggle to be faithful. The questioning here, as Rowan Williams explains, is "not our interrogation of the data, but its interrogation of us . . . the greatness of the great Christian saints lies in their readiness to be questioned, judged, stripped naked and left speechless by that which lies at the center of their faith."[47] It is the Christian vocation to be drawn by the Spirit out of a life of provisionality and into the mystery of the incarnation by this divine questioning: "Who do you say I am?" (Mark 8:27). It is this questioning that Christian spirituality carries within itself—"always carrying in the body the death of Jesus" (2 Cor 4:10)—as its animating source.[48]

Whenever the church's worship has been authentic it has drawn people into an encounter, namely, the encounter between Christ and the Father in their Spirit. The church's worship centers on Jesus Christ, "present as the One whom God has raised to Life, revealed as the Holy and Just One, and exalted in Glory."[49] It is as the Living and Risen One that

---

of spirituality and one of the main propositions of his work. McIntosh argues that theology is rooted in spirituality, that is, theology grows organically out of God's own knowing and speaking of Godself through the Spirit.

44. McCabe, *God Matters*, 20.

45. McIntosh, *Mystical Theology*, 123–5.

46. In the transcendental theology of Karl Rahner, the term of transcendence is the "holy mystery." It is "mystery" because it cannot be defined, and it is "holy" because transcendence does not refer exclusively to the condition of possibility for categorical knowledge as such but includes the transcendence of freedom, of willing, and of love (Rahner, *Foundations of Christian Faith*, 65–66).

47. Williams, *Wound of Knowledge*, 1.

48. McIntosh, *Mystical Theology*, 18.

49. Van Beeck, *Understanding Christian Faith*, 154. The author views the Christian

Christ can become in the Eucharist the "bread of life" (John 6:35, 48), the "living bread" (John 6:51).[50] Because of the paschal context—"Take, eat, this is my body"—of the Eucharist, it is situated within the sphere of reality of Christ's *gift of himself*, "through the eternal Spirit" (Heb 9:14). We should appreciate, as Edward Schillebeeckx has argued, that there exists an "essential bond between the real presence of Christ in the Eucharist and his real presence as Lord living in the Church."[51] Moreover, the eucharistic bread and wine not only signify Christ's real presence to his church, they also signify the real presence of the church to Christ. The eucharistic meal signifies both Christ's gift of himself and the church's responding gift of herself, of what the church is in Christ. The Eucharist therefore signifies "the *reciprocity* of the real presence."[52] The central Christian experience is essentially mystical and actualized in worship. The risen Christ, present in the Spirit, evokes participation in his divine identity, in his perfect self-abandonment and worship to the Father. The Spirit prompts and sustains worship as response to the living encounter between Christ and his Father. "The Eucharist leads to participation in the enfleshed Son who then raises the eucharistised, 'through him, with him and in him,' to the Father and in the love of the Holy Spirit."[53] The

---

faith as having a radically doxological essence: it is in worship that the church draws closest to its central mystery, which is the life of the Trinity. In worship the church experiences the fusion of *awe* and *intimacy* that prompts and sustains its life. Teaching is informed by worship and life, and life is informed by worship.

50. John Paul II, *Ecclesia de Eucharistia*, §14. The pontiff makes the point that Christ's passover is not limited to his passion and death but includes his resurrection. The eucharistic sacrifice includes the mystery of the resurrection, which crowned his sacrifice on Calvary. The pontiff's view is congruent, it is worth noting, with the thought of F. X. Durrwell who asserted that because Christ's death is a glorifying death (i.e., Christ's death is the means by which he goes to the Father), the principle of intelligibility of the eucharistic mystery is "the paschal Christ who comes into His earthly Church" (*Eucharist*, 15).

51. Schillebeeckx, *Eucharist*, 138.

52. Schillebeeckx, *Eucharist*, 139. This assertion about the reciprocity of the real presence is supported by the arguments in this study concerning the reciprocity of the divine-human relationship, which is especially highlighted by the theological category of the divine pathos. The covenant relationship consists not only of the human's commitment to God (hence human laments addressed to God) but of God's engagement to the human and to the world (thus divine laments due to the people's sin and rebellion). The theological interpretation of Jesus's cry proposed in ch. 3, which affirms both human and divine aspects to Jesus's cry, underscores the reciprocity of the divine-human relationship.

53. McEvoy and Hogan, *Mystery of Faith*, 200.

Eucharist, as Christ's giving of himself and the church's reciprocal gift of herself in response to Christ's paschal mystery, is directed towards a common surrender to the Father, "for the salvation of the world."

Those who participate in the Eucharist are drawn into the ineffable communion of the Blessed Trinity and live by grace in anticipation of the fullness of joy in the risen Christ, who is the "pledge of future glory."[54] Just as Christ became completely "poor" (2 Cor 8:9) on the cross as he gave himself fully into the hands of his Father, who alone could save him from death (Heb 5:7), those who are incorporated into Christ the Redeemer must become poor. This inward poverty is called humility or self-renunciation, abandonment to God. "Humility means accepting our poverty so as to be rich only in God."[55] We must identify with Christ in his death, in his total self-renunciation and abandonment to the Father, in order that we may share in the holiness of God by dying to ourselves, by humbly putting ourselves into the hands of the living God, who is true to his covenant promises. To live eucharistically as the body of Christ is no facile undertaking, however, for it requires ongoing conversion to that ineffable love of God displayed by Christ who surrendered the totality of his life in perfect obedience to the Father for the eschatological salvation of the world. It is this "art of loving"[56] that is required to effectively build up the church as the ongoing embodiment of Christ in the world. The Christian life is a straining forward in the eschatological hope of "a new heaven and a new earth" (Rev 21:1), but this glorious expectation "increases, rather than lessons, our sense of responsibility for the world today."[57]

This art of loving is also required to realize the vision of the church espoused by Pope Francis, who in his apostolic exhortation *Evangelii Gaudium* has urged Christians not to keep Christ's wounds at arm's length: Christ's followers must "touch human misery, touch the suffering flesh of others."[58] Just as God hears our cries which are joined to Jesus's cry, we are called to hear the cries of others, to respond to the needs and afflictions of others in the solidarity of compassionate and charitable love. As the basic sacrament of Christ's salvation in the world, the church cannot be turned

---

54. John Paul II, *Ecclesia de Eucharistia*, §18.

55. Durrwell, *In the Redeeming Christ*, 164.

56. McEvoy and Hogan, *Mystery of Faith*, 207.

57. John Paul II, *Ecclesia de Eucharistia*, #20.

58. Francis, *Evangelii Gaudium*, 270.

in on itself and confined to the security of its ecclesial structures but must go forth into the world and become "bruised, hurting, and dirty because it has been out on the streets."[59] As a people advancing on its pilgrim way towards God, the church cannot rest in the confines of ecclesial structures but must be a place where the merciful love of God can be encountered; where everyone can feel welcomed, loved, and forgiven; and experience the joy of being drawn into the new life of the gospel. The exhortation of the author of the Letter to the Hebrews expresses the pontiff's exhortation to the pilgrim people of God in the following words: "Therefore, Jesus died outside the gate, to sanctify the people by his own blood. *Let us go* to him outside the camp, bearing the insult which he bore" (Heb 13:12–13; emphasis added). To follow Christ entails our preparedness to go out to the Crucified One who "consecrated" himself outside the Holy City, that is, outside the sphere consecrated to God and reserved for the religious people. "One must therefore *dare* to leave the sacred where one feels secure in order to find Christ among the impious, among those without God, for it is there that God has decided to pitch his tent."[60] For Pope Francis, to evangelize is to make God's kingdom a concrete and visible reality in our world, that is, to affirm the truth that works of love and mercy are the most perfect manifestation of the grace of the Spirit indwelling us:

> When preaching is faithful to the Gospel, the centrality of certain truths is evident and it becomes clear that Christian morality is not a form of stoicism, or self-denial, or merely a practical philosophy or a catalogue of sins and faults. Before all else, the Gospel invites us to respond to the God of love who saves us, to see God in others and to go forth from ourselves to seek the good of others. Under no circumstance can this invitation be obscured! All of the virtues are at the service of this response of love. If this invitation does not radiate forcefully and attractively, the edifice of the church's moral teaching risks becoming a house of cards, and this is our greatest risk. It would mean that it is not the Gospel which is being preached, but certain doctrinal or moral points based on specific ideological options. The message will run the risk of losing its freshness and will cease to have "the fragrance of the Gospel."[61]

---

59. Francis, *Evangelii Gaudium*, 49.

60. Rossé, *Cry of Jesus*, 124; emphasis original.

61. Francis, *Evangelii Gaudium*, 39.

It is plain from this citation that if the church wishes to be credible in a world that continually experiences the absence of God and proclaims the death of God, then it must concretely radiate the reality of the God of love, manifested in Christ, who lived to the point of abandonment on the cross, for the salvation of a suffering world estranged from God. Only in a love similar to that lived by Christ "outside the gate" on Golgotha can the church go forth to proclaim the gospel, which means being the visible presence of the Risen One in the world, in whom all are one in a new creation (cf. John 12:32). While the pontiff's vision of the church as truly engaged with our suffering world is well and good, what is lacking in his statements, as well as those of Pope John Paul II, is the recognition of the essential role that lament plays in Christian life as the ongoing embodiment of Christ in the world. The disciples of Christ can all too easily become overwhelmed and demoralized by the magnitude of sin and suffering they encounter as they go forth into an unredeemed world to preach the good news of the gospel. This means they must be able to earnestly open their hearts to God in prayers of lament that serve the multifaceted functions outlined earlier in this chapter. The lament speech form is necessary for the rekindling of eschatological hope, which is rooted in the knowledge that our cries are joined to the cry of the Crucified One, whose cry was heard by the Father, who raised him from the dead in the power of the Spirit. Prayers of lament go hand in glove with the apophatic way of unknowing in theology, for the emphasis falls on mystical union with God, in Christ, through the Spirit, who empowers us to bear the redemptive death of Christ in our mortal bodies for our deification, as well as for the life of the world.

This mystical perspective is consistent with the encounters of God recorded in the Hebrew Bible, which is captured in the revelation of the divine name: "I am who I am" (Exod 3:14). This mystical name, as Ottmar Fuchs explains, contains no general or abstract quality that could be used to name God: "The name says 'only' that God is and will be there. It describes in this form a personal existence which cannot be obviously determined on a level which is detached from the concrete and real experience. In this respect the name . . . is open for a meaning which still has to be experienced."[62] The name Yahweh, to be sure, is associated with titles full of authority, but these titles are a result of the people's liberating encounters with "I am who I am." The biblical God is known

62. Fuchs, God's People, 31.

through the unique stories of divine-human encounters, that is, through testimonials of God's abiding presence in the midst of his people, but the God of Israel, supremely embodied in the person of Jesus Christ, is not definable and remains incomprehensible to the human mind. The mystical character of "I am who I am" is strongly bolstered by the event of the crucified Messiah, who is the new locus of encounter with the living God: "We have confidence to enter the sanctuary by the blood of Jesus, by the new and living way which he opened for us through the curtain, that is, through his flesh" (Heb 10:19–20). The indwelling of God in humankind is directed towards humankind's participation or dwelling in the ineffable God. As the Holy One, God alone can triumph over the troublesome realities of sin and death, transform the many kinds of sufferings (innocent and guilty) in this world, and establish final justice and enduring peace in a new creation of exalted joy that finally brings the covenant promises to fulfillment, to the everlasting praise of God.

The Doctrine of God: Eternal Event of Trinitarian Kenotic Love

The previous chapter of this study has argued that the ineffable love and unity between the Father and the Son, manifested through the Spirit, is the exegesis of the event of the cross. In the Gospel story, love of the Father is the motivating force in the Son's messianic mission (see John 14:31), and the Father reciprocates this love when he affirms Jesus as his "beloved Son" with whom he is well pleased (Matt 3:17, 17:5; Mark 8:7). The mission of proclaiming the Father's benevolent love for the people leads Jesus the Son to the climactic point of his passion, where the Father does not grant the Son's petition that the hour might pass from him; instead, the Father gives him up "for us all" (Rom 8:32) in order that "the world might be saved through him" (John 3:18).[63] The Father's forsaking of the Son to an unjust and violent death not only highlights what it cost the Son to accomplish his salvific mission and glorify the Father, it also sheds light on the Father's silence in surrendering the Son to the cruel

63. The view that the love between the Son and the Father is the exegesis of the cross is shared, for example, by Balthasar who places the abandonment within the eternal generation of the Son from the Father and asserts that on the cross we see "the highest union possible in love" between them (*Last Act*, 263); and Rossé who holds that "the extreme abandonment manifests the extreme communion of the Son with the Father" (*Cry of Jesus*, 116).

workings of a sinful and rebellious people. The cross is an event involving the *double surrender* both of the Father and of the Son.[64] We are to
understand, therefore, that the silence of the Father has not only redemptive significance but also revelatory significance in that it points to the
sacrifice and sorrow of the Father in his identification with the Crucified
One.[65] Once the unfathomable unity of love between the forsaken Son and
the forsaking Father is recognized as the exegesis of the event of the cross,
the nonintervention of the Father is to be seen in a positive light. That is
to say, the Father reveals himself on the cross precisely in his silence; he
manifests himself as the interiority of the event of the Son's crucifixion.
In the very act of abandoning the Son into the hands of his enemies,
the Father reveals himself by disappearing in the death of Christ.[66] The
silence of God on the cross should not be interpreted as meaning the loss
of divine presence—as if the divine being is rent asunder, as Moltmann
suggests—although clearly Jesus's cry of lament indicates a "felt" loss of
intensification of God's presence, which Jesus had earlier enjoyed as a figure of power and authority in proclaiming the kingdom of God to Israel.

The kenosis of the Son on Calvary requires us to recognize, at the
same time, the kenosis of the Father in forsaking the Son, and this mutual

64. Saint Paul makes it clear in his writings that the cross involves a double surrender. In Rom 8:32 he says that God "did not spare his own Son but gave him up for
us all," and in Gal 2:20 he speaks about the "Son of God who loved me and gave himself
for me." In both these texts the Greek word is *paradidonai*, which means "to hand over."
In this perspective, we can appreciate why Karl Barth in his *Church Dogmatics* presents
the Trinity as the prolegomenon to all Christian theology; the Trinity provides the
structure without which the nature of revelation and faith become unintelligible. For
Barth revelation involves a threefold distinction between God as revealer (Father),
God as revelation (Son), and God as revealedness (Holy Spirit).

65. Jüngel has made the identification of God with the crucified Jesus a central
theme of his theological writings, from which emerges the historical narrative of the
humanity of God and the death of God. God's identification with the crucified Jesus
defines God's own reality; namely, love, which is not something about God but God's
very definition (cf. 1 John 4:16). See Jüngel, *God as the Mystery*, 299, 314–96.

66. Many interpret Paul's statement that Christ was "made sin" (2 Cor 5:21) to
mean that Christ suffered *God*-abandonment, for that is precisely what sin is, namely,
separation from God. If sin is separation from God, then Jesus as sin-bearer must
suffer separation from God. The problem with this position is that Jesus is without sin,
which is to say that he is intimately united with the Father in unfathomable love; there
is no separation between Jesus the Son and his Father. Jesus is the sin-bearer in the
sense that he suffers the consequences of the people's sin and estrangement from God;
he assumes in his person the people's forsaking of God, thereby representing sinners
before the Father, with a view to offering, through the Spirit, the gift of redemption and
the fullness of salvation.

self-giving or self-emptying of Father and Son in the economy of salvation directs us to a corresponding kenosis within God. The work of Sergius Bulgakov is worth highlighting at this point of the discussion, for he is among a group of foremost Russian thinkers who have formulated the idea of the inner life of the Trinity as eternal self-renouncing love, which meshes especially well with the theological interpretation of Jesus's cry offered in this study.[67] Bulgakov understands the divine nature as "a *personal* self-positing, but one that is personally trihypostatic."[68] God's nature is the one nature of Father, Son, and Holy Spirit, with each hypostasis having the divine nature in its own way. The Father lives not in himself and for himself but in proceeding out of himself, in revealing himself, in the begetting of the Son. This begetting power is the ecstasy of a going out of oneself, of a kind of self-emptying: "For the Father, begetting is self-emptying, the giving of Himself and of His own to the Other; it is the sacrificial ecstasy of all-consuming jealous love for the Other."[69] The Son, the begotten, who is the revealed one, has himself and his own not as himself and his own but as the Father's, in the image of the Father (see John 8:30; 14:9). Bulgakov explains the Son's self-emptying in the name of the Father as follows:

> Sonhood is already *eternal kenosis*. . . . The Son's love is the sacrificial, self-renouncing humility of the Lamb of God, "foreordained before the foundation of the world" (1 Pet 1:20). And if the Father desires to have Himself outside Himself, in the Son, the Son too does not desire to have Himself for Himself: He offers His personal selfhood in sacrifice to the Father. . . . The sacrifice of the Father's love consists in self-renunciation and in self-emptying in the begetting of the Son. The sacrifice of the Son's love consists in self-depletion in the begottenness from the Father. . . . The *sacrifice* of love, in its reality, is pre-eternal suffering—not the suffering of limitation (which is incompatible with the absoluteness of divine life) but the suffering of the authenticity of sacrifice and of its immensity. . . . If God is love,

---

67. In modern Russian Orthodox theology, there has developed the idea that the divine kenosis is not confined to the event of the incarnation, which culminates in the passion of Christ, but is something eternal in the life of the triune God, in which case the divine kenosis is involved with the very act of creation and the whole divine economy of salvation. The main representatives of this school of thought are Vladimir Soloviev, M. M. Tareev, Sergius Bulgakov, and Vladimir Lossky.

68. Bulgakov, *Lamb of God*, 97.

69. Bulgakov, *Lamb of God*, 98.

He is also sacrifice, which manifests the victorious power of love
and its joy only through suffering.[70]

God, however, is not the dyad of Father and Son but the Trinity of Father,
Son, and Holy Spirit. For Bulgakov, the Spirit is the joy of sacrificial love,
the bliss and actualization of this love. The reality of the divine nature is
accomplished by the Holy Spirit who proceeds from the Father, reposes
upon the Son or proceeds "through" the Son, and unites the two of them.
The Holy Spirit is the mutual love of Father and Son and the joy of this
ineffable sacrificial love. What is accomplished in the Spirit is the self-
revelation of divinity in its nature, not only in Truth but also in Beauty.
"This is no longer the sacrificial act; it is the triumphant testimony about
itself of love and the self-knowledge of God's nature; it is not begetting
but procession."[71] In this view, there is *no self-emptying of the Spirit* on the
cross (see below). As the actualization of the mutual love of Father and
Son, one can say that the procession of the Spirit is not active but passive,
for the Spirit issues or flows out to proclaim that which the Son says in
the name of the Father. In and through the Spirit the depths of God in
Truth and Beauty become transparent.

Among Western theologians, Balthasar closely follows the thought
of Bulgakov, whom he explicitly acknowledges when he asserts that
the Father generates or begets the Son in an act of primal kenosis or
Urkenosis (self-giving or self-emptying), in which the Father gives all
that he has and is to the Son.[72] The eternal generation of the Son is a
"self-sacrificial" act in which the Father "abandons" his own divinity; "he
will not be God for himself alone."[73] The Father's letting go of his divinity
and the Father's letting be of the Son express a primordial "separation"
of God from Godself, which provides the "space" for the "Other" of the
Son, as well as the "other" of creation and the abuse of freedom given to
creaturely being. The Father *is* this movement of total self-donation that
holds nothing back, and in this primal kenosis we see the unity of power
and powerlessness: omnipotence since the Father can give all, the whole

70. Bulgakov, *Lamb of God*, 99.

71. Bulgakov, *Lamb of God*, 100.

72. Balthasar, *Action*, 323, 326, 331. Both Bulgakov and Balthasar envisage kenosis
as an eternal process within the immanent Trinity, which is the foundation of the
historical event of Jesus Christ. Barth, though, does not speak of kenosis in relation to
the inner life of the triune God; rather, he speaks of the Word's self-emptying in the
person of Jesus Christ; that is, kenosis is attributed only to the economic Trinity.

73. Balthasar, *Action*, 324.

divine essence to the Son; and powerlessness since "nothing is as truly powerful as the gift."[74] The Son receives all that he has and is from the Father and gives himself fully back to the Father. From eternity the Son has been a yes to the Father, a surrender of obedience, for the Son possesses the divine nature in the mode of receptivity, which includes "his filial thanksgiving (Eucharist) for the gift of consubstantial divinity."[75]

Given that the Son's self-surrender is just as full and complete as that of his Father, the two hypostases stand in a relation of mutual and reciprocal self-giving love, which is an "event" within God.[76] The Spirit is breathed forth (spirated) by both Father and Son as the communion of their love for one another, as the "We" in the identity of the gift-as-given and the gift-as-received in thanksgiving.[77] This implies that there is "no self-emptying (*exinanitio*) in the case of the Holy Spirit,"[78] who

74. Balthasar, *Action*, 326.

75. Balthasar, *Action*, 326. Traditionally, receptivity, as a passive potency proper to the human, was not attributable to God, who is perfect. Balthasar, though, regards receptivity as intrinsic to the perfection of the interpersonal relations within God, which leads him to posit an *active* receptivity in God, who is love. Cf. Hunt, *Trinity and Paschal Mystery*, 85.

76. Balthasar uses the term *event* to convey a liveliness and vitality within God, which traditional notions of immutability and impassibility fail to express. He qualifies the term, though, by the adjective "supra-temporal," so as to distance himself from any univocal attribution of change to God.

77. For both Balthasar and Bulgakov, the model of the eternal Trinity is one of interpersonal love, given and received among distinct persons. The explication of the immanent Trinity is not social in the sense of positing three divine wills or three centers of consciousness in God (cf. Bracken, "Holy Trinity as Community"; Hill, *Three-Personed God*, 272). The model of interpersonal love stresses that "person" in the Trinity signifies a relation, which alone provides the principle of distinction within the Trinity. Since this relation is not accidental but constitutive of the divine nature as absolute love, we can say, following the Thomistic tradition, that the divine persons are "subsistent relations." As subsistent relations, the divine persons share one divine consciousness because each person is identical with the divine nature. The stress on subsistence preserves the original Greek notion of *hypostasis*, that is, an objective presentation of the Godhead. The interpersonal model of the Trinity could also, however, be seen as picking up on the classical concept of *perichoresis*, that is, the persons of the Trinity so perfectly indwell each other that the being of the persons is their relationships.

78. Balthasar, *Spirit of Truth*, 227. Bulgakov also holds that there is no self-emptying in the case of the Spirit. He differs from Balthasar, though, in that he does not talk of a separation or distance between Father and Son, which is bridged over by the Holy Spirit. For Bulgakov the Holy Spirit is the actualization of the eternal act of sacrificial love between the Father and the Son.

from eternity maintains and bridges over the distinction and separation between Father and Son. Balthasar conceives of a twofold aspect of the Holy Spirit: "He is both the act of reciprocal love between Father and Son and the fruit of that act."[79] The immanent Trinity is portrayed as that eternal, absolute self-surrender whereby God is seen to be, in himself, absolute love (1 John 4:8, 16). This perspective is informed by the paschal mystery of the Son, where we see that "love alone is credible,"[80] because it is the only thing that is truly rational.

For Balthasar, the divine act of the Father's generation of the Son, who possesses a distinctly filial way of being divine that is irreducible to the Father's own way of being God, involves positing the Son as positively *other than* the Father. The Father's bringing forth of the Son involves "the positing of an absolute, infinite 'distance' that can contain and embrace all the other distances that are possible within the world of finitude, including the distance of sin."[81] The condition for the possibility of humanity's rejection of God in all its forms is the immanent Trinity: "It is the drama of the 'emptying' of the Father's heart, in the generation of the Son, that contains and surpasses all possible drama between God and the world."[82] Just as the Son eternally proceeds from the Father immanently, the Son is sent forth by the Father into the world economically, and both are kenotic in quality. The kenotic quality of the Son's economic mission is most clearly on display on Calvary, where the Son gives himself for the salvation of the world out of self-sacrificial love for the Father. For Balthasar, all forms of kenosis *ad extra* are contained with the primal kenosis *ad intra*.

Balthasar, like Barth and Moltmann, develops a doctrine of God as a Trinitarian theology of the cross. He seeks to show that the cross reveals the Trinity and can be interpreted only in terms of the Trinity. Balthasar

---

79. Balthasar, *Spirit of Truth*, 242.

80. Balthasar, *Love Alone*. Balthasar believes that the primacy of love and the sheer glory of God's love have been overlooked by much of the Latin theological tradition. He thinks of the divine processions not in terms of the categories of intellect and will but as the movement of eternal self-emptying love, which better reflects the biblical data of the event of salvation in Jesus Christ. Love is "that than which nothing greater can be thought" (Hunt, *Trinity and Paschal Mystery*, 58). This perspective explains God's self-giving to the world in love and freedom without suggesting that God needed the world in order to become himself—Balthasar is critical of Moltmann who entangles the immanent Trinity in the world process (Balthasar, *Action*, 321–23).

81. Balthasar, *Action*, 323.

82. Balthasar, *Action*, 327.

consistently links the salvific drama of the cross—by cross he means the entire paschal mystery—with the inner-Trinitarian drama of the relations among Father, Son, and Spirit. In the passion of Christ, the triune God is both *acting*, that is, performing the work of salvation, and *speaking*, that is, revealing the divine nature through the drama of salvation. The essential elements of the cross for Balthasar are the Father's gift of the Son, the Son's gift of himself, the "separation" between Father and Son, and the Spirit who maintains the distance and distinction of Father and Son while preserving the indestructible unity of the Trinity in the work of salvation. The Father gives his Son to the world out of love, because the Father eternally generates the Son out of love; the Son responds to the Father's love, both immanently and economically, with an equally total and full gift of self-donation; Father and Son can be "separated" on the cross because they are eternally distinct in the immanent Trinity; but the Spirit is "that love which, even in the form of 'separation' between the one who 'commands' and the one who 'obeys,' holds fast, undiminished."[83] The Spirit is the Spirit of both maintaining and bridging the personal distance and distinction between the Father and the Son. The cross of the Son compels us to speak in terms of the Lamb slain from the foundation of the world (Rev 13:8; 1 Pet 1:19–20). For Balthasar, as for Bulgakov, "the Cross of Christ is inscribed in the creation of the world since its basis was laid,"[84] which is to say that a fundamental kenosis is given with creation as such.

Balthasar's model of the immanent Trinity as the "event" of self-emptying love is very similar to Bulgakov's interpersonal model, although a notable point of difference is Balthasar's notion of "separation" or "distance" between the Father and the Son. It is the latter, to my mind, that is questionable and problematic. Is Balthasar on solid ground when he envisages a fundamental separation between the Father and the Son as integral to the difference-in-unity of the divine persons? His ontology of love has the merit of venturing beyond the traditional understanding of the being of God in Augustinian-Thomistic theology—i.e., a substance-based metaphysics or essentialist ontology—and is better able to contextualize and personalize the paschal mystery of Christ as a salvific event of triune love "for us." Bulgakov, though, also proposes an ontology of

83. Balthasar, *Spirit of Truth*, 244. It is as if the Spirit is witness that the "distance" between the Father and the Son can never be separation because the Spirit constantly bridges the distance.

84. Balthasar, *Mysterium Paschale*, 35, citing Bulgakov.

love, which, to my mind, is preferable to Balthasar's, inasmuch as he does not posit a primal separation or infinite distance between the Father and the Son. Instead, the dynamics of self-sacrificing love within God are described in a way that emphasizes the unity of God constituted by the perichoretic indwelling of the divine persons in one another: the sacrifice of the Father's love consists in self-renunciation in the begetting of the Son; the Son, too, does not desire to have himself for himself but offers his personal selfhood in sacrifice to the Father; but there is no self-emptying in the case of the Spirit, who is the actualization of mutual self-sacrificing love of the Father and the Son. This perspective better accords with the findings of this study regarding a theological interpretation of Jesus's cry on the cross: Jesus does not have himself for himself but lives wholly for the cause of his beloved Father, hence he offers his personal selfhood in sacrifice to the Father; the sacrifice of the Father's love "for us" consists in handing over his beloved Son into the custody of evildoers, which is an act of self-emptying on the part of the Father, which is rooted in the eternal begetting of the Son; and the suffering of the cross takes place in the power of the Spirit who upholds the ineffable communion of mutual self-sacrificing love of the Father and the Son. The reason Balthasar uses the language of distance or separation between the Father and the Son is that he subscribes to the God-abandonment thesis in his interpretation of the cross of Christ, which he sees as necessary to uphold the biblical datum that Christ was "made sin" (2 Cor 5:21) for our sake. Since sin is separation from God, Christ on the cross must suffer separation from God in order to conquer sin and death and offer new life to the world.

Unlike Moltmann, however, who conceives of this separation as a division or rupture in the very life of God, Balthasar locates the event of the cross in the inner-Trinitarian event of self-emptying love, which creates the space for the other of the Son, as well as the other of creation. Jesus's cry of God-forsakenness gives poignant voice to the separation between the Father and the Son that is now being played out on the historical plane for the sake of the salvation of the world, and it is precisely in the sacrifice of this separation that divine love unfolds its whole depth. Balthasar, in paradoxical fashion, contends that *the extreme abandonment manifests the extreme communion of the Son with the Father.* In the Son's abandonment by the Father, the Father does not leave the Son, and, moreover, the Son is united more and more to the Father in this separation "until he is nothing more on the Cross than the revelation of the will of the Father."[85] But if the Father does not leave the Son for a moment, does this not imply that the Father is present, not absent, on Calvary? How then can it be said that the Son suffers extreme abandonment by the Father?[86] If the Father, whose distinct identity emerges in the eternal begetting of the Son in self-emptying love, identifies with the crucified Son who is his gift of salvation to the world, does this not undermine the thesis of *God*-abandonment rather than support it? Is it not more plausible to hold that God is "for" the crucified and "with" Jesus in his cry?

Balthasar insists that the will of the Father is loved by Jesus for its own sake and that Jesus does not look to anything beyond the sacrificial death he is about to suffer. This means that Ps 22, which concludes with the glorification of the suffering righteous one, cannot be used to interpret the cross of the Son. The episode in Gethsemane, says Balthasar, shows that all expectation of glorification is walled off. A narrow perspective is in view where the will of the Father, which is opposed to the will of Jesus, is loved for its own sake.[87] This study has consistently repudiated the view that Ps 22 should not be used to interpret Jesus's cry on the cross. In contrast to Balthasar's narrow perspective, a broad perspective has been proposed that incorporates the totality of Ps 22 as a comprehensive depiction of Jesus's entire life and mission. The major components of Ps 22, it has been shown, capture the major thrust of the

85. Balthasar, *Last Act*, 263; *Mysterium Paschale*, 106.

86. The presence of God is easily affirmed in extraordinary concrete events, such as Moses and the burning bush, the Exodus event, the feeding of the people in the wilderness of Sinai with quails and manna from heaven, the giving of the Torah to Moses (to observe Torah is to be molded into the people of God and thus make God present), the appointment of judges once the people have entered the land, the sending of the prophets, and Jesus's Galilean ministry. With the prophets—Jesus stands in the line of prophets—something new emerges: the prophet suffers on account of fidelity to Torah and comes to know the prophetic condition as a suffering in sympathy with the divine pathos. In the confessions of Jeremiah, God falls silent to his lament cries, yet in this silence God is not absent but present, in the sense that the prophet embodies the suffering of God before the people. The prophet experiences a loss of intensification of God's felt presence, but this is not to say that God is absent; in fact, the silence of God allows the prophet to enter more deeply into the life of God, in the sense that the prophet's suffering mirrors the suffering of God before the people. The mode of silence can be an effective mode of God's self-communication.

87. Balthasar maintains that on the Mount of Olives and in the abandonment of Christ on Calvary, what is in view is "the opposition of the two wills of the Father and Son" (*Mysterium Paschale*, 203). This very opposition is what constitutes the saving action of God, yet the resurrection reveals that in their extreme separation, Father and Son are united in love.

Gospel depiction of Jesus's mission: Jesus's increasing trouble, isolation, and rejection by his own, which gives rise to his passion predictions and the expectation of being raised from the dead—i.e., his confidence that the Father will not abandon him but will deliver him out of death; his complete self-abandonment to the cause of God and utter trust in the Father who hears all his prayers, including his cry for help on Calvary; and Jesus's entire life and mission is directed towards the glory and praise of God, hence the universal praise of God with which Ps 22 concludes aptly conveys Jesus's expectations with respect to the accomplishment of his salvific mission as the Son. The episode in the garden of Gethsemane does indicate that perfect obedience to the will of the Father defines Jesus's mission as the Son, which entails his having to bear the great apocalyptic trial of the hour and the drinking of the cup. But this defining act of perfect obedience, far from suggesting the opposition of the two wills of Father and Son, actually reveals Jesus's unity with the Father in unfathomable love, which means that any expectation of glorification on Jesus's part is not walled off. In his passion predictions, for instance, Jesus instructs his disciples that he will be put to death but in three days he will rise again; in the narrative of the transfiguration (Matt 17:1–9), Jesus instructs Peter and James and John to tell no one the vision they have witnessed until he is raised from the dead, for only then will the law (Moses) and prophecy (Elijah) be fulfilled; and at the Last Supper, Jesus says that he will "not drink again of this fruit of the wine until that day when I drink it new with you in my Father's kingdom" (Matt 26:29), which is a reference to the glory of the eschatological banquet in the age to come (cf. Isa 25:6–8; Rev 19:9). Everything Jesus says and does as the Son is for the kingdom of glory and to the praise of the Father, so why should all expectation of glory be precluded as Jesus suffers the agony of his passion in bringing his mission as the Son to completion?

I would maintain that Jesus's death should be regarded as a glorifying death in three distinct but interrelated senses. (1) Jesus glorifies the Father by his total self-abandonment to the Father in perfect obedience, so as to accomplish his messianic mission as the Son. From eternity, Jesus as the Son receives the gift of divinity from the Father and gives himself fully back to the Father in a surrender of obedience and filial thanksgiving (Eucharist). On the cross, the Son's eternal surrender of obedience to the Father in self-sacrificial love is played out on the human historical plane, so as to glorify the Father within the world and proffer salvation to the world. (2) Jesus goes to his death as an act of abandonment to the Father in perfect obedience, but the Father also abandons and empties himself in giving up his Son. In the eternal begetting of the Son, the Father abandons his own divinity, he empties himself in the letting be of the Son, which means that the Father is the eternal dynamic of total self-donation that holds nothing back. On Calvary, what comes into focus is the Father's identification with the Son, who is the Father's gift of self-donation to the world. By fulfilling his mission as the Son in his surrender of obedience to the Father, Jesus expects that the Father will glorify him as the Holy and Just One by raising him from the dead. (3) Since Jesus suffers the agony of the cross through the eternal Spirit, who is the fruit and actualization of sacrificial love between the Father and the Son, this means that the Spirit is himself the power of the resurrection. The following discussion of the Holy Spirit will develop further the view of Jesus's death as a glorifying death, which seriously calls into question the understanding that Jesus on the cross suffers extreme abandonment by, or separation from, the Father.

It is the Easter faith in Jesus's resurrection from the dead that informs the whole of the New Testament witness to the Spirit of God. Saint Paul, for example, writes that Jesus Christ is "designated Son of God in power according to the Spirit of holiness by his resurrection from the dead" (Rom 1:4; also 1 Tim 3:16; 1 Pet 3:18). The resurrection of Jesus in the power of the Spirit is God's response to his cry of abandonment on the cross. The Father not only hears the Son's lament but responds by performing a new action in the Spirit that conquers death in the full sense and reveals the Crucified One as "the Holy and Righteous One" (Acts 3:14). The risen Jesus then bestows the Spirit on his disciples by "breathing" on them (John 20:22).[88] Yet this Easter faith in the risen Jesus in no sense contradicts the claim that it was the selfsame Spirit of God that brought about Jesus's conception in the womb of Mary (Matt 1:18; Luke 1:35) and descended upon him at his baptism (Mark 1:10; Matt 3:16; Luke 3:22; John 1:32), thereby empowering him to proclaim with divine force, "The time is fulfilled, and the kingdom of God is at hand; repent and believe in the gospel" (Mark 1:15). As bearer of the eschatological Spirit of God, Jesus speaks with great authority and performs many wondrous works,[89]

---

88. Jesus's death, resurrection, ascension, and sending of the Spirit form a single theological unity in the Gospel of John.

89. Jesus's own understanding of his mission in terms of the Spirit is clearly in view in his success as an exorcist: "But if it is by the Spirit of God that I cast out demons, then the kingdom of God has come upon you" (Matt 12:28; Luke 11:20). Jesus's

yet another distinctive feature of the Gospel story is the emphasis placed on Jesus's passion predictions and his increasing isolation and rejection as he seeks to advance his mission.[90] This trajectory of steadily increasing rejection of Jesus's proclamation of the kingdom of God reaches its zenith on Calvary, where the accomplishment of his mission requires him to endure the suffering of crucifixion "through the eternal Spirit" (Heb 9:14). This implies that suffering and sacrifice are also signs of the Spirit of God, although the identity of the Spirit, unlike that of the Father and the Son, is not to be understood in terms of self-sacrificing or self-emptying love for the other. There is no self-sacrificing or self-emptying in the case of the Spirit who is the fruit of the act of sacrificial love between the Father and Son. The salvific drama on the cross between the self-sacrificing Father and the self-sacrificing Son is played out in the Spirit who is the "We" of the gift-as-given (Father) and the gift-as-received in thanksgiving (Son). The consistent references to the workings of the Spirit to be found in the New Testament writings, from the birth of the Savior to his baptism by John to his paschal mystery, exposes the need to develop a Spirit-Christology in Western theology.[91] Balthasar, for instance, acknowledges this fundamental need in the following words:

> Jesus has the Spirit in him [he is conceived by the power of
> the Spirit] and over him [the Spirit descends upon Jesus at his

exorcisms indicate that the end-time reign of God is already effective in his ministry. Jesus's unique empowerment by the Spirit is also manifest in the consciousness of inspiration, which is evident in his astonishing "But I say to you" passages in the Sermon on the Mount (Matt 5:21ff). See Dunn, *Pneumatology*, 5–8.

90. Even in the Gospel of John, as early as the second chapter (2:13–17) Jesus enters the temple and expresses zeal for his Father's house in his capacity as the divine Son. His zeal is driven by his revulsion at the blighted worship being offered at the place where God had chosen to establish his name. The episode therefore serves as a pointer to Jesus's passion, for his messianic mission from the beginning sets him on a collision course with the Jewish leaders. The narration of the cleansing of the temple in John, note, supports the synoptic narratives in Matt 9:27–31 and Mark 3:1–6.

91. See Congar, *River of Life*, 165–73; Del Colle, *Christ and the Spirit*; Kasper, *Jesus the Christ*, 250–53; Rosato, "Spirit Christology"; and Durrwell, *Holy Spirit of God*. Much of Western theology in the past was nonhistorical in the sense that Christ was seen as possessing everything required for his mission as the Son from the time of his conception in Mary's womb. What are reported in the New Testament as institutive events, especially the theophany at the baptism of Jesus and Jesus's glorification, are interpreted as simply a manifestation *for others* of a reality that is already there. This amounts to a purely ontological approach to the Christ event that fails to give any room to historical thinking and to the role played by the Holy Spirit in the development of Jesus's consciousness of his identity and mission as the Son.

baptism], and now that he is expressly the one-who-is-sent, it is through this internal—not external—communication that he is in relationship with the Father in heaven. The fact that Jesus has the Spirit in him "without measure" and yet declares that the Spirit is above him expresses his humiliation . . . in this state . . . he becomes "obedient unto death" (Phil 2:8). But the Spirit of God above him, whom he obeys (for the Father's will is expressed in the Spirit) and in whom he discerns the here-and-now form of his mission, is also in him as the one who "drives" him . . . So the Spirit in him and above him is the manifest presence of his divine mission.[92]

It is clear from this citation that Jesus's attitude of total openness and complete receptivity to the Father, which allows him to perform the will of the Father for the good of Israel and the world, cannot be thought of apart from Jesus's personal relation to the Spirit. It is the Spirit who shows Jesus the Father's will, which constitutes his mission as the Son, and it is the Spirit in him who drives him to undertake and complete his mission. The relation between the "I" of Jesus the Son and the "Thou" whom he calls Father always points to their "We" (the Spirit), who is the internal principle of God's self-communication, that is, the opening of God outward to creation and history.[93]

The integral role of the Spirit in the Christ event is strongly reinforced by the writings of the biblical scholar François-Xavier Durrwell, who paints a picture of the Spirit as the "divine womb" from which Jesus is born Word of God in the world. The Spirit is the agent of every manifestation of God in the world; the Spirit is the "mouth" through which the Word is poured out into the world. "The Spirit has spoken through the prophets, he has spoken through Christ; he is not the word, he is the one through whom it is transmitted: 'He will not be speaking as from himself . . . all he tells you will be taken from what is mine'" (cf. John 16:13).[94] Like Balthasar, Durrwell maintains that Jesus's intimate knowledge of the Father's will should not be assumed simply on the basis of the ontological

92. Balthasar, *Dramatis Personae*, 520–21.

93. Kasper, *God of Jesus Christ*, 227–28. The Spirit as the internal presupposition of the communicability of God outside himself is reminiscent of the idea that was dear to many spiritual writers of the French school; namely, the Spirit as the end of the processions from the Father and the Son has no intra-divine fruitfulness of its own, hence it is made fruitful beyond God in creation, in the Incarnation, and in the sanctification of humankind. See Congar, *Lord and Giver*, 67, 72n2.

94. Durrwell, *Holy Spirit of God*, 1–2.

fact that Jesus is the eternal Word in human flesh, for there can be no communication of the Father's will to Jesus without the workings of the Holy Spirit. Durrwell's reflections are quite distinct from the thought of Balthasar, however, when we come to consider his portrayal of the life of the eternal Trinity. Durrwell says that while the Father is the principle of movement within the eternal Trinity, we should not fail to appreciate that *the Father eternally begets the Son in the Spirit.* When we say that the Spirit proceeds from the Father and (or through) the Son, this must not be taken to mean that the Spirit is not at the beginning of the divine activity: "He is at the beginning of the trinitarian movement of which the Father is the principle, he is also the final seal of divine perfection."[95] That the Spirit "proceeds" from the Father (cf. John 15:26) implies that the Spirit has its source in the Father but is not "begotten" by the Father as is the Son. Yet the Spirit's relationship to the Son is nevertheless profoundly intimate, for the Spirit "proceeds in the begetting of the Son, he is the Spirit of the Father in his fatherhood."[96] Now given that the Spirit proceeds from the Father whose mystery consists in begetting the Son, but the Spirit himself is not the Son, Durrwell concludes that the Spirit must be this begetting. The following paragraph captures the essence of his argument:

> On the one hand the Father is therefore the beginning and the Son is the end to which nothing is added; but the Spirit is at the beginning, in the Father who begets; he is at the end in the One Begotten. While proceeding from them, he does not come after the Father or after the Son, for it is in him that they are Father and Son. He is in the fatherhood of the Father in whom he has his source, and in the sonship of the Son from whom he wells up. The mystery of the resurrection of Jesus is an illustration of this: the Spirit is himself the power of the resurrection which enables Christ to be the channel of the Spirit.[97]

With respect to the world, Durrwell asserts that the Spirit was already active in the world before the event of the incarnation of the Son—the Spirit prepares the creation for the incarnation—however, the Spirit was not present as he is in the eternal Trinity. It is only with the unique event of Jesus's death, as a passover from this world to the

95. Durrwell, *Holy Spirit of God*, 56.

96. Durrwell, *Holy Spirit of God*, 140.

97. Durrwell, *Holy Spirit of God*, 146.

Father, which takes place "through the eternal Spirit" (Heb 9:14), that the *eternal begetting of the Son was fully "accomplished" within creation.*[98] And since the Spirit is this begetting of the Son by the Father, then the death of Jesus, as a glorifying death, emerges as *the fullness of the Spirit within creation.* Such a perspective calls into question the interpretation of Jesus's cry on the cross as "separation" from the Father, that is, *God-abandonment.* For when the death of Jesus is affirmed as taking place in and through the eternal Spirit, so that the Father's eternal begetting of the Son in the Spirit is fully accomplished within creation—the crucified Son is the "new creation" in person—the emphasis falls very much on the ineffable communion of the Father and the Son in their Spirit. Hence what is affirmed is God's presence, not absence, on the cross. The event of the cross emerges as something other for the Spirit than for the Son or the Father. For the Son, the cross is the enactment of perfect obedience to the Father—the Son possesses divinity in the mode of receptivity and thanksgiving—which entails his being forsaken by God into the hands of evildoers who execute their ungodly and brutal judgment upon him; while for the Father, the cross is the act of forsaking his beloved Son as his gift of salvation to a sinful and evil world—the Father possesses divinity in the mode of donation. The Spirit, on the other hand, suffers neither the grief of forsakenness nor the grief of forsaking but is the *presence of God* on the cross—the Spirit possesses divinity in the mode of the communion of mutual self-sacrificing love between the Father and the Son.[99] The identities of Father and Son both involve the eternal act of self-emptying love, but there is no self-emptying in the case of the Spirit who is in the fatherhood of the Father in whom he has his source and in the sonship of the Son from whom he wells up. What is revealed on the cross is the one single truth of the Son in the Father, and of the Father in the Son, and of the Spirit as the actuality of eternal self-emptying sacrificial love for the other, which brings into existence "the things that do not exist" (Rom 4:17). The contention that Jesus's cry should not be interpreted as

98. Durrwell, *Holy Spirit*, 141.

99. D. Lyle Dabney in his discussion of the cross as Trinitarian kenosis of God concludes that Jesus's passion should be thought of as "the sacrifice of the Father, the forsakenness of the Son, and the abnegation of the Spirit" (Dabney, "Naming the Spirit," 57). While Dabney acknowledges that the Spirit does not abandon Jesus on the cross—he talks of the Spirit as the presence of God on the cross—nonetheless he proceeds to uphold the notion of self-emptying ("abnegation") of the Spirit. Durrwell reaches quite a different conclusion: the death of Jesus is the "fullness" of the Spirit within creation.

God-abandonment, which is integral to the argument developed in the previous chapter 3, finds strong support in Durrwell's biblically based reflections on the Holy Spirit's role in the paschal mystery of Christ.

Kenosis as a Doctrinal Theory Revisited: Refutation of the Theory of Surrendered Divine Attributes

In light of the foregoing discussion regarding the interpersonal model of the Trinity as the eternal dynamic of self-emptying love between divine persons, it is necessary to revisit and critique the notion of kenosis in the theological tradition. As a doctrinal theory, kenosis was occasioned by the introduction into Lutheran dogmatics of a distinction between Christ's "two states," namely, his state of humiliation succeeded by his state of exaltation. The doctrine of the two states was introduced to give some vitality to the categories of classical Christology, which were perceived to be static. Chemitz and others explored the state of humiliation in terms of kenosis: the life of Christ was a state of emptiedness. But it was presumed that the eternal Word cannot have been emptied in the incarnation, hence a divine humiliation was not affirmed; instead, the kenosis was attributed to Christ's humanity, which was seen as renouncing the divine properties of majesty. The German theology of the nineteenth century offered a new interpretation of "self-emptying" in Christ in an endeavor to bring a new focus to the christological problem. The basic question that had occupied the minds of theologians for so long had been: Given the fullness of divinity in the person of Christ, how can his genuine humanity be upheld? The question of the union of divinity and humanity in the person of Christ was constructed in quite different terms in nineteenth-century German theology: Given the integrity of Christ's humanity, how is it possible to speak of his divinity? The humanity of Christ became the pivot of reconstruction.[100]

---

100. Hegel and Schleiermacher were the great figures that profoundly influenced the development of German theology in the nineteenth century. In addition to Hegel and Schleiermacher, the works of David Friedrich Strauss (*Life of Jesus*) and Ludwig Feuerbach (*Essence of Christianity*) were also influential in the rethinking of the christological problem. Straus held that it is inappropriate for the absolute to manifest itself in a single individual and thus proposed that the Gospel portrait of Christ is mythological. And Feuerbach questioned whether the idea of God is not itself altogether a projection of the human consciousness.

The Lutheran Gottfried Thomasius provided the most impres-
sive form of kenotic theory.[101] With respect to the state of humiliation,
Thomasius maintained that the person of the God-man is *completely*
given in the act of the incarnation, but it works itself out in the course
of a gradual development: "As consciousness concerning his innermost
nature arises for the growing and developing child Jesus, there opens up
for him at the same time the consciousness of his sonship to God, of
his relationship to the Father, and of his vocation as the redeemer of the
world."[102] There is a process of growing consciousness concerning the personal unity of humanity and divinity in his person, which is completely
given at the beginning. The process of growing consciousness in the God-
man is not conceived of as "a cumulative penetration of the two [natures]
. . . it only brings what is existent to consciousness."[103] The whole life of
Christ, as the divine-human continuation of the incarnation, is at once
"revelation" and "divesting."[104] It is revelation of the "immanent" divine
attributes, such as absolute power (i.e., the freedom of self-determina-
tion), truth (i.e., knowledge of the incarnate one concerning his own
essence and the will of the Father), holiness, and love. These attributes the
incarnate Son did not surrender, for they are inseparable from the essence
of God; nor did Christ withhold their use, for they shine throughout his
redemptive mission as recorded in the Gospels.[105] The act of humiliation is not only revelation but also divesting of those divine properties
that are "relative" to the world, such as omnipotence, omniscience, and
omnipresence.[106] The Son did not actively rule the world as he walked the
earth as a human being; the only lordship he exercised was the ethical
one of truth and love in his redemptive mission. Christ, furthermore,
was not the all-knowing human being, for his knowledge reached only as

---

101. The most extreme form of kenoticism was given by Wolfgang Gess, who contended that the incarnation involved not merely the laying aside of certain attributes of
the Logos but the eternal Son actually changing himself into a man. Other kenoticists
of the period, besides Thomasius and Gess, were Ebrard and Martensen. See Bruce,
Humiliation of Christ, 133–63.

102. Welch, *God and Incarnation*, 65.

103. Welch, *God and Incarnation*, 65.

104. The translator has rendered the German *Entäusserung* as "divesting" rather
than the usual "emptying." Thomasius rejects the idea of "emptying" (*Entleerung*) in favor of the idea of laying aside or divesting, which the word *Entäusserung* more directly
indicates (Welch, *God and Incarnation*, 19).

105. Welch, *God and Incarnation*, 67–68.

106. Welch, *God and Incarnation*, 70–71.

far as his redemptive mission required. And since the Son entered into a historical mode of existence, it cannot be said that he existed outside the limitations of space. "Accordingly, the humiliation is for us not a mere disguise, but an actual kenosis of the designated divine attributes, and surely not merely of their use but of their possession."[107] In this view, humiliation is indeed God's own act, but now the incarnation is conceived as the partial renouncing of divinity, so that the result of kenosis is "dedivinized divinity."[108] The fundamental problem with Thomasius's position is that it lacks a Trinitarian framework, where Christ's emptying of himself to take on the "form of a servant" (Phil 2:6–8) is interpreted from the standpoint of the "selflessness" of the divine persons in the inner-Trinitarian life of self-sacrificial love (as discussed above). In the utter powerlessness and weakness of the Crucified One, the full undiminished divinity of God is revealed and is at work. Thomasius's proposition that a distinction be made between the immanent and relative properties of divinity is ultimately "wholly unworkable."[109]

The developments in German theology flowed on to British theology, where kinetic theory is represented by theologians such as Peter T. Forsyth and Hugh R. Mackintosh. Forsyth is critical of a Greek metaphysic of being, which has traditionally been employed to expound the mystery of the incarnation. God is not God physically but morally, which is to say that the nature of divinity is Holy Love. "There lies the region, the nature, and the norm of its omnipotence."[110] The science of faith amounts to a metaphysic of ethics, for the moral is regarded as the real. The purpose of a world created by a holy God must be holiness, and salvation has to do with participating in God's own holiness. Some metaphysic is involved with respect to salvation in Christ, but it is "a metaphysic of the conscience."[111] Christ revealed that holiness *was* the divine power, that his omnipotence was not of the kingdom of nature but of grace. Forsyth is critical of Thomasius's kenotic theory and maintains that the relative attributes could not be parted with entirely and should be thought of as latent and potential. "Here we have not so much the renunciation of attributes, nor their conscious possession and concealment, as the *retraction*

---

107. Welch, *God and Incarnation*, 71.

108. Lewis, *Between Cross and Resurrection*, 171.

109. Balthasar, *Mysterium Paschale*, 32.

110. Forsyth, *Person and Place*, 313.

111. Forsyth, *Person and Place*, 222.

of their mode of being from actual to potential. The stress falls on the mode of existence of these qualities, and not on their presence or absence."[112] Instead of speaking of certain divine attributes as renounced, Forsyth suggests that we speak of a new mode of their being.

Ross H. Mackintosh proposes a view of the self-emptying of God in Christ that reinforces the thought of Forsyth. Mackintosh laments that christological relations that are in essence ethical and personal have been too much expressed in mechanical terms. He takes particular aim at the term "nature" (*physis*), which is not an ethical word at all. The problem with nonethical realities is that they are unable to establish the true unity of Christ, hence "we are not surprised to find that Godhead and manhood are contemplated here as being in essence so disparate, so utterly unrelated and heterogeneous, that a miracle of sheer omnipotence is needed to unite them."[113] Love is the driving force of the incarnation and gives it its significance, which means that ethical and personal terms are needed to explicate the Christ event. The categories employed in the incarnation, as Forsyth had argued, must be "genuinely moralized."[114] What is required is "a metaphysic of the conscience, in which not substance but Holy Love is supreme."[115] The essence of God is holy love, which is immutable. Once proper attention is given to Christ's life on earth as unequivocally human, it is difficult to avoid kenoticism in some form. The divine life in Christ finds expression through human faculty, "with a self-consciousness and activity mediated by His human *milieu*."[116] We must not look for the divine side by side with the human; rather, we must discern the divine *within* the human. No life of God in human flesh is possible, moreover, without some self-adjustment of deity, without a real surrender of the glory of deity in the life of Christ: "We are faced by a Divine self-reduction which entailed obedience, temptation, and death."[117] Mackintosh refutes Thomasius's distinction with respect to relative and immanent attributes of God and argues that the divine relations of omnipotence, omniscience, and the like, are as essential to the created order as righteousness and grace: "We cannot think away the relative attributes of God without at the

112. Forsyth, *Person and Place*, 308; emphasis added.

113. Mackintosh, *Person of Jesus Christ*, 214.

114. Mackintosh, *Person of Jesus Christ*, 472.

115. Mackintosh, *Person of Jesus Christ*, 472.

116. Mackintosh, *Person of Jesus Christ*, 470.

117. Mackintosh, *Person of Jesus Christ*, 470.

same time thinking away the relation."[118] No attributes of God are parted with in the incarnation, but they are *transposed*; that is, they function in new ways, they assume new forms of activity, "readjusted to the new condition of the Subject."[119] In the same manner as Forsyth, Mackintosh conceives of Christ as possessing all the attributes of God in the form of potency rather than full actuality. With regard to knowledge, for instance, Christ had divine knowledge by virtue of his relation to the Father, but his knowledge was limited to what was essential for his vocation as the Son. Since the life of divinity is mediated by Christ's humanity, "it is only by degrees that the full meaning of His relationship to the Father, with its eternal implicates, can have broken on Jesus' mind."[120] In Christ the deity is not omniscient, omnipresent, and omnipotent, as God absolute must be, but is "perfect Love and Holiness and Freedom in terms of perfect humanity."[121]

Unlike the first Lutheran kenoticists, Forsyth and Mackintosh are clear that God, not the human nature of Christ, is the subject of kenosis; and unlike the nineteenth-century German theologians they seek a self-emptying that is neither partial (Thomasius) nor so absolute (Gess) that it is no longer *God* who is in Christ. The guiding idea in their reformulation of the christological problem is that *the self-retraction of God from actuality to potentiality does not connote the cessation of deity*. With this idea the Scots anticipate further conceptual advance (e.g., Karl Barth) that will identify humiliation with the fullest expression of God's fullness. Yet there are defects here as well. The Scots have a revulsion of ontology

118. Mackintosh, *Person of Jesus Christ*, 476.

119. Mackintosh, *Person of Jesus Christ*, 477. This understanding is not unlike that of Bulgakov, who says that the kenosis consists in the change of form (*morphē*) of God. The humiliation refers not to the nature (*ousia*) but to the *morphē*, to the divine form, which Christ removes from himself in the incarnation. To possess the divine nature is also to possess the divine form of being, and it is this form or norm of divine life (i.e., glory) that Christ renounces in order to take on the form of a servant. God has the sovereignty to change for himself the mode of the living out of the fullness of his unchangeable essence (Bulgakov, *Lamb of God*, 213–46). What the kenosis expresses is the general relation of God to the world. The creation of the world is a kenotic act of God, and this kenosis is revealed in the humiliation of the Word in the event of the incarnation. Bulgakov repudiates the notion that the fullness of the divine life with its "properties" is present and actualized in Christ from the outset of the incarnation and argues instead that the divine humanity matures or progresses during the course of Jesus's earthly life, which culminates on the cross.

120. Mackintosh, *Person of Jesus Christ*, 481.

121. Mackintosh, *Person of Jesus Christ*, 486.

and insist that Chalcedon's ontological formula of the two natures in Christ must yield to the moral qualities of God's self-emptying. But by refusing ontology, they are refusing to "think" the faith and to seek an "understanding" of its deepest mysteries.[122] What is more, because the Scots think sequentially, so that the Son's descent of self-emptying (*kenosis*) in incarnation culminates in the ascent of exaltation (*plerosis*) in his resurrection, the divine attributes of power are resumed by Christ and the kenosis becomes a past episode. The form of the servant gives place again to the form of God, and the form of his servitude is left behind. "Thus are betrayed vestiges of the old immutability, an assumption that only in the renunciation, and not the fullest exercise, of Godness is it possible for God to be subject to our pain and death."[123] Contrary to the Gospel of John, the self-humiliation of God in Christ is not affirmed as the fullest self-manifestation of God. This robs Good Friday and Easter Saturday, and all that went before, of their mystery, as God's "with us" evaporates in the attempt to offer a better conceptual framework for reflection on the Gospel story. The old antithesis of divine and human, far from being overcome, is unwittingly reinforced. It is not inappropriate to speak of God's self-emptying in the person of Christ, "but only if it is understood in such a way as to be an *expression* rather than a 'retraction' of his deity."[124] The eternal Son humbled himself, but in his self-emptying in Jesus Christ he did not cease to be who he is. The interpersonal model of the Trinity as the eternal event of self-emptying love provides us with an effective conceptual framework for fathoming the kenosis of the Word of God in the event of the incarnation.

It was left to Barth to refute the theory of surrendered attributes, whether the partial self-emptying of Thomasius, or the absolute self-emptying of divinity postulated by Gess, or the self-retraction from actuality to potentiality suggested by Forsyth and Mackintosh. Barth broke new ground by talking of the fullness realized in that emptiedness itself, not merely in its aftermath.[125] The novelty of Barth's approach lies in that he reflected on the fullness of God made manifest in the very life of the incarnate Son: *the self-emptying of God in the event of the Incarnation is regarded as an expression, rather than retraction, of the fullness of*

122. Lewis, *Between Cross and Resurrection*, 174.

123. Lewis, *Between Cross and Resurrection*, 175.

124. Gunton, *Yesterday and Today*, 172.

125. Barth, *Church Dogmatics*, IV/1:179–80.

divinity.[126] In order to appreciate this, Barth insists that we begin with
a conception of God based not on an abstract ontology, an externally
determined metaphysic of pure, static essence, but on the grounds of
revelation; that is to say, the actuality of God's dynamic, triune being as
self-disclosed in the "event" that is Jesus Christ. Barth asserts that the
meaning of true deity can be learned only from what took place in the
event of Jesus Christ, that to dare to speak of God's identity with this man
"who was born like all of us in time, who lived and thought and spoke,
who could be tempted and suffer and die and who was in fact tempted,
and suffered and died" is something bold and astonishing. Christian theology must not allow itself to be centered on an "abstract God" and an
"abstract human being."[127] It is the person portrayed in the Gospels that
Barth is interested in. The point of departure for theology is the question
that Jesus addresses to us: Who do you say that I am? By listening to
the Gospel story—this is a methodology of hearing, as Bonhoeffer put
it—of the scandal of Christ's cross and burial, which is God's own way
of defining what true humanity and true divinity really are, we allow
our preconceptions of what the divine and human possibilities are to
be challenged and subverted. We must start with revelation, with God's
own self-revealing in Jesus Christ, for the one who precedes all human
presuppositions and theological inquiry is self-interpreting.[128]

For Barth, when we hear the word of God's self-revelation in the
person of Jesus Christ, we cannot affirm any disjunction or discrepancy
between God's "being" and God's "act." What God does is not separate
from what God is; rather, God's identity is constituted by God's action in
history.[129] God's act in becoming temporal, carnal, and vulnerable corresponds to the way God always is in his triune being.[130] Since God eternally

126. For a comprehensive treatment of Barth's reflections, see Jüngel, *God's Being.*

127. Barth, *Church Dogmatics*, IV/1:183, 186.

128. Barth, against liberal Protestantism influenced by the Enlightenment's anthropological emphasis, does not start with religious experience or moral values, nor
intellectual assumptions or cultural worldviews. The starting point is God's own self-
revealing Word in the temporal event of Jesus Christ.

129. See Barth *Church Dogmatics*, II/1:257–72. Note how Karl Rahner followed
Karl Barth on this fundamental point. Rahner talks of God who goes out of himself
in his fullness, subjecting himself to history, so that God expresses himself when he
empties himself, otherwise his humanity would amount to a masquerade (Rahner,
Foundations of Christian Faith, 136–37). In a Barthian or Rahnerian framework, God's
merciful love towards sinners is never regarded as the result of the cross of Christ but
as its cause and source.

130. Balthasar thinks in exactly the same way as Barth, although unlike Barth he

makes space for time, we should not think of temporality as eternity's polar opposite: "There is a way of being temporal, involved in the flux of events and happenings as a subject of history, which is not the negation but the expression of God's own manner of existing."[131] This movement of God's being from above to below, which is portrayed in terms of God's "one primal decision" with regard to the election of grace in Jesus Christ, the Elect One, cannot be thought of apart from the "human movement from below to above."[132] The encounter between God and humanity, which has its origin in the movement of God's being, is therefore first and foremost the encounter between the electing God and elected humanity, which is an event in Jesus Christ. "We cannot conceive ourselves and the world without first conceiving this man with God as the witness of the gracious purpose with which God willed and created ourselves and the world and in which we may exist in it and with it."[133] The primal decision of God to go into the "far country"—the pretemporal slaying of the Lamb of God as the foundation of the world (Rev 13:8)—with the view of bringing sinners home to God, is not something forced upon or foreign to God but God's free decision. And since this free decision to venture into the far country for the sake of our salvation (i.e., homecoming) is an act of boundless ineffable love, then God's primal decision, realized in history, allows us to perceive the being of God as "the One who loves in freedom."[134] That Barth allows his understanding of the divine nature to be wholly informed by the historical event of Jesus Christ is clear from the following citation:

> What is, then, the divine nature? It is the free love, the omnipotent mercy, the holy patience of the Father, Son and Holy Spirit . . . What does it mean that "God was in Christ" (2 Cor 5:19)? It obviously means that all that God is . . . is characterized by the fact that He is everything divine, not for Himself only, but also, in His Son, for the sake of man and for him. Col 2:9 tells us: "In him dwelleth all the fullness of the godhead bodily." Therefore

sees the life of the eternal Trinity as an eternal act of self-emptying love. For Balthasar, the kenosis of the Son of God in the event of Jesus Christ reveals the eternal kenosis in the very life of God. Barth, in contrast, does not talk of an eternal kenosis in the life of the immanent Trinity; only in relation to Jesus Christ does Barth talk of God's self-emptying or humiliation.

131. Lewis, *Between Cross and Resurrection*, 189.

132. Barth, *Church Dogmatics*, IV/2:32.

133. Barth, *Church Dogmatics*, IV/2:33.

134. Barth, *Church Dogmatics*, II/1:257. This perspective is shared by Balthasar.

the sovereignty of God dwells in His creaturely dependence as the Son of Man, the eternity of God in His temporal uniqueness, the omnipresence of God in His spatial limitation, the omnipotence of God in His weakness, the glory of God in His passibility and mortality, the holiness and righteousness of God in His adamic bondage and fleshniness—in short, the unity and totality of the divine which is His own original essence in His humanity.[135]

This is the freedom of God, to be not just our partner in eternity but our fellow creature in time, fulfilling deity within the bounds of a truly human life. God's freedom is not freedom *from* but freedom toward or *for* humankind; it is a freedom of intimate involvement with time and history, so that eternity and immutability encompass, rather than preclude, temporality and change and mortality. For Barth, divine immutability consists in the fact that God continues to be what God always is from all eternity, while being subjected to change and opposition in time and history.[136] To recognize the divine in the human is to acknowledge that there can be no evading the child in the crib at Bethlehem, the growing in wisdom and stature, the being tempted in the wilderness, the constant need for Jesus to pray to the Father, the episode in the garden of Gethsemane, and the genuine suffering in helplessness on the cross of Golgotha.[137] God's self-emptying in the event of the incarnation is regarded by Barth as an expression of the dynamic nature of God's triune being, which freely communicates itself to the non-divine other in time and history, so that we mortal sinners might be ontologically "transferred" (Col 1:13) from the reign of death to the kingdom of life in fellowship with God.

The thought of Barth has the great merit of demonstrating that the self-emptying of God in the event of Jesus Christ does not involve a

---

135. Barth, *Church Dogmatics*, IV/2:86.

136. God's being, as brought to expression by revelation, is a relationally structured being. The unified being of God is differentiated into three different "modes of being"—with the concept "mode of being" Barth takes up the patristic term "mode of subsistence" to replace the misleading concept of "person." God reveals himself as revealer (the being of the Father, by virtue of which God the Father is the Father of the Son), as revelation (the being of the Son, by virtue of which God the Son is the Son of the Father), and as revealedness (the being of the Spirit, by virtue of which God the Spirit is the Spirit of the Father and the Son). God is therefore the subject, the predicate, and the object of the event of revelation. As the mutual self-giving of the three modes of God's being, God's being is the pure event of love and thus may not be conceived as something abstract. See Jüngel, *God's Being*, 37–42.

137. Cf. Novello, *Passionate Deification*, 166–203.

self-restriction on the part of God; instead, we are required to acknowledge the fullness of deity dwelling bodily in Jesus Christ (Col 2:9). Barth turns classical Christology on its head by *attributing humiliation not to the human nature of Jesus Christ but to his divinity*, and exaltation not to divinity but to his, and therefore our, humanity. The attributing of humiliation to divinity means that in the person of Jesus Christ, God is "exposed to all the menaces and perils, the pain and opposition, which reciprocity with creatures represents. God risks, from the beginning, the threat of nonbeing and negation."[138] All human ideas of divinity are contradicted by the revelation which is the scandal of the cross, according to which God, in the person of Christ, embraces suffering and death while remaining God. The gospel of Christ declares this as an actuality and therefore challenges all human ideas concerning the character and being of God. The mystery of God in Christ must be allowed to stand: "In the undiminished humanity of Jesus, the whole power and glory of God are made present to us."[139]

Barth's refutation of the theory of surrendered attributes and his defense of the New Testament declaration that the fullness of deity dwells bodily in Jesus Christ (Col 2:9) find support in the main thesis of this study concerning a theological interpretation of Jesus's cry on the cross. According to the proposed thesis, it will be recalled, there are both divine and human dimensions to Jesus's cry, which accords with the view that the fullness of divinity in Christ is mediated and attested by his humanity. The divine dimension of Jesus's cry reveals the unfathomable depths of the divine pathos in relation to the world: that is, the crucified Jesus, out of God's ineffable love and boundless mercy and sovereign freedom, bears and internalizes in his tortured and broken body our sinfulness and rebellion against God—in his vicarious suffering "for us" is revealed the humiliation of the Son of God. This divine dimension of Jesus's cry is inseparable, though, from its human dimension according to the tradition of the righteous sufferer, where God is portrayed as hearing the lamenter's cry for help, as being in solidarity "with" the afflicted one, and as acting to deliver the afflicted one from the forces of evil that encircle him—what is in view here is the exaltation of the Son of Man. In the divine Son's condescension to the human temporal plane, humiliation is attributed not to his humanity but to his divinity, for only in this way can

138. Lewis, *Between Cross and Resurrection*, 191.

139. Balthasar, *Mysterium Paschale*, 33.

we credibly affirm the Pauline statement that the divine Son "emptied himself, taking the form of a servant" (Phil 2:7). According to the latter biblical text, the kenosis consists in a change of form: Christ was in the "form of God" but emptied himself to take the "form of a servant." By taking the form of a servant, we are to understand that what changed was not the immutable divine nature but the mode of the living out of the depths of the divine essence.[140]

The Son of God humbled himself to the extreme point of dying on a cross, yet it is precisely in his sheer humility, utter weakness, and perfect obedience to the Father, that we see the fullness of divinity dwelling bodily in him. We can think of the depths of the divine essence dwelling in the incarnate Son in the following ways:

1. The sovereignty of God should not be thought of as God holding on to what is proper to God, that is, as God dwelling in self-contained eternal perfection (aseity), totally removed and detached from the world. We must steer clear of the "monarchical" view of God as one-sidedly transcendent, separate from, and over and above the world. In light of the event of the incarnation of the eternal Word, God's sovereignty is to be understood in terms of *God's gift of giving away the divine life in perfect freedom*, which makes possible the divine economy of creation, redemption, and sanctification: "God sent forth his Son . . . so that we might receive adoption as sons" (Gal 4:4–5); "For God so loved the world that he gave his only Son . . . that the world might be saved through him" (John 3:16–17).

2. The omnipotence of God is the power by which God creates the world and continues to uphold it (God's creative action), the power through which God discloses the truth about his abiding relationship to the world (God's revelatory action), and the power through which God authenticates this truth in the certainty of faith and elevates human being to union with God (God's inspiring and perfecting action). The omnipotence of God expressed in these three types of divine action is a perfection of the Trinity, for it pertains to the inner-Trinitarian event of self-emptying love between the divine persons: the Father's total self-donation of his divinity in the begetting of the Son; the Son's perfect reception of the gift of divinity, which includes his filial thanksgiving (Eucharist); and the

140. Cf. Bulgakov, *Lamb of God*, 221–22.

Spirit breathed forth as the communion and joy of the mutual love of Father and Son. In this Trinitarian perspective, the omnipotence of God is understood in terms of absolute love (1 John 4:8, 16). Hence it becomes apparent in what manner it can be said that the *omnipotence of God dwells in Jesus's powerlessness and humility on the cross*. The weakness of Christ crucified is the "power of God and wisdom of God" (1 Cor 1:24).

3. In the traditional teaching regarding God's immutability and eternity, God has been said to be above time and immune from change. But God's eternity cannot be interpreted as mere timelessness or atemporality, for eternity is the creative ground of a temporal world. Barth underscores this fundamental point when he says that the covenant is the internal basis of creation, and creation is the external basis of the covenant. Eternity and immutability encompass, rather than preclude, temporality and change and mortality. The immutability of God means that God continues to be what God always is from all eternity—"the One who loves in freedom"—while being subjected to change and opposition in the person of Jesus Christ. God transcends the ravages of time in the sense that God remains constant and faithful, is not overwhelmed by suffering, and his love for the world does not diminish irrespective of what happens in the temporal realm, all of which is essential to underpinning a firm hope in God. Yet the struggles and sufferings of the world must be real for God, too, since the covenant implies that God has ultimate concern for his creation. The theological category of the divine pathos underscores God's genuine involvement, concern, and care for humanity and the world. While God is eternal and perfect, there is a real sense in which God's being is in becoming "all in all" (1 Cor 15:28). That *God's eternity dwells in Christ's temporal uniqueness* is affirmed by St. Paul when he writes: "For he has made known to us . . . the mystery of his will, according to his purpose which he set forth in Christ as a plan for the fullness of time, to unite all things in him, things in heaven and things on earth" (Eph 1:9–10).

4. With regard to the omnipresence of God, the event of the incarnation of the eternal Word does not mean that God ceases to be universally present to the world, upholding his creation. During the life and messianic mission of Christ, God continues to be present everywhere. But in order to plausibly affirm this position, it is

necessary to conceive of the divine nature of Jesus in terms of his modus of being related to the Father in unfathomable love, in the Spirit, who rests upon Jesus in eschatological fullness. Only then can it be said that God was not only wholly in Jesus but also wholly outside the flesh of Jesus. That the *omnipresence of God dwells in Jesus's spatial limitation*, yet at the same time God continues to be present everywhere beyond Jesus's bodiliness, enables us to relate the history of every single human being—past, present, and future—to the special history of Jesus Christ, the Savior of the world, who is the "way" (John 14:6) to the Father.

5. The pathos of God revealed in Jesus's life and mission, which culminates in his passion, takes issue with the traditional notion of divine *apatheia* associated with classical theism. God is not wholly external to the historical realm but is affected by what happens in the world and responds out of the depths of the divine pathos. The glory of God is revealed in the *way in which* God is involved with the world and is unwavering in his redemptive purposes. In the redemptive death of Christ, we see the extraordinary way in which God has transformed the grief of the world into the joy of the new creation. With Jesus's death on the cross, which takes place through the Spirit, the eternal begetting of the Son is fully accomplished within creation. And since the begetting of the Son by the Father takes place in the Spirit, the death of Jesus emerges as the fullness of the Spirit within creation. Jesus's death, as a passover from this world of death to the Father, is a glorifying death, hence it is perfectly legitimate to say that the *glory of God dwells in Jesus's possibility and mortality*. In John's Gospel in particular, we find this understanding that the sufferings themselves are a glorification: "The hour has come for the Son of Man to be glorified" (John 12:23). The glory properly belongs to the finishing of the work which the Father has given the Son to do: "It is finished" (John 19:30). The narration of the transfiguration of Jesus in the Synoptic Gospels, as well as Jesus's passion predictions, also point to Jesus's glorification through his sufferings. The riches and power of God are concealed in the weakness and poverty of Christ on the cross, and it is only with the raising of Christ from the dead that the power of God is labeled "glory" (Rom 6:4). At first glance, the crucifixion of Christ presents as a victory for the forces of darkness in the world, but the resurrection of Christ reveals the

triumph of the glory of God over the forces of evil: "For it is the God who said, 'Let light shine out of the darkness,' who has shone in our hearts to give the light of the knowledge of the glory of God in the face of Christ" (2 Cor 4:6).

6. With regard to the holiness of God, it is not so much an attribute of God as a reference to God's essential nature. "Holy, holy, holy is the Lord of hosts" (Isa 6:3). Thrice holy, holiness, accordingly, is the background for all else declared about God. In relation to the people of God, holiness refers both to the way God is distinct from the people and yet is steadfastly committed to their consecration as the people of God: "You shall be holy; for I the Lord your God am holy" (Lev 19:2; 1 Pet 1:16). Holiness is a synonym for God's transcendence, but God always remains related in his transcendence, which is manifested by the way in which God displays pathos towards his people: steadfast in love, always merciful and compassionate, slow to anger, long-suffering yet not overwhelmed by suffering, committed to justice and righteousness, unwavering in his redemptive purposes and promises, and having ultimate concern for Israel and the world. What the holiness of God brings into focus is the *relationship of reciprocity*: the covenant speaks not only of the requirement of commitment to God on the part of the people but of God's steadfast engagement to a sinful people. The discrepancy between God and the world is overcome not in humankind but in God, who participates in the predicament of his people, internalizes and bears their sinfulness, and suffers with them when the calamity of judgment strikes them, so as to redeem them and offer newness of life. Redemption, in this view, is grounded in a true communion of natures between God and the world—which is especially highlighted in the suffering of the prophet, who embodies the pathos of God. With respect to the event of the incarnation of the eternal Word, this perspective compels us to acknowledge that Jesus assumes not the "neutral" flesh of Adam prior to the first human transgression but adamic flesh; that is, flesh burdened with the consequences of Adam's sin, namely, suffering and mortality (not guilt). Since it is clear in Scripture that God's holiness emerges in the historical context of God's steadfast engagement with a rebellious people, in the case of Jesus the incarnate Word we are led to affirm that *God's holiness dwells in Jesus's adamic flesh*. In this way, Jesus's holiness

is affirmed as an "involved holiness." No Stoic notion of *apatheia* should be superimposed on the Savior so as to enforce a particular metaphysical conception of his divinity, which bears no relationship to his humanity.

Clarifications on God's Suffering in Relation to the World

The previous section has elaborated on ways in which the New Testament statement regarding the fullness of divinity dwelling bodily in the crucified Christ can be thought, in keeping with the lines of argument developed in the course of this study. It will be appropriate in bringing this chapter to a close to offer some important points of clarification on one particular aspect of the divine pathos in relation to the world, namely, the suffering of God. Given the proposition that the birthing of a new creation is inseparable from the suffering of God, this topic deserves some extra attention, not least because it seems to pose a real problem to the minds of many believers who find it difficult to ascribe suffering to divinity. Christ may have suffered in his humanity, they say, but in no wise can it be said that he suffered in his divinity, which is not becoming of God. This amounts to a form of docetism, which continues to exert its influence in the Christian churches today. There is also resistance, of course, from those who continue to adhere to classical theism, according to which God is pure act, so that in him there is neither passivity nor potency. God acts upon the creation, but there is no way in which the creation can affect God. No reciprocity at all is acknowledged in the God-world relation, which is a purely asymmetrical relation, in which the world is quite external to God. Therefore, given these persistent views on the doctrine of God's impassibility, it will be worthwhile to clarify in what ways it can intelligibly be held that God suffers in relation to the created world, which is indispensable to a credible Christian theodicy.

An appropriate place to begin is with the interpersonal model of the Trinity expounded by both Bulgakov and Balthasar, both of whom were discussed earlier. These two thinkers are distinct in that they both conceive of an eternal process of kenotic self-sacrificing or self-emptying love in the inner life of God, which is transposed onto the human historical plane in the event of Jesus Christ, who is the Lamb of God "foreordained before the foundation of the world" (1 Pet 1:20). Bulgakov speaks of the sacrifice of the Father's love in begetting the Son, and of the Son who offers his personal selfhood in sacrifice to the Father. At the heart of God is a reciprocal sacrifice of love, which manifests the victorious power of love and its joy only through suffering. Importantly, though, Bulgakov says that this sacrifice of love is *not the suffering of limitation*, "which is incompatible with the absoluteness of divine life." The suffering of God, in other words, is not like human suffering, which can overwhelm human beings and eventually lead to their destruction. Heschel, when discussing the divine pathos, also makes a point of stressing that God, unlike the human being, is not overwhelmed by suffering. In the Bible, the transcendence of God is always affirmed within God's relatedness to his people, never apart from them, thus it speaks of the way in which the divinity of God manifests itself in this relatedness. Any theology of the covenant that emphasizes God's concern for the salvation of humanity and the world, and any theodicy that depicts God as taking responsibility for the creation, cannot do otherwise than to affirm the suffering of God. However, care must be taken not to sacrifice God's transcendence by reducing God to a fellow sufferer who is unable to deliver afflicted humanity from their sufferings. For the result would be that hope in God is seriously undermined to the point that it ultimately vanishes, as the magnitude of evil and suffering in the world simply overwhelms the servants of God in their efforts to promote the good of "justice, peace, and joy" (Rom 14:17). So that we may abound in hope, it is imperative not to substitute God's immanence for God's transcendence. As Heschel puts it, "God remains transcendent in His immanence, and related in His transcendence."[141] God is deeply affected by everything that goes on in the world and is concerned for the fate of his people to whom he has opened up his heart, yet God is not overwhelmed by suffering: God has the capacity to internalize suffering and transform it through his merciful saving action, into newness of life.

The fundamental point shared by both Bulgakov and Heschel about not conceiving of God's suffering in terms of the suffering of limitation, is reinforced by Balthasar when he contends that the Father's eternal begetting of the Son involves an absolute, infinite "distance" that contains and embraces all the other distances that are possible within the created world, including the distance of sin. Just as the Son eternally proceeds from the Father immanently, the Son is sent by the Father into the world economically, and both are kenotic in quality. On the basis of

---

141. Heschel, *Prophets*, 486.

the primordial "separation" or "distance" of God from God in the Father's eternal begetting of the Son, Balthasar is able to attribute passibility and mutability to God in a qualified, analogical sense. The human properties of suffering and death are not attributed to God in a univocal sense. Here arises the second major point of clarification on the suffering of God: *God does not suffer univocally but analogically.* This is another way of upholding God's transcendence, while affirming God's immanence and radical engagement with the world. The Father's sending of the Son into the world, in their Spirit of mutual self-sacrificing love, shows that God stands in solidarity with his people and shares in their afflictions, with a view to absorbing their suffering and transforming it into unspeakable joy.

Elizabeth Johnson adds something more to this picture of God encompassing the suffering of the world, when she states that if the essence of God consists in the motion or dynamic of personal relations in the act of unfathomable love, then it is possible to conceive of suffering as "not necessarily a passive state nor a movement from potentiality to act. Rather, suffering can be conceived of ontologically as an expression of divine being insofar as it is an *act* freely engaged as a consequence of care for others."[142] If the essence of God's being is love, then God's love for the world must entail suffering in God. It is not sufficient to maintain, as the classical tradition teaches, that love is purely a matter of the will, that is, to love is simply to will the good of the one loved. As actually lived, Johnson explains, "love includes an openness to the ones loved, a vulnerability to their experience, a solidarity with their well-being, so that one rejoices with their joys and grieves with their sorrows."[143] This conception of divine suffering as an "act" provides a direct challenge to classical theism's teaching that God cannot be affected by the world because God is pure act, hence in God there is neither passivity nor potency. Johnson's reflections provide the basis for a third major point of clarification with regard to the suffering of God: *God's suffering in relation to the world is an "act" of ultimate concern and care for the creation, which is rooted in God's own life of relational participation in the eternal act that is love.* As an act, and not a passive state, God's suffering is purposeful since it is concerned with bringing to fullness the eternal covenant of grace: "And I will walk among you, and will be your God, and you shall be my people" (Lev

---

142. E. Johnson, *She Who Is*, 265.

143. E. Johnson, *She Who Is*, 266.

26:12). In the event of the Word of God being made flesh in Jesus Christ, God literally walks among his people, and Jesus's lament cry reveals what God is truly like in overcoming the obstacles to the kingdom of God, so that we might truly be his people, a holy people, always giving thanks to God who suffers "for us" and "with us," thereby transforming our grief (lament) into unspeakable joy (praise).

A final point on divine suffering can be made from the standpoint of the "communion of natures" in the one person of Jesus Christ, which pertains to the christological formula of the Council of Chalcedon (451 CE). Chapter 1 of this study has argued that the lament materials—both human and divine lament—in Scripture bring into focus the *reciprocity* of the divine-human relationship, which reaches a climactic point in Jesus's passion, where humanity and divinity are united in the ultimate agony. This reciprocity is implied by the Chalcedonian formula, which states that humanity and divinity in the one person of Christ are united "without confusion or change, without division or separation." One of the major intentions of this declaration is to dispel any suggestion that Christ is split or divided into two persons. Despite this intention, the formula has traditionally been interpreted in a way that does in fact split Christ into two persons, for his divinity is juxtaposed to his humanity: the divinity is in view when he performs miracles and forgives sins, and his humanity is apparent when he displays emotions and suffers on the cross. In no wise can it be said that Christ suffers in his divinity. Effectively, the theological tradition has failed to appreciate that unless we affirm that the person of Christ acts as the divine Son when he acts as a human, and as a human when he acts as the Son, then Christ is split into two persons and presents as a schizophrenic personality. The writings of Luther on this topic offer us a much more promising perspective, for Luther displays no dualistic modes of thought that regard divinity and humanity as unreconcilable opposites. By proposing that the properties of the two natures are communicated to the *concretum* of Christ's person, Luther avoids any suggestion of separation of the natures. In the event of the incarnation, the eternal Word has *in concreto* assumed humanity in the person of Christ, which means that divinity does in fact suffer on the cross. Luther writes: "God dead, God's passion, God's blood, God's death. According to his nature God cannot die, but since God and man are united in one person, it is correct to talk of God's death when that man dies who is one thing or one person with God."[144]

This extraordinary statement leaves us in no doubt about God's suffering in the event of the cross, which is one thing with Jesus's suffering as a human being. Luther pushes beyond the traditional unidirectional exchange of properties—i.e., the exchange occurs only from the divine to the human nature, just as fire permeates iron, but iron does not permeate fire—to include a real communication from the human to the divine nature of Christ. It is not sufficient to merely affirm the participation of the human in the divine; we must also uphold the participation of the divine in the human realm. This reciprocal communication of properties establishes a true communion of the natures, without, however, suggesting a commingling of the natures, since the properties are communicated to the concrete *person* of Christ, who is irreducible to either his divine or human nature. The common actualization of the divine and the human in the person of Christ does not blur the difference between the natures, for they actualize themselves as the one and the other as they confront and address one another in his person. The emphasis on the person of Christ, moreover, ensures that our reflections on the christological mystery are conducted in a strictly Trinitarian framework, for his identity as the Son emerges in his modus of being related to the Father in unfathomable love, through the Spirit, who comes to rest upon and indwell him in eschatological fullness. Since the inner life of the Trinity—conceived as the eternal event or act of self-sacrificing love between the divine persons—is the springboard of the historical event of Christ's saving cross, this means that the suffering of God on the cross is to be thought of analogically, not univocally, as stated earlier. God is in the paschal mystery what God is eternally. God does not become what God was not. Yet there is, nonetheless, a sense in which the cross of Christ introduces something new into the perfection of love that is the Holy Trinity: one of the Trinity has died on the cross! The upshot of all this is that the final point of clarification on the suffering of God can be stated thus: *Only the acknowledgment of a true communion of natures in the person of Christ can avoid splitting Christ into two persons. Yet such an acknowledgement means that Christ suffers not merely in his humanity but also in his divinity, for everything that is predicated of Christ is predicated of his one person. Christ did not do anything 'as God' or 'as man,' for he did everything as the God-man.* To affirm

---

144. Tappert, *Book of Concord*, 599.

the true humanity of Christ is to recognize the real participation of the divine in human historical realm, and to acknowledge the true divinity of Christ is to affirm the participation of the human in the divine. Therefore, when our sufferings are joined to the sufferings of Christ, when our cries are joined to Jesus's cry, they are taken up through the activity of the Spirit into the eternal Trinitarian event of self-sacrificing love between the divine persons and transformed into new life. The ineffable life of the Trinity has an infinite capacity for internalizing and transforming the suffering of the world, with a view to birthing a new creation of justice, peace, and joy, in the Spirit of the risen Christ.

CONCLUSION

T HE FOCUS OF THIS study has been on the ineluctable reality of evil and suffering in the world, which poses a serious challenge to belief in a benevolent and all-powerful God. If human reason is master, there is, as the book of Job persuasively demonstrates, no way of reconciling belief in God's justice with the reality of evil and suffering in the world. The evil that the blameless and upright Job is subjected to seriously undermines the "free will defense," which seeks to remove responsibility for evil from God by blaming it on the human being's misuse of freedom. Any potential rational explanation for the existence of evil, moreover, has to face the challenge put forward by Ivan Karamazov in Dostoyevsky's *The Brothers Karamazov*. Ivan claims that the suffering of even one innocent child is simply not worth the price, no matter what glorious end God may have in view.[1] To Ivan's mind, creation is not good, and he rejects the world that God has made. If reason alone is brought to bear on the existence of evil, then the weight of argument would be on Ivan's side or the side of Job's three friends.

The problem of evil, though, "is not at heart an intellectual one so much as an existential one."[2] As an existential reality, evil cannot be avoided, and we have to engage with it and wrestle with it. The Enlightenment, in its quest for truth and knowledge gained independently of the authority of revelation, dreamed of a golden age of civilization, prosperity, and world peace that would signal the triumph of human endeavor over the scourge of evil. But the modernist doctrine of progress, as the deeply troubled state of our twenty-first-century world all too plainly attests,

1. Dostoyevsky, *Brothers Karamazov*, 236–45.
2. Vardy, *Puzzle of Evil*, 202.

has proven to be shallow and incapable of realizing its utopic ideals. The kingdom of God has not materialized within history; on the contrary, it remains as elusive as ever. Postmodern thought, with its culture of suspicion that seeks to deconstruct the modernist ideology of progress, fares no better, for while it acknowledges evil as real and powerful, it gives no clues as to what should be done about this fundamental problem. And because it deconstructs human subjectivity, there is no moral dignity left inasmuch as there is nobody left to shoulder responsibility for evil.

The purpose of this study has been to offer a systematic *biblical* response to the problem of evil and suffering, informed by the voice of biblical lament which reaches its zenith with Jesus's lament cry, "My God, my God, why have you forsaken me?" (Mark 15:34). It was shown how the biblical materials reflect a development of thought on lament: lament is not confined to human lament as a posture of the suffering faithful before God but is broadened to include divine lament as a posture of God before a sinful and rebellious people. The latter pertains to the theological category of divine pathos, which serves to underscore the genuine *reciprocity* of the covenant relationship. The divine lament is especially emphasized in the prophetic writings, where we see a marked development of thought on the practice of lament. The advance in understanding consists in viewing the prophet not as the suffering representative of the people but one who embodies the sorrow and suffering of God before a rebellious people. The prophet is one who suffers in sympathy with the divine pathos, one whose life mirrors or embodies the suffering of God before the people. But the prophet's suffering is not vicarious in the sense that he makes himself "an offering for sin" (Isa 53:9–10). In Isa 52:13—53:12, there is no suggestion that the servant's life embodies the suffering of God, yet the reference in Isa 54:9-10 to God's covenant with Noah does imply that God's grief becomes embodied in the world in life of the servant. With the advent of Jesus Christ, he is both prophet and suffering servant of God, but as the eternal Word made flesh, he is the unique embodiment of God in the world, for in him "the whole fullness of deity dwells bodily" (Col 2:9). In the Crucified One is revealed how God truly internalizes the existential reality of sin and evil, so as to transform the grief of the world into the joy of the new creation.

No concept of God formulated independently of the Christ event may decide what is possible and impossible for God. The God of Jesus Christ, unlike the God of classical theism, is a God capable of suffering, for the inner-Trinitarian event of self-emptying love between the divine persons has an infinite capacity for the sacrifice of love. The benevolence and omnipotence of God, against all logical modes of thought, is definitively revealed in the crucified Christ, the God-man, who is "the power of God and the wisdom of God" (1 Cor 1:24). The most profound human wisdom is still preserved in the answers given by faith. The follower of Christ confesses that God is present among his afflicted people, mercifully bears their sin, and compassionately participates in their suffering—without being overwhelmed by it—with the good purpose of birthing a new creation and transforming lament into unutterable joy. In the final analysis, reason does not have the right to negate the astonishing revelation of God in the Crucified One, who lives as the Risen One in his church communities. The wisdom of God is truly inscrutable, as is the divine pathos, yet we humans are invited to taste this divine wisdom by participating in the Eucharist, where, in a special and unsurpassed way, the Spirit incorporates the baptized into Christ's relationship with the Father.

In the Eucharist, lament is integral to thanksgiving, for the crucified Christ is present as the Risen One; he speaks as the one who has been heard by the Father, and together they send their Spirit of new life, which is the power that saves and recreates out of suffering and death. Since lament has its place in how Christ dealt with his terrible suffering, it should also have its place among his followers, as they seek to persevere in the life of faith in a world that remains unredeemed. The happy ending of the journey of faith is something that is hoped for, it is not yet given, for we continue to wrestle with the existence of evil. There can be no doubt that the perennial "How long, O Lord?" and "Why, Lord?" questions of the biblical lament tradition will continue to find voice in Christian life, as we seek to give an emphatic response to the question that the Lord puts to us: "Who do you say I am?" (Mark 8:27). If our response is, "You are the Christ, the Holy and Just One, the Crucified and Risen One, the Savior of the world," then integral to this confession of faith is the requirement that we set our hearts upon the deep and leave our familiar shores behind, as we set out, in the Spirit of the risen Christ, on the *adventure of incarnation*. This adventure, though, is as daunting as it is wonderful, for incorporation into Christ means that we are to exhibit "the self-sacrificing, empowering love that Christ showed in his crucifixion. We must bear in our bodies the dying of Jesus in order that the life of Jesus may be manifested to the world. Crucifixion is what makes a Christian."[3] To bear in our bodies the dying of Jesus, so that the saving death of Jesus might be manifested to the world, is certainly no facile undertaking. Dietrich Bonhoeffer was right when he argued that "cheap grace" is the enemy of the Christian churches and amounts to a denial of the Incarnation of the eternal Word of God.[4] The "costly" nature of grace means that we will constantly be challenged and buffeted by waves of fear and doubt as we are overwhelmed by the extent of evil and suffering in the world, which is why the practice of lament is indispensable to "putting on Christ" (Rom 13:14). When faith is being sorely tested by the harsh realities of this world, prayers of lament enable us to persevere in faith, rekindle hope, and abandon ourselves to God who we know is with us and for us, because God was truly with Jesus and for the crucified when he cried out on Calvary. Since the lament cries of the faithful who make up the body of Christ are joined to the lament cry of the head, the faithful come to understand their suffering as taking on the meaningful aspect of participating in the paschal mystery of Christ. In the joining of our suffering to Christ's sacrificial suffering for our sake, we are drawn, through the indwelling Spirit, into Christ's relationship with the Father and thus divinized—i.e., we are lifted up into union with the Father, through the Son, in the Spirit.

The crux of the findings of this study is the proposed theological interpretation of Jesus's cry, which throws down the gauntlet to the *God-abandonment* thesis, which has risen to the level of an axiom in some theological circles.[5] From the perspective of the Gospel story—as well as the tradition of the suffering righteous in which Ps 22 stands—it is hardly credible to maintain that Jesus's cry reveals that he died in the despair of utter abandonment by God. We are on much firmer ground when we hold that Jesus's total and utter commitment to the cause of God is what carries him all the way to the cross, so as to accomplish his messianic mission as the Son in perfect obedience to the Father, with whom he is united in unfathomable love. In a sense, the cross does occur under the will of God, inasmuch as the Father does not intervene as Jesus is handed over into the custody of evildoers. But this should not be taken to mean that Jesus's cry expresses God's absence on the cross. The silence

3. Murphy-O'Connor, "Even Death on Cross," 43.

4. Bonhoeffer, *Discipleship*, 43–56.

5. My interpretation of Jesus's cry supports the contention of William Stacy Johnson that the divine abandonment thesis is marked by serious exegetical, theological, and pastoral flaws. See W. Johnson, "Jesus' Cry."

of the Father should not be interpreted as absence; rather, God's silence is a *self-concealing presence*, for the Father remains the interior reality of the event. In the Gospel story, God refers to Jesus as his "beloved Son" with whom he is well pleased, hence it is apparent that God fully identifies with the Son, who authoritatively proclaims in word and deed the kingdom of God. The Father, in other words, is the Father only in relation to the Son, and the Son is the Son only in relation to the Father, which means they are inextricably united with one another. On the cross, then, the Father also abandons himself in an act of self-sacrificial love for the world, when Jesus the Son is given over into the hands of sinners.

What Jesus's cry expresses is his total self-surrender and abandonment *to* the Father with whom he is united in love, not his abandonment *by* God. Jesus was not cut off from God, he did not suffer the loss of God, nor did he suffer rejection or extreme separation from God. Jesus is without sin, he is the Son who is perfectly obedient to the Father, so how can we say that he suffered the hell of separation from God on the cross?[6] By citing Ps 22 as his dying words, Jesus situates himself within the tradition of the suffering righteous one who suffers because of fidelity to the cause of God in an unredeemed world. The lament cry signifies that God will *not* abandon his suffering servant but will come to his aid and deliver him from affliction, thereby vindicating him as just and righteous. In the case of Jesus, he expects that his vindication will come in the form of his being raised from the dead, which is made very clear in his passion predictions that feature in the Synoptic Gospels. His death as the Son is no ordinary death, for it is a glorifying death, the saving benefits of which are spelt out in detail in the concluding section of Ps 22 (vv. 22–31). Jesus does not suffer *God*-abandonment, for the Father is with Jesus and for the crucified in the same Spirit of self-sacrificing love that enables Jesus to abandon himself totally to the Father in completing his salvific mission. And because God does not abandon Jesus in his hour of terrible suffering at the hands of evildoers, we can confidently say that God is with us and

---

6. That Jesus is without sin does not preclude his being subjected to the consequences of Adam's sin, namely, suffering and death. Since sin is understood as separation from God, Jesus on the cross cannot suffer separation from God. Jesus is the sin-bearer in the sense that he assumes the consequences of the people's sin—of which the cross is the consummate sign—while remaining united with the Father, hence he is our Representative before the Father, the Mediator between humanity and divinity. The Crucified One keeps sinners in relation to the Father, he always keeps open the offer of reconciliation and fellowship with God, which is the true vocation of the human being created in the image and likeness of God.

for us in our own cries, which are joined to Jesus's cry and thus redeemed. The gospel is the good news of unutterable joy, namely, the joy of the risen Christ who has triumphed over the powers of sin and death in the world. The joy of the gospel is no superficial worldly joy but the costly joy that has been hard won by Christ's cross. The followers of Christ are to be distinguished by their joy, but Christian joy must be a robust joy, inasmuch as praise of God is always intertwined with the existential reality of sin and evil in the world. If crucifixion is what makes a Christian, if the Christian bears in their mortal body the death of Christ so that the life of Christ might be manifested in the world, then we should think of Christian commitment to the cause of the Lord in terms of the ongoing transformation of lament (grief) into joy (praise): "Behold, I make all things new" (Rev 21:5).

Bibliography

Albright, William F. "A Catalog of Early Hebrew Lyric Poems." *Hebrew Union College Annual* 23 (1950) 1–39.

Allison, Dale C. *The End of the Ages Has Come: An Early Interpretation of the Passion and Resurrection of Jesus*. Philadelphia: Fortress, 1985.

Anderson, Bernhard W. *The Living World of the Old Testament*. 3rd ed. Essex, UK: Longman, 1978.

———. *Out of the Depths: The Psalms Speak for Us Today*. 3rd ed. Louisville: Westminster John Knox, 2000.

Aquinas, Thomas. *Summa theologica*. Translated by Fathers of the English Dominican Province. Britannica Great Books 19. Chicago: University of Chicago, 1952.

Athanasius. *Four Discourses against the Arians*. In *Nicene and Post-Nicene Fathers*, edited by Philip Schaff, 2nd ser., 4:303–47. Grand Rapids: Eerdmans, 1978.

Augustine. *City of God, XI–XXII*. Translated by William Babcock. Pt. 1, Vol. 7 of *The Works of Saint Augustine: A Translation for the 21st Century*. New York: New City, 2013.

———. *The Confessions*. Translated by Maria Boulding. Pt. 1, Vol. 1 of *The Works of Saint Augustine: A Translation for the 21st Century*. New York: New City, 2012.

———. *On the Creed*. In *Nicene and Post-Nicene Fathers*, edited by Philip Schaff, 1st ser., 3:369–75. Grand Rapids: Eerdmans, 1978.

———. *St. Augustine on the Psalms*. Translated by Scholastica Hebgin and Felicitas Corrigan. Ancient Christian Writers 29–30. New York: Newman, 1960.

Balentine, Samuel E. *The Hidden God: The Hiding of the Face of God in the Old Testament*. Oxford: Oxford University Press, 1983.

———. *Prayer in the Hebrew Bible: The Drama of Divine-Human Dialogue*. Minneapolis: Fortress, 1993.

Balthasar, Hans Urs von. *The Action*. Vol. 4 of *Theo-Drama: Theological Dramatic Theory*. Translated by Graham Harrison. San Francisco: Ignatius, 1994.

———. *The Dramatis Personae: The Person in Christ*. Vol. 3 of *Theo-Drama: Theological Dramatic Theory*. Translated by Graham Harrison. San Francisco: Ignatius, 1992.

———. *The Last Act*. Vol. 5 of *Theo-Drama: Theological Dramatic Theory*. Translated by Graham Harrison. San Francisco: Ignatius, 1998.

———. *Love Alone: The Way of Revelation; A Theological Perspective*. Edited by Alexander Dru. London: Burns & Oats, 1968.

———. *Mysterium Paschale: The Mystery of Easter*. Translated by Aidan Nichols, OP. Grand Rapids: Eerdmans, 1993.

———. *The Spirit of Truth*. Vol. 3 of *Theo-Logic*. Translated by Graham Harrison. San Francisco: Ignatius, 2005.

Barth, Karl. *The Doctrine of Creation*. Vol. III/3 of *Church Dogmatics*. Translated by G. W. Bromiley and R. J. Ehrlich. Edinburgh: T. & T. Clark, 1960.

———. *The Doctrine of God*. Vol. II/1 of *Church Dogmatics*. Translated by T. H. L. Parker et al. Edinburgh: T. & T. Clark, 1957.

———. *The Doctrine of Reconciliation*. Vol. IV/1 of *Church Dogmatics*. Translated by G. W. Bromiley. Edinburgh: T. & T. Clark, 1956.

———. *The Doctrine of Reconciliation*. Vol. IV/2 of *Church Dogmatics*. Translated by G. W. Bromiley. Edinburgh: T. & T. Clark, 1958.

———. *The Doctrine of the Word of God*. Vol. I/2 of *Church Dogmatics*. Translated by G. T. Thomson and Harold Knight. Edinburgh: T. & T. Clark, 1956.

Bauckham, Richard, and Trevor Hart. "The Shape of Time." In *The Future as God's Gift: Explorations in Christian Eschatology*, edited by David Fergusson and Marcel Sarot, 41–72. Edinburgh: T. & T. Clark, 2000.

Bayer, Oswald. "Toward a Theology of Lament." In *Caritas et Reformatio: Essays on Church and Society in Honor of Carter Lindberg*, edited by David M. Whitford, 211–20. Saint Louis: Concordia, 2002.

Beker, J. Christiaan. *Paul's Apocalyptic Gospel: The Coming Triumph of God*. Philadelphia: Fortress, 1982.

Ben-Zeèv, Aaron. "The Logic of the Emotions." In *Philosophy and the Emotions*, edited by Anthony Hatzimoysis, 147–62. Royal Institute of Philosophy Supplement 52. Cambridge: Cambridge University Press, 2003.

Betz, Otto. "Jesus and Isaiah 53." In *Jesus and the Suffering Servant: Isaiah 53 and Christian Origins*, edited by William H. Bellinger and William R. Farmer, 70–87. Eugene, OR: Wipf & Stock, 2009.

Beuken, W. A. M. "The Main Theme of Trito-Isaiah: 'The Servants of YHWH.'" *Journal for the Study of the Old Testament* 47 (1990) 67–87.

Billman, Kathleen D., and Daniel L. Migliore. *Rachel's Cry: Prayer of Lament and Rebirth of Hope*. Eugene, OR: Wipf & Stock, 1999.

Black, C. Clifton. "The Persistence of the Wounds." In *Lament: Reclaiming Practices in Pulpit, Pew, and Public Square*, edited by Sally A. Brown and Patrick D. Miller, 47–58. Louisville: Westminster John Knox, 2005.

Bonhoeffer, Dietrich. *The Cost of Discipleship*. New York, NY: Touchstone, 1995.

Braaten, Carl E., and Robert W. Jensen, eds. *Union with Christ: The New Finnish Interpretation of Luther*. Grand Rapids: Eerdmans, 1998.

Bracken, Joseph. "The Holy Trinity as a Community of Divine Persons." *Heythrop Journal* 15 (1974) 166–82.

Briggs, Charles A., and Emilie G. Briggs. *A Critical and Exegetical Commentary on the Book of Psalms*. 2 vols. Edinburgh: T. & T. Clark, 1906.

Brock, Brian. "Augustine's Incitement to Lament, from the *Enarrationes in Psalmos*." In *Evoking Lament: A Theological Discussion*, edited by Eva Harasta and Brian Brock, 183–203. London: T. & T. Clark, 2009.

Brown, Peter R. *Augustine of Hippo: A Biography*. London: Faber & Faber, 1967.

Brown, Raymond E. *The Death of the Messiah*. 2 vols. New York: Doubleday, 1994.

Brown, Sally A., and Patrick D. Miller, eds. *Lament: Reclaiming Practices in Pulpit, Pew, and Public Square*. Louisville: Westminster John Knox, 2005.

Bruce, Alex B. *Humiliation of Christ*. Edinburgh: T. & T. Clark, 1900.

Brueggemann, Walter. "The Costly Loss of Lament." *Journal for the Study of the Old Testament* 36 (1986) 57–71.

———. *The Psalms and the Life of Faith.* Edited by Patrick D. Miller. Minneapolis: Fortress, 1995.

———. "The Psalms as Limit Expressions." In *Performing the Psalms*, edited by Dave Bland and David Fleer, 31–50. St. Louis: Chalice, 2005.

———. "A Shape for Old Testament Theology, I: Structure Legitimation." *Catholic Biblical Quarterly* 47 (1985) 28–46.

———. "A Shape for Old Testament Theology, II: Embrace of Pain." *Catholic Biblical Quarterly* 47 (1985) 395–415.

———. *Theology of the Old Testament.* Minneapolis: Fortress, 1997.

Bulgakov, Sergius. *The Lamb of God.* Translated by Boris Jakim. Grand Rapids: Eerdmans, 2008.

Calhoun, Cheshire. "Subjectivity and Emotion." In *Thinking about Feeling: Contemporary Philosophers on Emotions*, edited by Robert C. Solomon, 107–21. Oxford: Oxford University Press, 2004.

Calvin, John. *Commentary on the Book of Psalms.* Vol. 1. Translated by James Anderson. Edinburgh: Calvin Translation Society, 1845.

———. *Commentary on the Book of Psalms.* Vol. 5. Translated by James Anderson. Edinburgh: Constable, 1849.

———. *Institutes of the Christian Religion.* Edited by Tony Lane and Hilary Osborne. London: Hodder & Stoughton, 1986.

Carey, Holly J. *Jesus' Cry from the Cross: Towards a First-Century Understanding of the Intertextual Relationship Between Psalm 22 and the Narrative of Mark's Gospel.* London: Bloomsbury, 2009.

Chrysostom, John. *Homilies on the Gospel of Saint Matthew.* Edited by Philip Schaff. Vol. 10 of *Nicene and Post-Nicene Fathers of the Christian Church*, 1st ser. Grand Rapids: Eerdmans, 1983.

Clifford, Richard J. *Psalms 1–72.* Nashville: Abingdon, 2002.

Collins, John J. *Daniel: With an Introduction to Apocalyptic Literature.* Grand Rapids: Eerdmans, 1984.

Congar, Yves. *Lord and Giver of Life.* Vol. 2 of *I Believe in the Holy Spirit.* Translated by David Smith. New York: Seabury, 1983.

———. *The River of Life Flows in the East and in the West.* Vol. 3 of *I Believe in the Holy Spirit.* Translated by David Smith. London: Chapman, 1983.

Crenshaw, James L. *Defending God: Biblical Responses to the Problem of Evil.* Oxford: Oxford University Press, 2005.

———. "The Human Dilemma and Literature of Dissent." In *Tradition and Theology in the Old Testament*, edited by Douglas A. Knight, 235–58. Sheffield, UK: Journal for the Study of the Old Testament, 1990.

———. *Reading Job: A Literary and Theological Commentary.* Macon, GA: Smyth & Helwys, 2011.

———, ed. *Theodicy in the Old Testament.* Philadelphia: Fortress, 1983.

Crook, Paul. *Darwinism, War and History: The Debate over the Biology of War from the 'Origin of Species' to the First World War.* Cambridge: Cambridge University Press, 1994.

Cyril of Alexandria. "Second Letter to Succenus." In *Cyril of Alexandria: Select Letters*, edited by Lionel R. Wickham, 84–93. Oxford: Clarendon, 1983.

Dabney, D. Lyle. "Naming the Spirit: Towards a Pneumatology of the Cross." In *Starting with the Spirit*, edited by Stephen Pickard and Gordon Preece, 28–58. Hindmarsh, Aus.: ATF, 2001.

Danchev, Alex, ed. *Fin de Siècle: The Meaning of the Twentieth Century*. London: Tauris, 1995.

Declaissé-Walford, Nancy, et al. *The Book of Psalms*. Grand Rapids: Eerdmans, 2014.

Del Colle, Ralph. *Christ and the Spirit: Spirit-Christology in Trinitarian Perspective*. Oxford: Oxford University Press, 1994.

Dostoyevsky, Fyodor. *The Brothers Karamazov*. Tranlated by Richard Pevear and Larissa Volokhonsky. New York: Farrar, Straus and Giroux, 1990.

Driver, Samuel R. *Studies in the Psalms*. London: Hodder & Stroughton, 1915.

Duff, Nancy J. "Recovering Lamentation as a Practice in the Church." In *Lament: Reclaiming Practices in Pulpit, Pew, and Public Square*, edited by Sally A. Brown and Patrick D. Miller, 3–14. Louisville: Westminster John Knox, 2005.

Dunant, Sarah, and Roy Porter, eds. *The Age of Anxiety*. London: Virago, 1996.

Dunn, James D. G. *Pneumatology*. Vol. 2 of *The Christ and the Spirit: Collected Essays of James D. G. Dunn*. Edinburgh: T. & T. Clark, 1998.

Durrwell, François-Xavier. *The Eucharist: Presence of Christ*. Translated by Salvator Attanasio. Deville, NJ: Dimension, 1974.

———. *Holy Spirit of God: An Essay in Biblical Theology*. Translated by Benedict Davies, OSU. London: Chapman, 1986.

———. *In the Redeeming Christ*. Translated by Rosemary Sheed. London: Sheed & Ward, 1963.

———. *The Resurrection: A Biblical Study*. Translated by Rosemary Sheed. London: Sheed & Ward, 1960.

Feuerbach, Ludwig. *The Essence of Christianity*. Translated by Marian Evans. 2nd ed. New York: Blanchard, 1855.

Fiddes, Paul S. *The Creative Suffering of God*. Oxford: Clarendon, 1988.

Forsyth, Peter T. *The Person and Place of Jesus Christ*. London: Hodder & Stoughton, 1909.

Francis, Pope. *Evangelii Gaudium*. Vatican City: Libreria Editrice Vaticana, 2013.

Frei, Hans. *The Identity of Jesus Christ*. Philadelphia: Fortress, 1975.

Fretheim, Terence E. "The Character of God in Jeremiah." In *What Kind of God? Collected Essays of Terence E. Fretheim*, edited by Michael J. Chan and Brent A. Strawn, 294–311. University Park: Pennsylvania State University Press, 2015.

———. "Some Reflections on Brueggemann's God." In *What Kind of God? Collected Essays of Terence E. Fretheim*, edited by Michael J. Chan and Brent A. Strawn, 71–83. University Park: Pennsylvania State University Press, 2015.

———. "Suffering God and Sovereign God in Exodus." In *What Kind of God? Collected Essays of Terence E. Fretheim*, edited by Michael J. Chan and Brent A. Strawn, 104–23. University Park: Pennsylvania State University Press, 2015.

———. *The Suffering of God: An Old Testament Perspective*. Philadelphia: Fortress, 1984.

Fuchs, Ottmar. *God's People: Instruments of Healing*. Bern: Lang, 1993.

Gabriel, Andrew K. *Barth's Doctrine of Creation*. Eugene, OR: Cascade, 2014.

Grayston, Kenneth. *Dying, We Live: A New Inquiry into the Death of Christ in the New Testament*. New York: Oxford University Press, 1990.

Gregory of Nyssa. *Funeral Oration on Melitius*. In *Nicene and Post-Nicene Fathers*, edited by Philip Schaff and Henry Wace. 2nd ser., 5:513–17. Grand Rapids: Eerdmans, 1979.

———. *The Life of Moses*. Translated by De vita Moysis. Classics of Western Spirituality. New York: Paulist, 1978.

———. "On Perfection." In *Ascetical Works*, translated by Virginia Woods Callahan, 95–122. Fathers of the Church 38. Washington, DC: Catholic University of America Press, 1967.

———. "On What It Means to Call Oneself a Christian." In *Ascetical Works*, translated by Virginia Woods Callahan, 81–89. Fathers of the Church 38. Washington, DC: Catholic University of America Press, 1967.

Gunkel, Hermann. *The Psalms: A Form-Critical Introduction*. Translated by Thomas M. Horner. Philadelphia: Fortress, 1967.

Gunton, Colin E. *Yesterday and Today: A Study of Continuities in Christology*. Grand Rapids: Eerdmans, 1983.

Harasta, Eva. "Crucified Praise and Resurrected Lament." In *Evoking Lament: A Theological Discussion*, edited by Eva Harasta and Brian Brock, 204–17. London: T. & T. Clark, 2009.

———, and Brian Brock, eds. *Evoking Lament: A Theological Discussion*. London: T. & T. Clark, 2009.

Heim, Mark. *Saved from Sacrifice: A Theology of the Cross*. Grand Rapids: Eerdmans, 2006.

Heinemann, Mark H. "An Exposition of Psalm 22." *Bibliotheca Sacra* 147 (1990) 286–308.

Hengel, Martin. *Crucifixion in the Ancient World and the Folly of the Message of the Cross*. Translated by John Bowden. Philadelphia: Fortress, 1977.

Heschel, Abraham J. "The Divine Pathos: The Basic Category of Prophetic Theology." In *Faith and Reason: Essays in Judaism*, edited by Robert Gordis and Ruth B. Waxman, 33–58. New York: Ktav, 1973.

———. *The Prophets*. New York: Harper & Row, 1962.

Hick, John. *Evil and the God of Love*. London: Collins, 1968.

Hicks, John Mark. "Preaching Community Laments: Responding to Disillusionment with God and Injustice in the World." In *Performing the Psalms*, edited by Dave Bland and David Fleer, 67–81. St. Louis: Chalice, 2005.

Hill, William. *The Three-Personed God: The Trinity as a Mystery of Salvation*. Washington, DC: Catholic University of America Press, 1982.

Hunt, Anne. *Trinity and the Paschal Mystery: A Development in Recent Catholic Theology*. New Theology 5. Collegeville, MN: Liturgical, 1997.

Irenaeus. *Against Heresies*. In *The Ante-Nicene Fathers*, edited by Alexander Roberts and James Donaldson, Apostolic Fathers 1, 309–567. Grand Rapids: Eerdmans, 1981.

Janzen, J. Gerald. "Eschatological Symbol and Existence in Habakkuk." *Catholic Biblical Quarterly* 44 (1982) 408–12.

Jenson, Robert. *The Triune God*. Vol. 1 of *Systematic Theology*. New York: Oxford University Press, 1997.

Jersak, Brad, and Michael Hardin, eds. *Stricken by God? Nonviolent Identification and the Victory of Christ*. Grand Rapids: Eerdmans, 2007.

John of Damascus. *Exposition of the Orthodox Faith*. Edited by Philip Schaff and Henry Wace. Vol. 9 of *Nicene and Post-Nicene Fathers*, 2nd ser. Grand Rapids: Eerdmans, 1979.

John Paul II, Pope. *Ecclesia de Eucharistia*. Strathfield, Aus.: St Paul's, 2003.

Johnson, Elizabeth A. *She Who Is: The Mystery of God in Feminist Theological Discourse*. New York: Crossroad, 1992.

Johnson, William Stacy. "Jesus' Cry, God's Cry, and Ours." In *Lament: Reclaiming Practices in Pulpit, Pew, and Public Square*, edited by Sally A. Brown and Patrick D. Miller, 80–94. Louisville: Westminster John Knox, 2005.

Jüngel, Eberhard. *God as the Mystery of the World: On the Foundation of the Theology of the Crucified One in the Dispute between Theism and Atheism*. Translated by Darrell L. Guder. Grand Rapids: Eerdmans, 1983.

———. *God's Being Is in Becoming: The Trinitarian Being of God in the Theology of Karl Barth*. Translated by John Webster. Edinburgh: T. & T. Clark, 2001.

Juvin, Hervé. *The Coming of the Body*. Translated by John Howe. London: Verso, 2010.

Kasper, Walter. *The God of Jesus Christ*. Translated by Matthew J. O'Connell. New York: Crossroad, 1992.

———. *Jesus the Christ*. Translated by V. Green. London: Burns & Oates, 1976.

Keck, Leander. *A Future for the Historical Jesus: The Place of Jesus in Preaching and Theology*. London: SCM, 1972.

Koch, Klaus. "Is There a Doctrine of Retribution in the Old Testament?" In *Theodicy in the Old Testament*, edited by James L. Crenshaw, 57–87. Philadelphia: Fortress, 1983.

———. *The Rediscovery of Apocalyptic*. Translated by Margaret Kohl. London: SCM, 1972.

Kraus, Hans-Joachim. *Psalms 1–59: A Commentary*. Minneapolis: Augsburg, 1988.

LaCugna, Catherine M. *God for Us: The Trinity and Christian Life*. New York: HarperCollins, 1993.

Lakeland, Paul. *Postmodernity: Christian Identity in a Fragmented Age*. Minneapolis: Fortress, 1997.

Lakkis, Stephen. "Have You Any Right to Be Angry? Lament as a Metric of Socio-Political and Theological Context." In *Evoking Lament: A Theological Discussion*, edited by Eva Harasta and Brian Brock, 168–82. London: T. & T. Clark, 2009.

Lathrop, Gordon W. *Holy Ground: A Liturgical Cosmology*. Minneapolis: Fortress, 2003.

———. *Holy Things: A Liturgical Theology*. Minneapolis: Fortress, 1993.

Lauber, David. *Barth on the Descent into Hell: God, Atonement and the Christian Life*. Surrey, UK: Ashgate, 2004.

Lehmann, Martin E. *Luther and Prayer*. Milwaukee: Northwestern, 1985.

Lewis, Alan E. *Between Cross and Resurrection: A Theology of Holy Saturday*. Grand Rapids: Eerdmans, 2001.

Levenson, Jon D. *Creation and the Persistence of Evil: The Jewish Drama of Divine Omnipotence*. Princeton, NJ: Princeton University Press, 1994.

Lienhard, Marc. *Luther: Witness to Jesus Christ*. Minneapolis: Augsburg, 1982.

Lindström, Fredrik. "Theodicy in the Psalms." In *Theodicy in the World of the Bible*, edited by Antti Laato and Johannes C. de Moor, 256–303. Leiden: Brill, 2003.

Lombardo, Nicholas E. *The Father's Will: Christ's Crucifixion and the Goodness of God*. Oxford: Oxford University Press, 2013.

Luther, Martin. *The Christian Society III.* Edited by Robert C. Schultz. Vol. 46 of *Luther's Works.* Philadelphia: Fortress, 1967.

———. *Devotional Writings.* Edited by Gustav K. Wiencke. Vol. 43 of *Luther's Works.* Philadelphia: Fortress, 1968.

———. *Lectures on Romans.* Edited by Hilton C. Oswald. Vol. 25 of *Luther's Works.* St Louis: Concordia, 1972.

———. *Selected Psalms I.* Edited by Jaroslav Pelikan. Vol. 12 of *Luther's Works.* St Louis: Concordia, 1955.

———. *Selected Psalms III.* Edited by Jaroslav Pelikan. Vol. 14 of *Luther's Works.* St Louis: Concordia, 1958.

———. *Sermons I.* Edited by John W. Doberstein. Vol. 51 of *Luther's Works.* Philadelphia: Muhlenberg, 1959.

Lyons, Michael A. "Psalm 22 and the 'Servants' of Isaiah 54; 56–66." *Catholic Biblical Quarterly* 77 (2015) 640–56.

Mackintosh, Ross H. *The Doctrine of the Person of Jesus Christ.* 2nd ed. Edinburgh: T. & T. Clark, 1913.

Macquarrie, John. *In Search of Deity: An Essay in Dialectical Theism.* Gifford Lectures 1983–1984. London: SCM, 1984.

Marcus, Joel. "'The Evil Inclination in the Letters of Paul." *Irish Biblical Society* 8 (1986) 8–21.

Markus, Robert. *The End of Ancient Christianity.* Cambridge: Cambridge University Press, 1990.

Marttila, Marko. *Collective Reinterpretation in the Psalms: A Study of the Redaction History of the Psalter.* Tübingen, Germ.: Mohr Siebeck, 2006.

Martyr, Justin. *Dialogue with Trypho.* In *The Ante-Nicene Fathers,* edited by Alexander Roberts and James Donaldson, Apostolic Fathers 1, 194–270. Grand Rapids: Eerdmans, 1981.

Mays, James L. "Prayer and Christology: Psalm 22 as Perspective on the Passion." *Theology Today* 42 (1985) 322–33.

———. *Psalms.* Louisville: John Knox, 1994.

McCabe, Herbert. *God Matters.* London: Chapman, 1987.

McEvoy, James, and Maurice Hogan. *The Mystery of Faith: Reflections on the Encyclical Ecclesia de Eucharistia.* Dublin: Columba, 2005.

McIntosh, Mark A. *Mystical Theology: The Integrity of Spirituality and Theology.* Oxford: Blackwell, 1998.

McIntyre, John. *The Shape of Christology.* London: SCM, 1966.

McKinnon, James W. "On the Question of Psalmody in the Ancient Synagogue." *Early Music History* 6 (1986) 159–91.

McKnight, Scot. *Jesus and His Death: Historiography, the Historical Jesus, and Atonement Theory.* Waco, TX: Baylor University Press, 2005.

Miller, Patrick D. *Sin and Judgment in the Prophets: A Stylistic and Theological Analysis.* Society of Biblical Literature Monograph Series 27. Chico, CA: Scholars, 1982.

———. *They Cried to the Lord: The Form and Theology of Biblical Prayer.* Minneapolis: Fortress, 1994.

Moingt, Joseph. "Montre-nous le Père." *Recherches de science religieuse* 65 (1977) 305–37.

Moltmann, Jürgen. *The Crucified God: The Cross of Christ as the Foundation and Criticism of Christian Theology*. Translated by R. A. Wilson and John Bowden. London: SCM, 2001.

———. *God in Creation: An Ecological Doctrine of Creation*. Translated by Margaret Kohl. London: SCM, 1985.

———. *The Source of Life: The Holy Spirit and the Theology of Life*. Translated by Margaret Kohl. London: SCM, 1997.

———. *The Trinity and the Kingdom: The Doctrine of God*. Translated by Margaret Kohl. Minneapolis: Fortress, 1993.

Mowinckel, Sigmund. *The Psalms in Israel's Worship*. Translated by Dafydd Rhys Ap-Thomas. 2 vols. Nashville: Abingdon, 1962.

Murphy-O'Connor, Jerome. "Even Death on a Cross: Crucifixion in the Pauline Letters." In *The Cross in Christian Tradition: From Paul to Bonaventure*, edited by Elizabeth A. Dreyer, 21–50. New York: Paulist, 2000.

Murphy, Roland E. *The Psalms, Job*. Proclamation Commentaries. Philadelphia: Fortress, 1977.

Nagel, Norman. "Martinus: Heresy, Doctor Luther, Heresy! The Person and Work of Christ." In *Seven-Headed Luther: Essays in Commemoration of a Quincentenary 1483–1983*, edited by Peter Newman Brooks, 25–49. Oxford: Clarendon, 1983.

Neiman, Susan. *Evil in Modern Thought: An Alternative History of Philosophy*. Princeton, NJ: Princeton University Press, 2002.

Neusner, Jacob. *The Mishnah: A New Translation*. New Haven, CT: Yale University Press, 1988.

Ngien, Dennis. "Chalcedonian Christology and Beyond: Luther's Understanding of the *Communicatio Idiomatum*." *Heythrop Journal* 45 (2004) 54–68.

Novello, Henry L. *Death as Transformation: A Contemporary Theology of Death*. Surrey, UK: Ashgate, 2011.

———. "God's Action of Furthering Nature in the Resurrection of Jesus Christ." *Pacifica: Australasian Theological Studies* 25 (2012) 217–38.

———. "The Nature of Evil in Jewish Apocalyptic: The Need for Integral Salvation." *Colloquium* 35 (2003) 47–63.

———. *Passionate Deification: The Integral Role of the Emotions in Christ's Life and in Christian Life*. Eugene, OR: Pickwick, 2019.

———. "The Sexual Abuse of Minors in the Church: Reform through the Practice of Lament." *Worship* 92 (2018) 222–40.

Nussbaum, Martha C. *Upheavals of Thought: The Intelligence of the Emotions*. Cambridge: Cambridge University Press, 2001.

O'Collins, Gerald. *Jesus Our Redeemer: A Christian Approach to Salvation*. New York: Oxford University Press, 2007.

O'Donnell, John. *The Mystery of the Triune God*. London: Sheed & Ward, 1988.

Öhler, Markus. "To Mourn, Weep, Lament and Groan: On the Heterogeneity of the New Testament's Statements on Lament." In *Evoking Lament: A Theological Discussion*, edited by Eva Harasta and Brian Brock, 150–65. London: T. & T. Clark, 2009.

Otzen, Benedikt. *Judaism in Antiquity*. Sheffield, UK: JSOT, 1990.

Pannenberg, Wolfhart. *Jesus—God and Man*. Translated by Lewis L. Wilkins and Duane A. Priebe. London: SCM, 1968.

———. *Systematic Theology*. 3 vols. Translated by Geoffrey W. Bromiley. Grand Rapids: Eerdmans, 1997.

Patterson, Richard D. "Psalm 22: From Trial to Triumph." *Journal of the Evangelical Theological Society* 47 (2004) 213–33.

Peake, Arthur S. "Job: The Problem of the Book." In *Theodicy in the Old Testament*, edited by James L. Crenshaw, 100–108. Philadelphia: Fortress, 1983.

Pleins, J. David. *The Psalms: Songs of Tragedy, Hope, and Justice*. Maryknoll, NY: Orbis, 1993.

Power, David N. *The Eucharistic Mystery: Revitalizing the Tradition*. New York: Crossroad, 1992.

———, and Michael Downey. *Living the Justice of the Triune God*. Collegeville, MN: Liturgical, 2012.

Rahner, Karl. *Foundations of Christian Faith: An Introduction to the Idea of Christianity*. Translated by William V. Dych. New York: Crossroad, 1994.

Reumann, John H. "Psalm 22 at the Cross: Lament and Thanksgiving for Jesus Christ." *Interpretation* 28 (1974) 39–58.

Ricoeur, Paul. *Evil: A Challenge to Philosophy and Theology*. Translated by John Bowden. New York: Continuum, 2007.

Rosato, Philip. "Spirit Christology: Ambiguity and Promise." *Theological Studies* 38 (1977) 423–49.

Ross, Allen P. *A Commentary on the Psalms, Volume 1 (1–41)*. Grand Rapids: Kregel, 2011.

Rossé, Gérard. *The Cry of Jesus on the Cross: A Biblical and Theological Study*. Translated by Stephen Wentworth Arndt. New York: Paulist, 1987.

Rowley, H. H. *Job*. New Century Bible. 2nd ed. London: Oliphants, 1976.

Sanders, John, ed. *Atonement and Violence: A Theological Conversation*. Nashville: Abingdon, 2006.

Schaefer, Konrad. *Psalms*. Collegeville, MN: Liturgical, 2001.

Schillebeeckx, Edward. *The Eucharist*. Translated by N. D. Smith. London: Sheed & Ward, 1968.

Schnackenburg, Rudolf. *The Gospel According to St. Mark*. 3 vols. London: Sheed & Ward, 1971.

Schreiner, Susan. "'Through a Mirror Dimly': Calvin's Sermons on Job." *Calvin Theological Journal* 21 (1986) 175–93.

Schweitzer, Albert. *The Mystery of the Kingdom of God: The Secret of Jesus' Messiahship and Passion*. New York: Dodd & Mead, 1914.

Schwöbel, Christoph. *God: Action and Revelation*. Kampen, Neth.: Kok Pharos, 1992.

Selderhuis, Herman J. *Calvin's Theology of the Psalms*. Grand Rapids: Baker Academic, 2007.

Senior, Donald. *The Passion of Jesus in the Gospel of Mark*. Wilmington, DE: Glazier, 1984.

———. *The Passion of Jesus in the Gospel of Matthew*. Wilmington, DE: Glazier, 1985.

Sobrino, John. *Christology at the Crossroads: A Latin American Approach*. London: SCM, 1978.

Sponheim, Paul. "Transcendence in Relationship." *Dialog* 12 (1973) 264–71.

Stanley, David M. *Jesus in Gethsemane: The Early Church Reflects on the Suffering of Jesus*. New York: Paulist, 1980.

Strauss, David Friedrich. *The Life of Jesus, Critically Examined*. New York: Blanchard, 1855.

Studer, Basil. *The Grace of Christ and the Grace of God in Augustine of Hippo*. Collegeville, MN: Liturgical, 1997.

Stuhlmacher, Peter. "Vicariously Giving His Life for Many, Mark 10:45 (Matt 20:28)." In *Reconciliation, Law, and Righteousness: Essays in Biblical Theology*, edited by Peter Stuhlmacher, 16–29. Philadelphia: Fortress, 1986.

Stuhlmueller, Carroll. *Psalms 1–72*. Wilmington, DE: Glazier,1983.

Suggs, M. Jack. "Wisdom 2:10—5: A Homily Based on the Fourth Servant Song." *Journal of Biblical Literature* 76 (1957) 26–33.

Tappert, Theodore G., ed. *The Book of Concord: The Confessions of the Evangelical Lutheran Church*. Philadelphia: Fortress, 1959.

Terrien, Samuel. *The Psalms: Strophic Structure and Theological Commentary*. Grand Rapids: Eerdmans, 2003.

Tertullian. *Against Marcion*. In *The Ante-Nicene Fathers*, edited by Alexander Roberts and James Donaldson, Apostolic Fathers 3, 269–475. Grand Rapids: Eerdmans, 1981.

Tucker, Gene M. "Sin and Judgment in the Prophets." In *Problems in Biblical Theology: Essays in Honor of Rolf Knierim*, edited by Henry T. C. Sun and Keith L. Eades, 373–88. Grand Rapids: Eerdmans, 1997.

Van Beeck, Frans Jozef. *Loving the Torah More than God? Towards a Catholic Appreciation of Judaism*. Chicago: Loyola University Press, 1989.

———. *Understanding the Christian Faith*. Vol. 1. of *God Encountered: A Contemporary Catholic Systematic Theology*. San Francisco: Harper & Row, 1989.

Vardy, Peter. *The Puzzle of Evil*. London: Fount, 1992.

Volf, Miroslav. *Exclusion and Embrace*. Nashville: Abingdon, 1996.

Von Rad, Gerhard. "The Confessions of Jeremiah." In *Theodicy in the Old Testament*, edited by James L. Crenshaw, 88–99. Philadelphia: Fortress, 1983.

———. *Old Testament Theology*. 2 vols. Edinburgh: Oliver and Boyd, 1962.

Wallace, Alfred Russel. *The Wonderful Century: Its Success and Its Failures*. New York: Dodd, Mead, 1898.

Welch, Claude, ed. *God and Incarnation in Mid-Nineteenth Century German Theology*. New York: Oxford University Press, 1965.

Welz, Claudia. "Trust and Lament: Faith in the Face of Godforsakenness." In *Evoking Lament: A Theological Discussion*, edited by Eva Harasta and Brian Brock, 118–35. London: T. & T. Clark, 2009.

Westermann, Claus. *Creation*. Translated by John J. Scullion. Philadelphia: Fortress 1974.

———. *Praise and Lament in the Psalms*. Translated by Keith R. Crim and Richard N. Soulen. Edinburgh: T. & T. Clark, 1981.

Whitehead, Alfred North. *Process and Reality: An Essay in Cosmology*. Edited by David Ray Griffin and Donald W. Sherburne. Corrected ed. New York: Free, 1978.

Wickham, Lionel R. *Cyril of Alexandria: Select Letters*. Oxford: Clarendon, 1983.

Williams, Rowan. *The Wound of Knowledge: Christian Spirituality from the New Testament to St. John of the Cross*. 2nd ed. Cambridge, MA: Cowley, 1991.

Wright, N. T. *Evil and the Justice of God*. Downers Grove, IL: InterVarsity, 2006.

———. *Jesus and the Victory of God*. Christian Origins and the Question of God 2. Minneapolis: Fortress, 1992.

Wüthrich, Matthias. "Lament for Naught? An Inquiry into the Suppression of Lament in Systematic Theology: On the Example of Karl Barth." In *Evoking Lament: A Theological Discussion*, edited by Eva Harasta and Brian Brock, 60–76. London: T. & T. Clark, 2009.